AMERICAN INDIAN POLICY

Theodore W. Taylor

Lomond Publications, Inc.
Mt. Airy, Maryland 21771
1983

Second Printing, 1986

Library of Congress Catalog Number: 83-81947

ISBN: 0-912338-41-5 (Clothbound)
      0-912338-42-3 (Microfiche)

Printed in the United States of America.

Published by
Lomond Publications, Inc.
P.O. Box 88
Mt. Airy, Maryland 21771

ACKNOWLEDGMENTS

Officials of the Interior Department and other Federal agencies, leaders of Indian interest groups, and state governors and other state employees concerned with Indian matters have all been generous in providing information essential to the preparation of this book. Kenneth Payton, when he was Acting Assistant Secretary of the Interior Department in charge of the operations of the Bureau of Indian Affairs, wrote to state governors for information about their state Indian programs and many states responded with essential information used in chapter 4. I queried 60 Indian interest groups for information which is reported in Chapter 5. My letter to the various Federal agencies with programs for American Natives resulted in much of the information included in Chapter 3, along with Richard S. Jones' report of *Federal Programs of Assistance to American Indians*. Officials of Indian interest groups, Federal agencies, and states also were courteous and helpful in responding to numerous telephone inquiries following up on questions raised or for clarification of material submitted.

I am indebted to many for information and understanding of the Maine Indian land claims case settled in 1980: officials of the Penobscot tribe whom I visited in Old Town, Maine; Thomas Tureen, attorney for the Maine Indians; staff of the Senate Select Committee on Indian Affairs, particularly Peter Taylor; various Maine officials contacted by telephone; and Tim Vollmann in the Solicitor's Office, Department of the Interior. For the Alaska material Robert D. Arnold's book, *Alaska Native Land Claims*, proved to be invaluable. Dennis Tiepelman, while a Washington representative of the Alaska Federation of Natives, helped with the material on Alaska Native Land Claims as well as providing information on the organization and accomplishments of the Alaska Federation of Natives.

Ronald P. Andrade, Executive Director of the National Congress of American Indians (NCAI), and Annette Traversie Bagley, then with NCAI, graciously arranged for a personal meeting and provided material on the NCAI. Phillip Martin, Chief, Mississippi Band of Choctaw Indians and President of the National Tribal Chairmen's Association (NTCA), read portions of the manuscript included in Chapters 2 through 5 and provided information on NTCA. For his help and encouragement I am deeply grateful.

The Division of Tribal Government Services in the Bureau of Indian Affairs received the material sent in by the state governors, provided information and counsel on the Sioux Black Hills case, and reviewed parts of the manuscript. Bradley Patterson on the White House staff at the time of the Trail of Broken Treaties furnished valuable information on this incident. Cecil Hoffman, while on the staff of the Assistant Secretary for Indian Affairs in the

Interior Department, reviewed the cases in Chapter 2 and offered helpful suggestions. Thomas Oxendine and his information staff in BIA have helped in innumerable ways. S. Lyman Tyler, American West Center, University of Utah, read drafts of Chapters 2 through 5 and gave much needed encouragement.

The material in Chapters 2, 3, 4 and 5 was originally prepared for inclusion in a book on *The Bureau of Indian Affairs* to be published by Westview Press, but had to be omitted because of the lengthy manuscript. I greatly appreciate the permission of Westview Press to use this material in this book, especially the sections on the Indian Health Service, the Department of Justice, and the Maine case which are included in the Westview book.

For whatever merits this book may have I am deeply indebted to those mentioned above and many others too numerous to mention individually. However, I must accept responsibility for any errors or shortcomings.

Theodore W. Taylor

TABLE OF CONTENTS

LIST OF TABLES

LIST OF FIGURES

LIST OF ABBREVIATIONS

AFN   Alaska Federation of Natives

AIPRC   American Indian Policy Review Commission. This commission was established by the Congress and included three senators, four members of the House of Representatives, and five Indian members. The commission's *Final Report* was issued May 17, 1977.

BIA   Bureau of Indian Affairs, U.S. Department of the Interior.

HRC 108   House Concurrent Resolution 108, adopted August 1, 1953; frequently referred to as the "termination policy."

IHS   Indian Health Service, Health Services Administration, U.S. Department of Health and Human Services.

IRA   Indian Reorganization Act of 1934, 48 Stat. 984. Authorized the organization of Indian tribes with a large degree of self government; stopped the allotment policy and authorized the purchase of land for Indian people.

JOM   Johnson-O'Malley Act of 1934, 48 Stat. 596. Authorized the Secretary of Interior to enter into contracts with states or their subdivisions for education, medical attention, agricultural assistance, and social welfare for Indians.

NCAI   National Congress of American Indians

NTCA   National Tribal Chairmen's Association

PL 280   Statute giving the consent of the United States for any state to assume civil and criminal jurisdiction over their Indian citizens, 1953, 67 Stat. 588; amended to require Indian consent in 1968, 82 Stat. 78.

PL 638   Indian Self-Determination and Education Assistance Act, January 4, 1975, 88 Stat. 2203.

CHAPTER 1
AMERICAN INDIANS TODAY

INTRODUCTION

American Indian policy is a crazy quilt of varying and inconsistent law and administration. Administration of the laws and operation of active programs is divided among several Federal agencies, more than half the states, and many local governments. Interest groups are active throughout the administration of Indian programs and related legislative and judicial processes.

This book is intended to provide a comprehensive overview and description of *programs* and *participants* uniquely related to American Indians, and to serve as a reference source to identify specific *roles* of Federal and state and local governments and of major interest groups.

Equally if not more important the book provides a base for understanding the *process* of formulating Indian policy.

This extremely complex, and flawed, pattern of law, judicial decision and administrative action is derived from a congeries of interest group involvement, legislative process, judicial decision, public opinion influence and administrative decision. How to provide the basis for understanding this intricate and dynamic pattern of influence and action is a formidable challenge.

Interrelationships of official and unofficial institutions and individuals and of public opinion (influenced by the communications media) are critical to the way in which policy and administration have been formulated; likewise they are critical to improvement, rationalization and reform.

I have chosen to approach this challenge of providing perspective first with a set of case studies: Alaska Native Claims; Maine Indian Claims; Trail of Broken Treaties; Wounded Knee and the Longest Walk; Western Washington Treaty Fishing Rights; the Sioux and the Black Hills. These instances of controversy, with description of official and unofficial participants, relevant policies, events, actions and outcomes reflect the realities of American Indian policy issues and problems. It is only within this context of interinstitutional dynamics that the straightforward description of government and interest group policy and program can be appreciated.

Subsequent chapters present a catalog of Federal Government Services (Chapter 3), State and Local Government Services (Chapter 4) and Indian Interest Groups (Chapter 5).

Thoughts on the future are presented in the final chapter.

There is general agreement that the condition of Indian policy and administration on reservations is unsatisfactory. The Indian economy and quality of life are afflicted (though unevenly) by high unemployment, poverty, high birth rates, low motivation, health problems including alcoholism and mental health, hostilities toward the system, and uncertainties of role between internal Indian culture and outside national society.

That Indians can compete successfully outside the reservation is well proven. That ethnic groups can retain a sense of ethnicity and maintain traditions is demonstrated by other groups in our society.

There is a national concensus that European invasion of what is now the United States, inhabited only by the Indians, was accompanied by wrongs and inequities. Equitable recompense and the appropriate time frame for compensation are very difficult issues. They are issues in which deep self-interests are involved and for which there are many and continuously changing variables.

Solutions are especially difficult too because attitudes are based on partial, distorted and erroneous facts. This imperfect information base is a problem not only for the general public but also for principals in policy formation and administration—government officials, Indian leaders and interest group activists.

Information about existing policies and the policy-making process will be at the base of improvement in the present unsatisfactory reservation system and in the quality of life for American Indian citizens. But there has been no ready access source of such information.

This book contributes to the information base and should be useful to all concerned—Indians, children in the schools, Indian leaders, interested citizens, writers about Indian affairs, academicians, attorneys, business leaders and others who serve Indian communities and groups, legislators, judges and government program administrators.

The book should also be very useful to students and analysts of public policy for its cases and descriptions of policy formulation and execution.

American Indians have contributed a great deal to this nation—a love of the out-of-doors, many of our foods such as potatoes and corn, a concern for the earth and all living things, the wisdom in Indian philosophy, and inspiring examples of individual and group self-sufficiency, independence and direct contributions to society.

Indians helped the original European settlers survive the harsh winters and participated with distinction in World Wars I and II in both the military and in defense industry. Today citizens of Indian blood are leaders in local, state, and Federal governments, in business and industry, and they enrich our culture through the arts. As a result of the contacts between Indian and

European cultures both have been changed and, hopefully, both have profited.

Indians, originally members of independent and self-supporting Indian groups, are now citizens of the United States and the states wherein they reside. They have all of the rights, privileges, and responsibilities of citizenship.

Some members of tribal groups live on Federal Indian reservations while others live with non-Indian neighbors off the reservation, often in metropolitan areas. Since the establishment of the reservation system in the 19th century the Bureau of Indian Affairs (BIA) of the U.S. Interior Department has historically been concerned primarily with reservation-based Indians.

THE FEDERAL RESERVATION SYSTEM

For years some reservations have been described as rural slums. With 56 percent of those able to work (16 years of age or older) unemployed on the reservations in Montana, 68 percent in Wyoming, 59 percent in Arizona, and 74 percent in South Dakota, as examples, the idleness, aimlessness, and resultant lack of purpose cannot help but have a disintegrating effect. [1]

Many reservations are overpopulated and cannot possibly provide opportunity for economic self-sufficiency for all current residents. Why do so many remain under these circumstances? It may be in part due to the perverse economic incentives involved in the current reservation system: Indian lands and homes are not taxed by states as a result of their Federal trust status; subsidized housing is often available; free medical and hospital care is provided by the U.S. Public Health Service; free management of lands is available from BIA and income from such lands may be forthcoming without any personal effort; sharing in claims awards to the tribe and in income from tribally owned resources is more certain, many believe, if they remain on the reservation; economic security is available through the extended family; and welfare payments are assured if no other means of support are available.

In the Allotment Act period of the 1890s and the trust termination period of the 1950s the emphasis was on transfer of Federal Indian functions to the Indians themselves and to the states. This has been supplanted by the current emphasis on self-determination. However, the same basic thrust remains of placing more responsibility on the Indians themselves. In the 1950s the transfer of responsibility generally was without a transfer of Federal funding for fiscal support. In the 1980s the transfer of responsibility under "self-determination" is only partial and the Federal funding is actually increased to cover not only the program function but also to pay for tribal overhead involved in administering the activity. The secretaries of Interior and Health and Human Services still retain responsibility for oversight.

Self-determination contracts or agreements are required by law to be monitored to assure compliance with the purpose of the specific program funded, assure accurate accounting and avoidance of graft or theft, and to take back the operation if the tribal effort fails. There is little emphasis on state responsibility or transferring additional responsibilities to the states. Although in the 1980s the goal of transfer of responsibility is still present, it is different than in the 1950s in that it is Federally subsidized and is accompanied by an underlying Federal responsibility.

The current policy may result in increased ability of Indian groups to manage their own affairs which is an obvious objective. But it also may result in the continuance of a dependent-paternalistic relationship. It may, indeed, add to perverse incentives. Will there be a development of self-governing ability without the discipline of having to be economically self-sufficient? Reservation economies, with a few exceptions such as Palm Springs and Osage, are largely based on Federal subsidies. Take away this Federal and state fiscal underpinning and most reservations would collapse into even worse economic problems than at present.

The public is tolerant of group diversity and pluralistic differences and accommodates to variations in culture and ways of living within reason, but tends to be intolerant if such groups are not self-supporting. American Indians have been somewhat excepted from this requirement of self-sufficiency because of history and the public view of Indians. But the moves in the 1890s and the 1950s to put Indians on their own were expressions of the fundamental belief of many Americans that no group should continue indefinitely on a subsidy. This underlying view will probably resurface from time to time.

Even though most persons with some Indian blood are already operating in the larger society, reservation populations recently have been increasing at the rate of about four percent a year. Indian birthrates are two or three times as high as the average in the United States.

WHERE DO INDIANS LIVE?

Federal Indian reservations are not the only places Indians live. Indians live in every state as indicated in column 1 of Table 1.1. Those served in one way or another by the Bureau of Indian Affairs, who constitute 53 percent of those identifying as Indians, live in only 27 states (column 3 of Table 1.1). Even fewer states have tribal or individual Indian land under trust administered by the Bureau of Indian Affairs (columns 6 and 7 of Table 1.1). Indian trust land is often located in isolated rural areas and Federal Indian reservations are generally related to such Indian owned land. However, the Agua Caliente Indians of Palm Springs, California, own alternate sections of the town and, of course, their real estate holdings are very valuable. A map which shows Indian lands and communities and indicates Federal Indian reservations and other Indian groups is provided in Appendix A.

Most of the estimated 20 million people in the United States with some Indian blood do not identify as Indians and are scattered throughout the land. Even many of the 1,400,000 identifying as Indian do not live on reservations; many of them, in fact, live in metropolitan areas as indicated in Table 1.2. All of the metropolitan areas listed have 5,000 or more Indians. Interestingly, compared to these 19 metropolitan areas there are 26 Indian reservations with 5,000 or more Indians (Table 1.3). In Florida the Miccosukees (495) and Seminoles (1426) served by BIA number together 1921 persons as compared to the total number of Indians in Florida of 19,000. The metropolitan or urban areas in Florida with 1000 or more Indians have a total Indian population of approximately 11,000 Indians, including Miami with 3,000, Jacksonville with 1,500, Orlando 1,770, Pensacola 2,140, and Tampa-St. Petersberg with 2,650. Approximately 23,600 (12 percent) of California's 201,400 Indians are served by BIA and are mostly in the rural areas. The Los Angeles urban complex has 81,900 and San Francisco 32,000 Indians. The only reservation with an Indian population greater than the number of Indians in the Los Angeles area is Navajo with an estimated 158,900 residents, about four times the size of the next largest Indian group.

Although most persons with some Indian blood do not identify as Indians, such identification as far as the Bureau of Census is concerned is up to the individual. In view of the open-ended nature of the number of persons who could identify as Indians, criteria for eligibility for BIA or other government services are important. BIA's services are generally restricted to Federally recognized Indian tribes and their members and to tribes and individual Indians owning land held in trust by the Federal government. Some statutes restrict services to Indians with at least 25 percent Indian blood; such is the case for eligibility for Indian schools, for example. BIA's requirements are generally more stringent than those of other Federal agencies.

CULTURE CHANGE

The romanticized Indian warrior and hunter represented an aspect of Indian culture that has largely faded from the current scene. The Navajo sheep and horse culture was borrowed from the Spanish. Their centralized governmental structure of today is in stark contrast to the roving Navajo bands encountered by the Spanish adventurers. There are estimated to have been 800,000 to 2,000,000 natives in what is now the United States when the colonists started coming to these shores. From 1850 to 1900 it appeared that

Table 1.1   Indian Population and Land by State

State	Population					Trust land (acres)	
	Indian	% Indian of total	Eligible for BIA service	% of total Ind. pop.	% Unemployed BIA elig.	Tribal	Individual
	1	2	3	4	5	6	7
U S Total	1,421,400	.6	755,201	53	51	42,032,871	9,989,041
Alabama	7,583	.2	-	-	-	-	-
Alaska	64,103	16.0	64,970	100	62	86,759	361,523
Arizona	152,745	5.6	194,818	100	59	19,555,036	252,474
Arkansas	9,428	.4	-	-	-	-	-
California	201,369	.8	23,625	12	64	500,285	68,556
Colorado	18,068	.6	2,661	15	61	752,462	3,623
Connecticut	4,533	.1	-	-	-	-	-
Delaware	1,328	.2	-	-	-	-	-
District of Col.	1,031	.2	-	-	-	-	-
Florida	19,257	.2	1,921	10	36	79,014	-
Georgia	7,616	.1	-	-	-	-	-
Hawaii	2,768	.3	-	-	-	-	-
Idaho	10,521	1.1	7,108	68	66	461,543	332,240
Illinois	16,283	.1	-	-	-	-	-
Indiana	7,836	.1	-	-	-	-	-
Iowa	5,455	.2	662	12	68	4,164	-
Kansas	15,373	.6	2,243	15	23	5,768	22,433
Kentucky	3,610	.1	-	-	-	-	-
Louisiana	12,065	.3	717	6	33	-	-
Maine	4,087	.4	2,261	55	43	416	-
Maryland	8,021	.2	-	-	-	See notes	-
Massachusetts	7,743	.1	-	-	-	-	-
Michigan	40,050	.4	5,829	15	60	12,085	9,186
Minnesota	35,016	.9	18,260	52	65	713,076	50,914
Mississippi	6,180	.2	4,487	73	32	17,635	19
Missouri	12,321	.2	-	-	-	-	374
Montana	37,270	4.7	27,529	74	56	2,220,383	3,016,409
Nebraska	9,195	.6	4,404	48	74	22,656	42,339
Nevada	13,308	1.7	8,259	62	59	1,138,462	78,567

	1	2	3	4	5	6	7
New Hampshire	1,352	.1	-	-	-	-	-
New Jersey	8,394	.1	-	-	-	-	-
New Mexico	106,119	8.2	105,973	100	47	6,483,483	675,986
New York	39,582	.2	11,167	28	55	See notes	-
North Carolina	64,652	1.1	5,971	9	57	56,461	-
North Dakota	20,158	3.1	21,552	100	63	207,820	643,959
Ohio	12,239	.1	-	-	-	-	-
Oklahoma	169,459	5.6	159,852	94	23	86,684	1,127,752
Oregon	27,314	1.0	4,301	16	48	620,412	139,045
Pennsylvania	9,465	.1	-	-	-	-	-
Rhode Island	2,898	.3	-	-	-	-	-
South Carolina	5,757	.2	-	-	-	-	-
South Dakota	45,968	6.5	46,101	100	74	2,621,228	2,473,118
Tennessee	5,104	.1	-	-	-	-	-
Texas	40,075	.3	-	-	-	-	-
Utah	19,256	1.3	7,140	37	57	2,251,749	33,647
Vermont	984	.2	-	-	-	-	-
Virginia	9,454	.2	-	-	-	-	-
Washington	60,804	1.5	39,726	65	63	2,014,238	481,547
West Virginia	1,610	.1	-	-	-	-	-
Wisconsin	29,499	.6	18,279	62	53	328,887	80,795
Wyoming	7,094	1.5	5,385	76	68	1,792,166	94,536

Notes on columns 1 through 7:

1 U. S. total and state population of Indians (American Indian, Eskimo, Aleut) 1980 Census, General Population Characteristics, PC80-1-B, Table 15. Differs from 1980 Census Total, last column, Table 1, Appendix B, due to rounding of "Other States" figure in that table.

2 Indian percent of total population, U. S. total and each state.

3 Eligible for BIA services: Indians living on Federal reservations or nearby who are considered part of the service population of the Bureau of Indian Affairs. See Appendix B.

4 Percent of Indians eligible for BIA services compared to total number of Indians.

5 Percent unemployed of BIA eligible 16 years of age or older able to work. See Appendix B.

6 Tribal land under the trusteeship of the Federal government and under the jurisdiction of the BIA as of September 30, 1981. From Annual Report of Indian lands, September 30, 1981, published by BIA. Figures rounded and may not add precisely. This column does not include the 40,000,000 acres transferred to Alaska Natives under the Alaska Native Claims Settlement Act of 1971 and amendments (85 Stat. 688) since that land is not in trust. The Maine Indian Claims Act of 1980 (94 Stat. 1785) authorized the purchase of 300,000 acres of land in trust and over 100,000 acres had been purchased as of July, 1983. New York reservation land, other than the Poospatuck and Shinnecock reservations, cannot be alienated without Federal approval but is not considered as trust land.

7 Acres of trust land under the jurisdiction of BIA owned by Indian individuals, Annual Report of Indian lands.

TABLE 1.2

METROPOLITAN AREAS WITH 5000 OR MORE INDIANS
(figures rounded to nearest hundred)

Location	Number of Indians
Arizona: Phoenix	22,800
Tucson	14,900
Colorado: Denver	9,000
District of Columbia (D.C., Md., Va.)	6,400
California: Los Angeles (Long Beach, Anaheim)	81,900
San Francisco (Oakland, San Jose)	32,000
Illinois: Chicago (Gary, Kenosha)	11,600
Minnesota: Minneapolis-St. Paul	15,800
Michigan: Detroit (Ann Arbor)	13,000
New York: New York City	20,500
Oregon: Portland	8,500
New Mexico: Albuquerque	20,700
Oklahoma: Oklahoma City	24,700
Tulsa	38,500
Pennsylvania: Philadelphia (Wilmington, Trenton)	6,000
Texas: Houston - Galveston (SCSA)	6,900
Dallas - Ft. Worth	11,000
Washington: Seattle - Tacoma (SCSA)	20,800
Wisconsin: Milwaukee	6,500

Source: 1980 Census, Table 30, General Characteristics for Selected Racial Groups
for Areas and Places, Standard Metropolitan Statistical Areas. SCSA refers to
a Standard Consolidated Statistical Area.

TABLE 1.3

FEDERAL INDIAN RESERVATIONS WITH 5000 OR MORE INDIANS
(figures rounded to nearest 100)

BIA Area	Agency or Reservation	Number of Indians
Aberdeen	Pine Ridge (SD)	18,400
	Rosebud (SD)	9,700
	Standing Rock (SD-ND)	8,200
	Turtle Mountain (ND)	9,600
Albuquerque	Laguna (NM)	6,500
	Zuni (NM)	7,300
Anadarko	Citizen Potawatomi (OK)	6,400
Billings	Blackfeet (MT)	6,600
	Crow (MT)	5,300
	Ft. Peck (MT)	5,000
	Wind River (WY)	5,400
Eastern	Cherokee (NC)	6,000
	Seneca (NY)	5,500
Muscogee	Ardmore (Chickasaw) (OK)	8,800
	Okmulgee (Creek) (OK)	39,400
	Osage (OK)	6,000
	Tahlequah (Cherokee) (OK)	43,000
	Talihina (Choctaw) (OK)	19,900
Navajo	Navajo (AZ, NM, UT)	158,900
Phoenix	Ft. Apache (AZ)	8,100
	Hopi (AZ)	8,800
	Papago (AZ)	17,700
	Gila River (Pima) (AZ)	9,800
	San Carlos (AZ)	6,700
Portland	Payallup (WA)	7,000
	Yakima (WA)	8,400

Source: *Local Estimates of Resident Indian Population and Labor Force Status.*
(Washington, DC: Bureau of Indian Affairs, January, 1983). Appendix B.

the Indians were a vanishing race as disease, wars, and other ravages caused by a disruptive interaction with the European invaders took their toll. The "Vanishing American" was reduced to around 300,000 during this period, but in the 20th century the trend has reversed.

World Wars I and II found many Indians in the armed forces and in factories. A considerable number moved from poverty striken reservations to urban areas. Indians on the reservations of any size today not only have doctors and hospitals, but have axes and chain saws in place of stone cutting tools, pick-up trucks and cars instead of relying entirely on their feet and later on the horse and wagon. Now there are TVs, radios, and telephones in place of runners and smoke signals. Most Indians today are educated in public schools and some have entered the professions and the arts. William Keeler was a former Chief of the Cherokees in Oklahoma and was successively President and Chairman of the Board of Phillips Petroleum. Ben Reifel, Rosebud Sioux, represented South Dakota in the U.S. House of Representatives for 12 years. Marvin Franklin, former Chief of the Iowa Indians, is an attorney and was formerly Assistant to the Secretary for Indians in the Department of Interior. Others are Vine Deloria, Jr., Standing Rock Sioux, author of *Custer Died for Our Sins* and other books, and N. Scott Momaday, Kiowa-Cherokee, Pulitzer Prize winning author of *A House Made of Dawn*. Well-known individuals of Indian descent include Charles Curtis, Vice President of the United States (1929-1933), whose mother was half Indian, and Will Rogers, the humorist, who had Cherokee ancestry. Indians have been elected to local school boards, county offices, and state legislatures. There are Indian artists with national reputations. Jim Thorpe, whose mother was a Sac Indian, was one of the greatest athletes of all time.

Indian culture, like all cultures, is in a process of continual change. Chief Joseph, Nez Perce, who outwitted U.S. army generals in the Pacific Northwest, said in 1879:

> I know that my race must change. We cannot hold our own with white men as we are. We only ask an even chance to live as other men live. . . . We ask that the same law shall work alike on all men. . . .
>
> Let me be a free man—free to travel, free to stop, free to work, free to trade where I choose, free to choose my own teachers, free to follow the religion of my fathers, free to think and talk and act for myself—and I will obey every law, or submit to the penalty. [2]

Today most persons with some Indian blood live with non-Indian neighbors and work with non-Indians in the workplace. Almost 50 percent of those identifying as Indians have no association with the Bureau of Indian Affairs. As in the case of most cultures Indians retain that which is useful from their traditional culture and adopt practically useful aspects from other cultures.

Indians residing in the United States not already U.S. citizens as a result of previous treaties or acts of Congress became citizens in 1924. They also became citizens of the states wherein they reside. American Indians are Indian Americans. Yet some of these Indian American citizens are also members of Indian tribes and, if living on a reservation, may be subject in some respects to tribal governments.

TRIBAL GOVERNMENT

The bands, groups, and occasionally confederations of various groups of natives inhabiting North America in what is now the United States had their own governmental systems. Many were roving bands with individual leaders and others lived in villages or adobe pueblos. The basic social fabric was kinship. The European invaders negotiated with and made agreements and treaties with various groups. As the balance of power shifted and Indian groups largely lost their former independence many were placed on reservations and furnished food rations as their traditional subsistence economy eroded. Treaty making ceased in 1871 and the Bureau of Indian Affairs reservation superintendent often became the center of government on various reservations during the latter part of the 19th and early part of this century.

The Indian Reorganization Act of 1934[3] reversed the trend and emphasized strengthening tribal government and the Indian Self-Determination and Education Assistance Act of 1975[4] gave additional impetus to this policy. Most of the constitutions and bylaws of the larger tribal governments are based on western ideas patterned on model documents furnished by BIA after 1934. There are a few traditional governments, as in some of the pueblos in New Mexico.

Tribal membership is determined by each tribe and criteria vary from one group to another. Uintah and Ouray Utes in Utah require over 50 percent Indian blood with at least 50 percent Ute blood, while other tribes, such as the Cherokee in Oklahoma, may include persons who are lineal descendents of tribal members who may have a small fraction of Indian blood. The Santa Clara pueblo in New Mexico considers the children of a Santa Clara Indian man married to a non-Indian as eligible for membership, but children of a Santa Clara Indian woman married to a non-Indian as ineligible.

Tribal governments constitute a fourth level of government in the United States and pose many anomalies. Some have police power and tribal court authority within their reservation boundaries and some do not, such functions in the latter instances being performed by the state in which they reside. Approximately 80 percent are served by the state public school system, but some have tribal schools under contract with the Bureau of Indian Affairs and some have BIA operated schools.

Jurisdictional problems relating to police, taxing powers, water rights, and hunting and fishing rights keep the tribal, state, and Federal governments busy and uncertain and many issues end up on the docket of the Supreme Court of the United States. The area of jurisdiction for whatever powers a tribal government may have is generally within the exterior boundary of the reservation and may not apply to non-Indians in many instances. Major crimes committed by Indians on Indian reservations are under the jurisdiction of the Federal government.

The aspects of the jurisdictional relationships among Federal and state agencies, tribal governments, and Indian citizens will be noted in the chapters that follow.

FOOTNOTES

[1]Resident Indian Population by BIA Area Office, State, and BIA Reservation Agency, August 1983 (Appendix B).

[2]Wayne Moquin, ed., *Great Documents in American Indian History* (New York: Praeger Publishers, 1973), p. 251.

[3]48 Stat. 984, 1934.

[4]88 Stat. 2203, Jan. 4, 1975.

CHAPTER 2
CASES IN INDIAN POLICY

INTRODUCTION

The President, the Congress and the states often avoid controversial policy matters until a crisis forces action. Sometimes the refusal of the executive and legislative branches to act forces the courts to, in effect, legislate. This is illustrated in Indian policy issues such as treaty rights regarding fishing and aboriginal land claims. The executive and legislative branches at both state and national levels did not come to grips with the resolution of Maine land claims and Indian fishing rights in the state of Washington until forced by court action. The courts also were a major factor in the Black Hills settlement.

Courts do not initiate cases. However, Indian tribes and interest groups have learned how to use the courts as well as how to put pressure on the executive and legislative branches in other ways. The discovery of oil on the North Slope of Alaska and the demands of the oil companies and the state for a resolution of land ownership provided a basic impetus to governmental action on the land claims of Alaskan Natives which had been pending for years. The natives and Interior Secretary Stewart Udall took full advantage of this pressure to achieve desired action.

Chapters 3-5 describe Federal and state and local programs and Indian interest groups. These descriptions do not fully illumine the interaction between Indian citizens and their governments, other citizens, and the interplay of various parts and levels of government with one another. The examples of Indian policy resolution which follow give a view of the process and illustrate how the actors described in the following chapters actually behave in the resolution of intransigent problems and challenges. These cases present the involvement of citizens with their government and the multitudinous factors, influences, personalities, institutions and public views concerned in the resolution of specific policy issues. Fig. 2-1 portrays the Indian Policy Environment.

The case examples presented here do not by any means include all the important unresolved issues in Indian Affairs. Some of the problems not included in these cases and urgently requiring resolution will because of their highly controversial nature tend to be avoided by the executive and the legislature for as long as possible. They are: quantifying Indian water rights, firming up Indian land boundaries, legislative definition of an Indian, solving the Indian land heirship tangle, clarification of Federal trust responsibility

FIGURE 2.1. INDIAN POLICY ENVIRONMENT:
BIA RECOGNIZED GROUPS

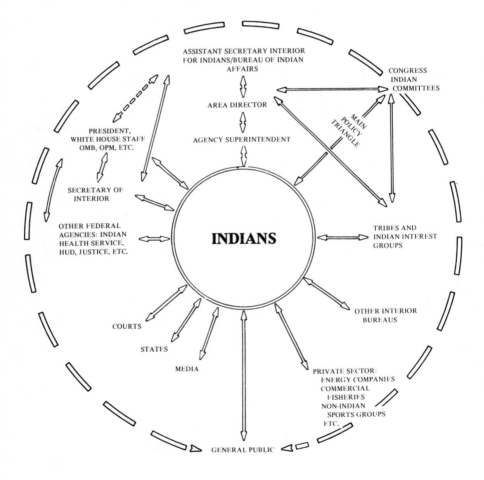

including how long it should exist, and specific legislation on the exact nature of tribal governments and the relationships of such governments to local, state and Federal governments.[1]

ALASKA NATIVE CLAIMS

History and Background

The first Native organization in Alaska with more than a local basis was the Alaska Native Brotherhood (ANB). It was founded in 1912 by a Tsimshian and nine Tlingits from Southeastern Alaska whose goal was citizenship. In addition they sought education in the white man's way and abandonment of aboriginal customs. The full goal of citizenship was achieved in 1924.[2]

The Alaska Statehood Act of 1958 granted about 103 million acres of land to the new state. Selections of land from the Federal domain by the state under this authority threatened the continued subsistence use by the Natives. Likewise, proposed additions to national parks, national forests, and wildlife areas implied possible reduction in land available for Native subsistence living. "Project Chariot" was suggested to blast a harbor at Cape Thompson by a nuclear device and the proposed Rampart Dam would have flooded the lands of surrounding villages. There were also restrictions on hunting in the Barrow area under migratory bird treaties which created great concern among the Natives. The assistance of the Association on American Indian Affairs in New York City was sought and a conference was held in Barrow in November 1961. The Inupiat Paitot, a Native organization, was established to unite in defense of Native rights and to discuss how to obtain legal ownership of the land used by Natives. The *Tundra Times*, first published on October 1, 1962, was a vehicle to express Native views and problems, among them the land rights of Natives.

Secretary of Interior Stewart Udall's Alaska Task Force on Native Affairs in 1963 cited the failure in the Organic Act of 1884 to provide a means for Natives to acquire title to land, and also pointed to Congressional avoidance of the controversial task of defining Native entitlement. The Natives wanted land which was also desired by the state, business interests, and non-Natives. Tremendous values were involved. The Natives' desire for subsistence use of large areas of land obviously posed a threat to other uses by the state and its citizens. Any attempt to arrive at a resolution would involve a difficult fight and members of Congress wondered if the political costs were worth it.

Various approaches to the problem were offered—from settlement of claims by the U.S. Court of Claims (by Senator Ernest Gruening of Alaska) to extinguishment of Native rights by Congress and reimbursement by cash (by

Representative Ralph Rivers of Alaska). The Udall task force had recommended granting 160 acres to individuals for their homes, small acreages for village growth, and designation of areas for Native use, not ownership. These proposals were considered inadequate by the Natives and with the help of the Association on American Indian Affairs, an Indian interest group headquartered in New York City, they prevented action on the recommendations. According to Robert Arnold the Natives had four alternatives: establishment of reserves, resolution by Court of Claims, obtain state legislation to protect their land rights, or obtain a Congressional settlement.[3]

The various Native regional and local organizations made several attempts to get together to strengthen their voice during the early 1960s but suspicion, distance, and lack of effective communication stymied these efforts. U.S. Office of Economic Opportunity (OEO) funds supported the growing community and regional organizations and since one of the major objectives of these organizations was to obtain title to land these funds in effect supported the increase in land rights activity.[4]

In October 1966, Emil Notti, president of the Cook Inlet Native Association, called a meeting with representatives from seventeen Native organizations. Helping organize this session were Chief Albert Kaloa, Jr. of Tyonek village, Stanley J. McCutcheon who helped Tyonek win almost $13 million from oil leases (Tyonek helped with the costs of the meeting) and Thomas Pillifant of the Bureau of Indian Affairs. The following positions were adopted: (1) a "land freeze" on all Federal lands until Native claims were resolved; (2) Congressional legislation to settle claims; and (3) consultation with Natives prior to settlement of claims. These recommendations blazed the path that would be followed to achieve a final resolution in 1971. This meeting also received a great deal of attention from political and other leaders in the state, and in November three Native leaders active at the meeting were elected to the Alaska House of Representatives, making a total of seven Natives in the state legislature. In 1967 the group adopted "The Alaska Federation of Natives" (AFN) as its name and elected Emil Notti as a full-time president.

In 1966 Secretary of the Interior Stewart Udall stopped land transactions on Federal land (a "land freeze") until Congress could act upon the claims. Alaska objected since it halted transfer of lands to the state as authorized by the Statehood Act, and also prevented issuance of oil leases on Federal lands. Since the state was to receive 90 percent of Federal revenues from such leases, it wanted to obtain this income. The election of Richard Nixon in 1968 resulted in the nomination of Alaska Governor Walter Hickel as Secretary of the Interior. Governor Hickel had opposed the freeze. The AFN asked Hickel to state his stand on the freeze and how he would protect Native rights. Conservation groups opposed the nomination and Hickel needed AFN support. So he agreed to extend the land freeze until December 1970 and the AFN endorsed his nomination. As Arnold points out this victory indicated the increasing strength of the AFN and its ability "to influence the processes of government."[5]

Another pressure that helped AFN get its proposals before Congressional leaders and the White House came from oil companies who wanted to capitalize on Alaska north slope oil. As long as there was a land freeze, Interior would not grant permits for a proposed oil pipeline to carry oil from the northern fields in the Artic near Barrow to Valdez on the South coast in the Gulf of Alaska.

As summed up by Guy Martin, legislative assistant to Alaska's Congressman Nick Begich:

> The Natives had a good cause. It was an election year. The Indian rights movement was gaining strength and acceptance. Still, none of these factors could have been a controlling influence at the White House, or even made it possible for Native leaders to see the White House staff without other assistance. This assistance came largely from the oil industry and related business interests, and from the only Republican in Alaska's delegation, Senator Ted Stevens. This was the first of many times that the shared fates of the land claims and the trans-Alaska pipeline would produce a strange coalition of support for the Native cause.[6]

Senator Henry Jackson, Chairman of the Senate Committee on Interior and Insular Affairs, had requested a study by the Alaska Federal Field Committee as a basis for a comprehensive proposal. In 1968 this Committee produced a report, *Alaska Natives and the Land*, which gave definitive information on the relation of Natives to their resources. [7]

In May 1969 AFN adopted the following points for a land settlement: the Natives should receive 40 million acres, an appropriation of $500 million, Native corporations should be the instruments used, and the Natives should receive a two percent perpetual share of the revenues produced from lands given up. At the Prudhoe Bay oil lease sale later in 1969 oil companies paid over $900 million to the state of Alaska, demonstrating the value of the mineral estate. This helped support the legitimacy of the AFN proposals and also whetted the appetites of the state and the oil companies to get on with the exploitation of the oil.

Senator Henry Jackson (D-Washington) had introduced a bill in 1969 based on recommendations of the Alaska Field Committee providing for only 10 million acres to be transferred to the natives plus subsistence use of other lands and a cash settlement. Jackson As chairman of the Senate Committee on

Interior and Insular Affairs was in a key position and AFN was worried that his bill might pass.

Publicity efforts of the AFN and the Association on American Indian Affairs had secured support for AFN proposals by national media. AFN also secured the services of Arthur J. Goldberg, a former Justice of the Supreme Court, and Ramsey Clark, former U.S. Attorney General.

However, Keith Miller, the new governor of Alaska replacing Hickel, was opposed to the 40 million acre transfer and the mineral revenue sharing proposal as were many business interests in Alaska. In April 1970 Jackson's committee reported his bill with a compensation award of $1 billion, revenue sharing for a limited number of years, and approximately 10 million acres. Alaska's new senator, Ted Stevens, supported the Jackson bill.

Alaska had requested the courts to reject Udall's land freeze. The lower courts had supported the Interior Department freeze and in 1970 the Supreme Court declined to review the lower court's decision. Without the pressure of the land freeze the chances of a settlement would have dimmed.

Not only had AFN obtained able counsel but it secured the necessary funds to carry on the battle without which they would surely have had to settle for less. The Yakima Indian Nation loaned AFN $225,000 in 1970. Up to this time the Tyonek loan of $100,000 and voluntary donations had been their sole support. AFN was in the big league and resources were necessary to operate effectively in taking advantage of the various pressures to maximize results for the Alaska Natives. The National Congress of American Indians gave full support to AFN, and the Alaska elections in 1970 put William A. Egan in the governor's chair and Nick Begich became Alaska's congressman, both more amenable to the Native position.

Three bills were introduced in the early days of the 92nd Congress in 1971: AFN's bill providing full title to 60 million acres, initial payment of $500 million, perpetual sharing in minerals from lands given up, and establishment of regional corporations; Senator Henry Jackson's bill which had passed the Senate in 1970; and Chairman of the House Committee on Interior and Insular Affairs Wayne Aspinal's bill providing for Native ownership of about 100,000 acres, subsistence use of other lands on a permit basis, and administration of the settlement through a state agency on which Natives would be represented. With the chairmen of the responsible committees in the House and Senate against the AFN proposals, prospects looked poor. However, pressure from the oil companies, favorable testimony from the new Alaskan governor and congressman, and effective presentation and followup by AFN and its lobbyists, resulted in a Nixon special message in April recommending: 40 million acres to the Natives, $500 million in compensation from the Federal treasury, and another $500 million from mineral revenues.

With pressure upon Congressmen growing from the Native lobby, oil interests, and the Nixon administration, there was increasing agreement that a settlement had to be achieved. Begich called together AFN president Don Wright, Aspinall's staff assistant, and Alaska Attorney General John Havelock, and agreement was reached on the specific terms of the settlement. 8

The House Subcommittee bill contained provisions closely paralleling the administration proposal and, after a fight with environmentalists on the floor, passed the House. The Senate, observing the House action, upped its ante, providing more compensation, but a different number and arrangement for the Native corporations that were to administer the settlement. The Conference Committee report was adopted by both houses. President Nixon asked AFN if the bill was satisfactory to the Natives, and at a meeting on December 16, 1971, 600 delegates met in Anchorage and voted to accept the settlement and the President signed the bill.

The Alaska Claims Settlement Act of December 18, 1971,9 is 29 pages long and very complex, but essentially followed the main AFN recommendations and the administration proposal: title to 40 million acres, compensation of $962.5 million, and authorization of 12 regional corporations. 10

AFN did not stop there. It participated actively in the 1976 amendments, often referred to as the Omnibus Act of 1976, which provided, among other things, for: the late enrollment of certain Natives; the establishment of escrow accounts for income from lands withdrawn for Native selection so that pertinent income would go to the corporations when land was finally transferred; authorized mergers within regions of village corporations with each other or with the regional corporation [subject to the laws of the state]; and authorized the consolidation of ownership by agreement among the U.S., the Native region, and the state in some instances. 11 Special provisions for Klukwan were provided on October 4, 1976. 12 Further amendments in 1977 provided additional criteria for selection and conveyance of land in southeastern Alaska and authorized regional corporations to assign their rights to income from the Alaska Native Fund. 13

AFN was also active in the consideration of the Alaska National Interest Lands Conservation Act of December 2, 1980 14 designating additions to national parks, national forest, national wild and scenic rivers, and national wilderness preservation systems in the state of Alaska. One of the key purposes stated in this act was "to provide the opportunity for rural residents engaged in a subsistence way of life to continue to do so." Title VIII dealt with subsistence uses of the withdrawn areas and Title IX contained additional provisions for implementation of the Alaska Native Claims Settlement Act and the Alaska Statehood Act, and Title XIV provided desirable and clarifying amendments to the Alaska Native Claims Settlement Act.

AFN Internal Struggles

The various Native groups were not all of one mind on the provisions desired in the AFN proposal for settlement. For example, the Arctic Slope group opposed the majority's view of distribution of land and money obtained in the settlement on the basis of a region's population. Arctic Slope executive director Charles Edwardsen, Jr. termed the majority view as "welfare legislation," and insisted that benefits be divided on the basis of a region's land area. A compromise was finally hammered out and the AFN agreed to the Arctic Slope argument. As President Joseph Upickson of the Arctic Slope Native Association said: "We realize each of you has pride in his own land. By an accident of nature, right now the eyes of the nation and the world are centered on the North Slope. . .without intending to belittle your land, the real reason for the entire settlement is oil, which by accident is on our land, not yours."[15]

Analysis

Differences from the Lower 48 States

Based on the request of Alaska Natives the Alaska Native Claims Settlement Act provides that the settlement should be accomplished "without establishing any permanent racially defined institutions" and "without creating a reservation system or lengthy wardship or trusteeship, and without adding to the categories of property and institutions enjoying special tax privileges. . . ."

One Native view was expressed by Sam Kito, executive vice president of Doyon, Ltd., in 1973:

> The Native people of Alaska have long been victims of an archaic bureaucratic philosophy that they are unable to regulate their own affairs. Yet the Government who 'sees all, knows all' and 'knows what is best for its Indian people' has been the progenitor of a trustee system of stewardship over American Native peoples, which has succeeded only in robbing them of their heritage, divorcing them from their culture, made them outcasts in their own land, and left them naught but apathy, alcohol, and forgotten graves.[16]

Both Natives and non-Natives were opposed to reservations in Alaska authorized by the extension of Indian Reorganization Act (IRA) authority to Alaska in .1936. [17] Only seven reservations were established between 1941 and 1946. However, because the influx of non-Natives during World War II threatened their subsistence economy, by 1950 "80 additional villages had submitted petitions to the Secretary requesting reservations of 100 million acres." No action was taken and Arnold reports that "The likely reason for inaction was that public opinion in the 1950s seemed opposed to reservations and what they represented: racial segregation and discrimination." [18]

In cooperation with the state of Alaska the AFN supported a state Lands Claims Task Force, chaired by Willie Hensley and with participation by leaders of Native organizations. One of the three recommendations in its report in 1968 was that the settlement of Native land claims "be carried out by business corporations organized by villages, regions, and by one which would be statewide." [19]

As noted earlier, the Alaska Native Brotherhood (ANB) sought participation in the life of the state, not isolation, and in 1924 William L. Paul, a Tlingit attorney and an active member of ANB. was the first Native to be elected to the Alaska House of Representatives. [20] Other natives followed, and as noted, three leaders of the new AFN were elected to the state legislature shortly after organizing.

The U.S. House of Representatives Subcommittee [after the meeting between Begich, Don Wright, Aspinal's staff assistant, and John Havelock in 1971, noted earlier] reported a bill on August 3, 1971, incorporating "the concept of regional corporations sought by the AFN." [21]

Thus a new direction was set and incorporated in the final act. Land is owned in fee simple title. A corporate structure under the laws of the state of Alaska is the vehicle for managing both the land and the money obtained in the settlement.

Influence of Native Population in Alaska

Natives are a higher percentage of the total population in Alaska than is the case in the lower 48 states. In 1880 there were only 430 non-Natives and 33,000 Natives, almost 100 percent Native. In 1970 there were approximately 52,000 Natives and 250,000 non-Natives, or approximately 17 percent. In 1980 there were 64,000 Natives according to the 1980 census out of a total of 400,000 population for the state, or approximately 16 percent. New Mexico's 8.2 percent Indian population is the highest in the lower 48. As Arnold points out, in the rural parts of Alaska the Natives are generally the majority.

The regional corporation enrollments as of June 30, 1978, were higher than the 1980 census figure, for a total of 78,400—including 4000 Natives in the Thirteenth Regional Corporation who live outside Alaska in other states.

The Natives cooperate with other rural area residents and utilize a "bush caucus" in the state legislature and frequently have considerable bargaining power. If a political candidate is obviously opposed to AFN goals he has a disadvantage to overcome because of the percentage of Native voters. In recent history governors and members of Alaska's Congressional delegation have had short careers if they did not obtain Native support. This is indicative of Native power.

However, with the increase in non-Natives, especially in the cities, there are signs of a lessening of this power. Two recent candidates for the state legislature in Anchorage ran on a platform of opposition to liberal subsistence provisions for Natives and won. They had the backing of sportsmen who wanted more opportunity for hunting as a sport.

Importance of Subsistence Economy

The threat to the subsistence economy of many Natives, posed by the increase in non-Natives and the interest of the business community and the state in exploiting Alaska's vast natural resources, was one of the primary forces causing the Natives to band together in the AFN. "Protection of subsistence opportunities—the theme of the 1977 convention (AFN)—was looming as the largest single issue for Natives in 1978."[22] As indicated earlier, one of the purposes of the Alaska National Interest Lands Conservation Act of December 2, 1980, was to provide for a continued subsistence way of life for rural residents who wished to maintain it. Title VIII, Subsistence Management and Use, contains nine pages and declared the purpose of the title ". . .to provide the opportunity for rural residents engaged in a subsistence way of life to do so," and outlined criteria for subsistence use of lands withdrawn for national forests, parks, and wildlife refuges. Obviously, AFN was still getting its message across in the halls of Congress.

Able Leadership

One of the obvious aspects of the development of Native policy in Alaska is the able leadership of the Native groups and, in turn, in the AFN. The officers of separate area and regional groups did not all see eye to eye in the beginning, but then they recognized that working together was a necessity if they were to protect and enhance the major Native objectives. They hammered out compromises, employed able assistance from the non-Native world, secured necessary funds, and won most of their objectives. It was a phenomenal accomplishment. They used the pressure of the oil companies and the state, with the cooperation of Secretary Udall in imposing a land freeze to get the attention of the White House and Congressional leaders. They helped elect a governor, Egan, and a congressman, Begich, who favored their aims and in particular proved to be an able strategist who assisted in turning the House Subcommittee around to favor AFN proposals. They extracted a promise from Walter Hickel that he would continue Udall's land freeze before they would endorse his nomination as Secretary of the Interior. Without the freeze a large part of their leverage would be lost. Alaska's attempt to get Udall's freeze declared illegal failed in the courts. The merits of the case from the Native point of view were presented effectively.

This, of course, was against almost insurmountable odds. In the beginning both the House and Senate subcommittee chairmen had different and much less generous ideas about settlement; the governor succeeding Hickel, Alaska business interests, and big oil were against the freeze, and generally against a large land settlement as it reduced the options of others in the state. For example, the Alaska Miners' Association stated at a Congressional hearing in Anchorage in 1968 that the Natives had their opportunity under the 1946 Indian Claims Commission Act. If they had not filed before the 1951 deadline of that act, "neither the United States, the State of Alaska, nor any of us here gathered as individuals owes the Natives one acre of ground or one cent of taxpayer's money. . . ." This could easily have provided a rationale to negate the whole Native effort if the Natives had not led the fight supported by many others in key places.

The Future

For the future, the Natives, in the tradition of all special interest groups, may succeed in not only the large land and money settlement already obtained but also continuing or increasing special Federal trust and other services. There are statements in the Omnibus Act of 1976 [23] which may be setting a trend: (1) "The payments and grants authorized under this Act constitute compensation for the extinguishment of claims to land, and shall not be deemed to substitute for any governmental program otherwise available to the Native people of Alaska as citizens of the United States and the State of Alaska;" (2) section 5 provided that the Alaska Native Fund would be held in trust by the Federal government until distributed, and indicated "That nothing in this section shall be construed to create or terminate any trust relationship between the United States and any corporation or individual entitled to receive benefits under the Settlement Act;" (3) section 3 exempted Native Corporations from Federal statutes controlling corporations including SEC oversight through December 31, 1991; (4) section 4 also provides that Settlement Act income is not to be considered in eligibility for food stamps; and (5) section 13 of the act provides that "Until January 1, 1992, stock of any Regional Corporation. . .or any Village Corporation. . .shall not be includable in the gross estate of a decedent" for Internal Revenue Service purposes.

As of November 1981, the Bureau of Indian Affairs had received 29 applications from Native groups for incorporation or organization under the Indian Reorganization Act of 1934 (IRA). Many of the groups are already organized as local governments under Alaska state law; some are also a part of Village Corporations organized under the Settlement Act. The Governor of Alaska has written to the Interior Department about the policy implications of these recent requests and to determine the Interior Department's view. Jurisdictional questions are unavoidably involved and unless some resolution as to a single jurisdictional authority for governmental purposes is developed, the same complications could develop in Alaska as exists in many areas in the Lower 48.

The 1980 Act providing lands for national parks, forests, and wildlife areas, also demonstrated the apparent ease with which the 1971 Settlement Act can be amended and amplified. Title VIII of the 1980 act provides criteria for Native subsistence use of Federally-owned lands, which, of course, limits their use in certain respects by others.

Summary

The Alaska Native Claims policy setting procedure illustrates the actions and influence of elements diagrammed in Figure 2-1. The Alaska Federation of Natives (AFN) was the primary interest group on the Native side, assisted by the Association on American Indian Affairs and the National Congress of American Indians. AFN was also assisted financially by Tyonek, a native village with oil money, and the Yakima Indian Nation from the state of Washington. Arrayed on the other side were business interest groups such as the Alaska Miners' Association, sportsmen, and environmental groups.

Elected officials were on both sides of issues, but as the time for decision grew closer, the Natives helped elect officials as Governor and Congressman who were more favorable to their interests.

The AFN succeeded in getting a good press. The Interior Department through the BIA area office in Anchorage helped in the initial organization efforts of the AFN and clamped on a land freeze that exerted pressure for settling the Native Claims issue. This caused the state and oil interests to urge resolution. The state attempted to cut this pressure by going to court, but the courts supported Interior's land freeze. OEO, as a grassroots advocacy fund, helped to establish Native village organizations in their beginning efforts to fight for a land settlement, although this was not the primary purpose of the funds.

The Natives and the Interior Department with the help of the oil interests got the President's attention. Capable strategy by Alaska's new Representative brought AFN, the state, and the key staff person for the House committee together for an informal meeting with favorable results for AFN. The President sought the concurrence of AFN before he signed the Alaska Native Claims Settlement Act.

The relative influence of the various forces at work is largely a subjective judgment. It is clear that the AFN had able leadership, employed competent advisers, and helped elect supportive officials. AFN played a key role and was supported by other Native groups. Interior's action in stopping land transactions was vital in creating the economic pressures for settlement from the state and big oil. This got everybody's attention. This, in effect, created a sufficient "crisis" to force the Congress and the President to act.

The public perception of this issue as reflected in the press indicated a basic "good will" toward a fair settlement which probably supported a generous rather than a meager settlement. The result was a compromise. Nobody was completely happy, but most believed they could live with the results. This particular policy decision was a major one for the Alaska Natives, the state of Alaska, and the non-Native business interests and individuals directly effected. It also set the stage for the consideration of the Alaska National Interest Lands Conservation Act of December 2, 1980, discussed earlier, by resolving the Native land claims issue.

MAINE INDIAN CLAIMS

History and Background

In 1777, Colonel John Allen, director of the Federal government's Eastern Indian Department, negotiated a treaty with the Maine Indians to obtain their assistance in the Revolutionary War in return for the protection of their lands by the United States and provision of supplies in times of need. This treaty was never ratified and the Federal government did not protect the Indians followng the war. In 1791, the Passamaquoddy Tribe and the Commonwealth of Massachusetts (which had jurisdiction over what is now Maine) entered into an agreement in which the tribe ceded all but 23,000 acres. Subsequent sales and leases by the state of Maine reduced the acreage to about 17,000 acres. The Penobscot Nation through treaties in 1796 and 1818 and a sale in 1833 ceded most of its aboriginal territory.

A Senate Report in 1980 indicated that the validity of these agreements with the tribes was not seriously questioned until 1972. Thus, for nearly 200 years the Indians, the state, and the Federal government were all of the belief that the state had the responsibility for Maine Indians and the Federal government was not involved.

Thomas N. Tureen, an attorney, convinced the Passamaquoddys that the lack of approval by the Federal government of the treaties and agreements with the state (Massachusetts and later Maine) was a violation of the Trade and Intercourse Act of 1790, which, as amended, is now found in 25USC 177.[24] This act required the approval of the United States for any transfer of lands from Indian ownership.

In 1972 the Passamaquoddy Tribe asked the United States to sue the State of Maine on the basis that the treaties and agreements had never been approved by the Federal government. The Secretary of the Interior at the time did not agree and did not sue. He argued that the Trade and Intercourse Act did not apply to nonrecognized tribes and that there was no trust relationship between the United States and the Maine tribes. The tribe went to court. Since the Indians were claiming about two-thirds of the State of Maine this issue was considered critical by the state and its citizens as well as by the Indians. Maine was allowed to intervene in the case. The issues were: (1) whether the Nonintercourse Act applied to the Passamaquoddy Tribe; (2) whether the Act established a trust relationship between the United States and the tribe; and (3) whether the United States could deny the tribe's request for litigation on the sole ground that there is no trust relationship. The District Court ruled in the tribe's favor on all points, holding that the language of the Nonintercourse Act protected the lands of "any. . .tribe of Indians" and that the Passamaquoddy Indians were a tribe.[25]

So too thought the Circuit Court to which the case was appealed.[26] However, the decision was narrowly defined, affirming "that the United States never sufficiently manifested withdrawal of its protection so as to sever any trust relationship. In so ruling, we do not foreclose later consideration of whether Congress or the Tribe should be deemed in some manner to have acquiesced in, or Congress to have ratified, the Tribe's land transactions with Maine."

The state of Maine had maintained that: (1) the Nonintercourse Act "was never intended to apply to the original thirteen colonies after they became states;" (2) that "the Indians transferred the lands in question before the Revolution and thus before 1790;" and (3) that "in ratifying the Articles of Separation, by which Maine was separated from Massachusetts and admitted to the Union in 1820, Congress implicitly approved all treaties concluded by Massachusetts up to that time."[27]

This court action brought about by the Passamaquoddy Tribe forced the Federal Government to act. The President, the Congress, the state, and the tribes were all interested in a more speedy and less costly solution than the judicial route.

Peter Taft, who had been appointed to the Justice Department under President Gerald Ford as an Assistant Attorney General, Interior Solicitor Greg Austin and Timothy A. Vollmann of Austin's staff met at the White

House with members of the White House staff on November 4, 1976. Taft indicated that it looked as if the Maine Indians had a claim. Agreement was reached that an effort should be made to settle the claim by negotiation to avoid the festering, delay, and cost of a judicial settlement.

In March 1977 President Jimmy Carter appointed William Gunter, a retired Georgia Supreme Court Justice, to study the case and make recommendations. Gunter and his staff delved thoroughly into the issue. On July 15, 1977, Justice Gunter recommended to the President:

I have given consideration to the legal merits and demerits of these pending claims. However, my recommendation is not based entirely on my personal assessment in that area. History, economics, social science, justness, and practicality are additional elements that have had some weight in the formulation of my recommendation.

My recommendation to you is that you recommend to the Congress that it resolve this problem as follows:

(1) Appropriate 25 million dollars for the use and benefit of the two tribes, this appropriated amount to be administered by Interior. One half of this amount shall be appropriated in each of the next two fiscal years.

(2) Require the State of Maine to put together and convey to the United States, as trustee for the two tribes, a tract of land consisting of 100,000 acres within the claims area. As stated before, the State reportedly has in its public ownership in the claims area in excess of 400,000 acres.

(3) Assure the two tribes that normal Bureau of Indian Affairs benefits will be accorded to them by the United States in the future.

(4) Request the State of Maine to continue to appropriate in the future on an annual basis state benefits for the tribes at the equivalent level of the average annual appropriation over the current and preceding four years.

(5) Require the Secretary of Interior to use his best efforts to acquire long-term options on an additional 400,000 acres of land in the claims area. These options would be exercised at the election of the tribes, the option-price paid would be fair market value per acre, and tribal funds would be paid for the exercise of each option.

(6) Upon receiving the consent of the State of Maine that it will accomplish what is set forth in numbered paragraphs (2) and (4) above, the Congress should then, upon obtaining tribal consent to accept the benefits herein prescribed, by statutory enactment extinguish all aboriginal title, if any, to all lands in Maine and also extinguish all other claims that these two tribes may now have against

any party arising out of an alleged violation of the Indian Nonintercourse Act of 1790 as amended.

(7) If tribal consent cannot be obtained to what is herein proposed, then the Congress should immediately extinguish all aboriginal title, if any, to all lands within the claims area except that held in the public ownership by the State of Maine. The tribes' cases could then proceed through the courts to a conclusion against the state-owned land. If the tribes win their cases, they recover the state-owned land; but if they lose their cases, they recover nothing. However, in the meantime, the adverse economic consequences will have been eliminated and Interior and Justice will have been relieved from pursuing causes of action against private property owners to divest them of title to land that has heretofore been considered valid title.

(8) If the consent of the State of Maine cannot be obtained for what is herein proposed, then the Congress should appropriate 25 million dollars for the use and benefit of the tribes (see paragraph numbered (1)), should then immediately extinguish all aboriginal title, if any, and all claims arising under an alleged violation of the 1790 Act as amended, to all lands within the claims area except those lands within the public ownership of the State. The tribes' cases could then proceed through the courts against the state-owned land. If the tribes win their cases they recover the land; but if they lose their cases they recover nothing against the state of Maine. However, in the meantime, they will have received 25 million dollars from the United States for their consent to eliminate economic stagnation in the claims area, and their consent to relieve Interior and Justice from pursuing causes of action against private property owners to divest them of land titles that have heretofore been considered valid.

It is my hope that the Congress can resolve this problem through the implementation of numbered paragraphs (1) through (6) above. Paragraphs (7) and (8) are mere alternatives to be utilized in the event consensual agreement cannot be obtained. [28]

This recommendation required negotiation and the President immediately appointed a negotiating team for the government consisting of Eliot Cutler, Associate Director of the Office of Management and Budget for Energy, Natural Resources and Science; Leo Krulitz, Solicitor of the Department of the Interior; and A. Stephens Clay, Judge Gunter's law partner. Negotiations between this work group and the tribes produced an agreement between the tribes and the administration in February 1978. In essence it proposed extinguishment of all tribal claims for parcels of land under 50,000 acres for a monetary payment of $25 million. This would have cleared title to an estimated 9.2 million acres of the 12.5 million acres claimed. This agreement left the big landowners, about 14 in number, and the state of Maine subject to suit and they would have to defend themselves in court. After several months, Attorney General Griffin Bell said he believed all owners should be treated alike which torpedoed the recommendation.

Meanwhile, other people seeking solutions to the Maine land problem had been active. In 1977 Senator William S. Cohen of Maine introduced a bill to extinguish the claim of aboriginal right asserted by the Penobscot and Passamaquoddy Indians. The purpose was to remove the cloud over real estate in Maine, and also to authorize court action to review whether or not a wrong had been done and damages were due. In his remarks in the *Congressional Record*, Senator Cohen made the following points, among others:

1. Maine had abided by its treaties with the tribes, and the tribes never questioned their validity, substance, or adequacy until five years before.

2. There is no equitable way of forcing the return of land which had been "settled, developed and improved in good faith by Maine people for two centuries."

3. One solution would be for the Federal government "to guarantee" state and local bonds and land transactions; however, OMB and Congress would not "be eager to undertake a contingent liability of undefined proportions." It would also set a precedent for other states with land claims.

4. Another solution was "that if the claim by the two tribes can remain viable for over 180 years, then it follows that Congress retains the power to ratify and confirm the very treaties which the tribes now claim are null and void." This, of course, would have resolved the issue.

Senator Cohen concluded: "Surely if the passage of time cannot bar the Indian tribes' complaint, then it follows that it cannot bar congressional review and ratification of the treaties if Congress finds they were properly negotiated at the time and were free from fraud and unfairness."[29]

Congressman Lloyd Meeds, Vice Chairman of the American Indian Policy Review Commission and Chairman of the House Subcommittee on Indian Affairs, recommended that Congress "adopt legislation that extinguishes for all time all tribal or Indian claims to interests in real property, possessory or otherwise, grounded on aboriginal possession alone. Indian lands held under treaty, statute, Executive order or deed would not be affected."[30] No compensation would be due under the 5th Amendment for such extinguishment.

This recommendation by Meeds made in May 1977 was stimulated by the Maine land claims. He emphasized that claims based on aboriginal possession cannot be asserted against the United States: Indian title is not good against the sovereign; the Nonintercourse Acts are not applicable to the United States; and all pre-1946 claims not brought before the Indian Claims Commission prior to 1951 were barred by section 12 of the Claims Commission Act. [31]

Meeds pointed out that entities such as states do not have similar protection as the United States against "ancient and stale Indian claims based on aboriginal possession." Thus the Maine Indians sought the aid of the United States in suing the state of Maine for violation of the Non-Intercourse Acts. Meeds recommended also "the enactment of a statute of limitations that all such claims not yet reduced to judgment shall be forever barred." As to morality, Meeds stated:

> Neither the Passamaquoddys whose possessory rights may have been interferred with, nor the people of the State of Maine or Massachusetts who may have dealt with them in the absence of a Federal treaty, are now alive. There is nothing unfair about denying the descendents of the Passamaquoddys a windfall and preventing the imposition of a bizarre and unjust burden on the descendents of the people of the States of Maine and Massachusetts.
>
> It seems to me that this is the correct solution because history clearly shows that the tribes for almost 200 years acquiesced in their land transactions with Maine and that the Congress had ratified Maine's and Massachusett's actions. [32]

In March 1978 the American Land Title Association (ALTA) issued a memorandum stating that Congress had the authority to (1) approve the transfer of lands made by the tribe as of the date of the transfer, (2) extinguish Indian title as of the date of the transfers, and (3) extinguish any claims for trespass. ALTA indicated that Congress might compensate the Indians for the extinguishment of claims. [33]

In opposition to proposals such as those made by Cohen, Meeds, and ALTA, Indian advocates contended that such action would constitute a taking of property without just compensation. Large claims would be filed as a result. ALTA, however, maintained that Congress could extinguish Indian aboriginal title without liability, and cited *Tee-Hit-Ton Indians v. United States*. [34]

This policy issue for other states continued to be debated in Congress when this book went to press in connection with proposed ALTA-type legislation to settle aboriginal land claims. The ALTA bill was not favored by either the House or Senate Committees in 1978 and was never subject to hearings.

Negotiation

The Gunter recommendation had an effect on subsequent negotiations. The pressure for a negotiated settlement was not only the result of the desire to avoid a costly and drawn-out judicial process over a long period of time and the economic stagnation that would be involved pending the outcome, but there was also the threat of Gunter's options (7) and (8) which closely paralleled some of the suggestions of Cohen, Meeds and ALTA. Since these options were regarded as undesirable by the Indians and the state, they were undoubtedly a factor in encouraging serious negotiation.

Since the Federal agencies were not coordinated and had been unable to come up with any proposal to which both the state and the tribes could agree, the Indians and the state took action. The result was a state act for implementing the settlement of the Indian claims approved by the governor on April 3, 1980. This state act was contingent on the enactment by the Federal government of legislation to extinguish the Indians' claims and provide the necessary funds, as well as provision for the "ratifying and approving this Act without modification" by the Federal government.

State and Indian representatives brought this state legislation to Washington and presented it to the White House, the Secretary of the Interior, the Office of Management and Budget, and the Committees on Capitol Hill. The first formal meeting took place in late June 1980, in Washington. There were differences between Senate Committee staff and others. Those representing the Federal government did not appreciate the "take it or leave it" attitude of the state and the Indians. It was reported that the meeting ended on a bitter note. Those involved from time to time in this and other meetings were: Timothy C. Woodcock and Peter Taylor from the Senate Select Committee on Indian Affairs; Thomas N. Tureen and Suzanne Harjo from the Native American Rights Fund; Barbara Cohen of the Justice Department; Maine Attorney General Richard Cohen; James St. Clair, Special Counsel for Maine; John Paterson from the Maine Attorney General's office; Dave Flanagan from the Governor's Office; John Hull, Legislative Counsel for the State Legislature of Maine; Bonny Post, Chairperson of Indian Affairs Committee of the state legislature; Reid Chambers for the Houlton Band of Maliseets; and Timothy A. Vollman of the Interior Department's Solicitor's Office. Also involved in sessions from time to time were Senators Cohen, Mitchell and Melcher, officials of the Office of Management and Budget and members of the House Committee on Interior and Insular Affairs.

A July 10, 1980 meeting in Portland, Maine, had representatives from Interior, Justice, the State of Maine, the Maine legislature, the Senate Select Committee on Indian Affairs, legal counsel to the private land owners, and special counsel to the State of Maine. According to Peter Taylor, the July 10 meeting "may well have been the most important. We spent an entire day reviewing the bill, exchanging views. Out of that meeting everyone realized agreement was possible and that everyone genuinely wanted a settlement. From that point on we all pulled in harness and worked diligently toward solutions."35

The general procedure during the ten or so meetings through September 10, 1980, was to discuss the issues and agree on adjustments. Tim Vollmann, from the Department of the Interior, assumed the redrafting responsibility all the way through these sessions and clearly was a key person.

The issues that were the most difficult to resolve were: (1) the extent to which Federal support would supplant the support the state would normally give the tribes as a result of their status as municipalities under the new state law; the exchange of correspondence on this issue was made a part of the record (some discussion of the accommodation reached is presented in Chapter 4); (2) the benefits, if any, to the Houlton Band of Maliseet—the bill presented to Congress would have extinguished any claim it might have but would not have provided trust status for the land involved; this issue was not resolved until the final drafting sessions; and (3) the date upon which Indian claims would be extinguished—the date of the Act or the date Congress appropriated money to implement the Act; the latter date was finally put in the bill.

Analysis

Settlement of the Maine Land Claims demonstrated the interactions of Indian tribes, attorneys, outside interest groups, courts, the state, Maine land owners, Interior, Justice, OMB, the President, an outside consultant (Gunter) and the Congress. BIA was not an active participant.

President Carter at the signing of the Maine Indian Claims Settlement Act of 1980 on October 10 stated:

> It's a reaffirmation that our system of government works. A hundred and ninety years after the Passamaquoddy and Penobscot Indians and Maine settlers fought side by side to protect Maine's borders, to help defend all thirteen colonies in the Revolutionary War, the people of Maine have again shown themselves to be an example to us all, by working together, by acting with patience and fairness and understanding. This should be a proud day for. . .the tribes who placed their trust in the system that has not always treated them fairly, the leaders of the state of Maine who came openly to the bargaining table, the landowners who helped make the settlement a reality by offering land for sale that they might not otherwise have wanted to sell, the members of Congress who realize the necessity of

acting and all the citizens of Maine who have worked together to resolve this problem of land title.[36]

However it took a great deal of pushing, crisis creating, compromise and hard work to achieve this result. As at the Constitutional Convention in Philadelphia, nobody was completely happy. Many involved in the Maine claims case undoubtedly thought they should have done better for themselves.

The Indians and their attorneys, assisted by the courts, created an action-forcing situation. The Federal government had to sue the state or change the law. There were proponents of both courses. Evidently it would have been legal to follow the suggestions of Cohen, Meeds and ALTA. This approach had the apparent advantage of a speedy removal of the cloud on land title which would eliminate that barrier to free economic activity. Depending on the wording of the legislation, it could also have provided for compensation to be determined through the courts. It is, of course, impossible to predict what might have been the end result of this process in terms of costs and benefits to the Indians and the state. This approach, however, might have turned out to be poor public relations, with a potential for leaving bitter feelings between two groups of Maine citizens. Undoubtedly Justice Gunter considered the social, economic, and political aspects of this case in arriving at his recommendations. Writing in 1979 before the settlement, Vollmann, in support of negotiation rather than unilateral action, stated that if the ALTA or Meeds concept were to approach enactment

> . . .the affected tribes may well seek to unite with the national Indian leadership and its allies, and take all political steps necessary to defeat it. Indeed, Indian leaders are likely to view such a battle as a struggle to the death, characterizing the legislation as a perverse culmination of 200 ill-starred years of Federal Indian policy, as a proclamation of a new rule that courts of law are accessible to all but Indian land claimants, and as a classic example of the principle that "might makes right." Such an ugly confrontation is unnecessary.[37]

Had not the President or the Secretary of the Interior Department taken the lead in seeking a consensus, a long and costly court process or unilateral action by the Congress might have resulted. However, President Carter seized the initiative by appointing Justice Gunter, and followed up Gunter's recommendations by appointing a team to represent the Federal government in negotiations with the Indians and the state. This, in effect, forced the Indians and the state to negotiate.

Nobody likes to recede from a pre-announced position, but the state and the Indians did so, as did the Federal government in agreeing to modification of Gunter's recommendations. In the background was the possibility of resorting to Gunter's options (7) and (8). The concepts involved in these options had strong supporters (Meeds, Cohen, ALTA, among others) and the Indians and the state knew this. The Indians or the state were aware that if they appeared to be unreasonable in the negotiation process, they would greatly strengthen the hand of the proponents of either unilateral action to extinguish alleged aboriginal rights or the payment of an indemnity without any return of land. The state also had the economic pressure of needing to clear land titles and thus wanted a speedy resolution. The negotiating team for the Federal government knew that the president wanted a consensus solution that would not be too costly to the Federal treasury. If it were too expensive, the Congress probably would not go along.

All of these factors, plus the generally pro-Indian attitude of a large segment of the U.S. citizenry, played a part in forcing the consensus. Further, if the negotiators had not been skillful, the whole effort could have come to naught. But the environment made it possible for the negotiators of all three parties to succeed in developing a workable compromise.

Had the president opted to support abrogation of aboriginal rights or "approval after the fact" of the land transfers between the tribes and the state, he might have succeeded in getting Congress to take this approach. Had the courts put a different interpretation on the Nonintercourse Act, ruling that it did not apply to non-Federally recognized Indians or to the original thirteen states, there would have been no action-forcing situation created, since this would have affirmed the belief of the state of Maine and the Interior Department. So the courts played an important part, too, in determining this particular policy outcome. Indian matters within each state under the Articles of Confederation were the responsibility of each state. Thus, it is easy to see how the Federal government and the states along the eastern seaboard arrived at policies for Indians different from those in the western states where the states were established after the adoption of the U.S. Constitution with its specific Indian provisions.

The Maine Indian Claims Settlement Act of 1980 resolved the Maine case. But it did not resolve at one stroke old aboriginal land claims issues arising in other states on the fulcrum of the Trade and Intercourse Act. Meeds had sought this result. It did set a precedent which may influence the resolution of other cases.[38]

THE TRAIL OF BROKEN TREATIES, WOUNDED KNEE, AND THE LONGEST WALK

Three events in the 1970s illustrate the influence of a militant minority, the reactions of governmental institutions, the participation of interest groups, and the power that anticipation of public reaction has on decisions.

The Trail of Broken Treaties

The stated purpose of the leaders of the Trail of Broken Treaties meeting on October 2, 1971 in Denver, Colorado, was to bring national attention to the conditions of the native peoples, and included seven points: (1) the fulfillment of treaty obligations; (2) moral and legal fulfillment of trust responsibility for Indian lands and resources, and the rights of individual Indians; (3) the placement of Indian affairs directly under the President; (4) no termination of Federal service for any Indian group without referendum; (5) appropriated funds increased to the same level as for the rest of American society; (6) a special law "guaranteeing education at the highest level for every Indian who wishes to attain it;" and (7) both presidential candidates meet with the Trail leaders and pledge adherence to the previous six objectives.[39]

Reportedly supporting the Trail of Broken Treaties in August 1972 were: the National Congress of American Indians; the National Council on Indian Work; the American Indian Movement; National Indian Leadership Training; the Native American Legal Defense and Education Fund; the National Indian Lutheran Board; the National Indian Brotherhood (Canada); the National Indian Youth Council; the Native American Rights Fund; the National American Indian Council; the American Indian Commission on Alcohol and Drug Abuse; Americans for Indian Opportunity; the Native American Women's Action Council; United Native Americans; and the Coalition of Indian Controlled School Boards.[40] On October 18, 1972 the National Congress of American Indians (NCAI) Convention declined to endorse the Trail group. How many of those listed who actually endorsed the effort is not known. The American Indian Movement (AIM) turned out to be the dominant participant.

Members of many different tribes participated in the Trail of Broken Treaties Caravan, a march on Washington. Only one tribal chairman, Trail Co-Chairman Robert Burnett of Rosebud, was involved and he renounced the Trail effort after it commandeered the BIA building, destroyed property, and defied the police and the government.

After the Trail group arrived in Washington, D.C., Bradley Patterson, who worked with Leonard Garment in the White House, and Robert Robertson, Executive Director of the National Council on Indian Opportunity, and Harrison Loesch, Assistant Secretary of Interior responsible for Indian Affairs, met with Trail leaders in Secretary Loesch's office on the evening of November 2, 1972. The Indians refused to talk with Loesch present, so he left. In effect, he was forced from his own office.[41]

The Indians decided to stay in the building (BIA) that night. The Interior Department wanted to eject the Indians by force if necessary if they would not leave voluntarily on the afternoon or evening of November 2. But the White House was concerned. As stated by Bradley Patterson:

> White House officials. . .apprehensive at the heavy use of force which would be required to oust the group (which included women and children), favored restraint and negotiations. The AIM bunch, unrepresentative though it was of Indian leaders, had managed to get into a position where it was staging guerilla theater at a strategic time and place, and the White House knew the whole world was the audience. They overruled Interior, decided to use the route of going to the Federal courts for an eviction order. . .;restraint and negotiations with the Trail leaders took priority over the use of police power.[42]

The Trail leaders sought to meet with the President and did succeed in meeting with several high officials during the 7-day occupation.

On November 6, during the occupation, Secretary of the Interior Rogers C.B. Morton released a statement, saying ". . .all Americans should understand that the protestors are a small splinter group of militants. They do not represent the reservation Indians of America." Morton said that every effort had been made to cooperate with the advance men of the Trail group, including the location of temporary housing, and a list of 20 demands was received "with the promise to study them carefully." He continued: "It is obvious to me that the seizure and continued occupation of the building are nothing more than a form of blackmail by a small group who seek to achieve through violence objectives which are not supported by a majority of reservation Indians."

The Secretary noted: "Doors have been ripped off and office machinery destroyed through use as barricades. A large quantity of furniture has been destroyed beyond repair to make clubs for use as weapons. Priceless and in many cases irreplaceable Indian art and artifacts have been destroyed, or unlawfully taken. . . .it is a shame that a small willful band of malcontents should attempt to wreck the headquarters of the Government's chief instrument for serving the Indian Community."[43]

The aftermath of the occupation resulted in the firing of Interior Department officials, relocation of BIA offices, final recovery of most of the stolen land records of vital importance to Indians on trust land, Congressional hearings, and an unknown impact on official and general public attitudes. The cost figure of the ransacking of the BIA headquarters was set at about $2.3 million by General Services Administration (GSA). The government paid $66,650 to the Caravan to help finance the return home.[44]

The Trail's 20-point position paper, an expansion of the seven goals originally stated, was reviewed by an Interagency Task Force co-chaired by Leonard Garment of the White House and Frank Carlucci of the Office of Management and Budget. The principal negotiator for the Trail group, Hank Adams, indicated that the Administration's response to the 20 points was "virtually devoid of positive content and reflects the hostile attitude which Federal agencies and officials have maintained against independent and creative Indian thought, expressions and proposals. . . ."[45]

Review of the Trail's 20 points, the response of the Administration Task Force and comments on the Administration's reply by Hank Adams is fascinating reading and indicates that the two parties were far apart. Space prevents a complete analysis but Point One will be used as an illustration.

Point One requested the restoration of constitutional treaty-making authority so that Indian nations could again become sovereign political entities which would contract treaties with the United States.

The Task Force response explained that Congress by law had stopped all treaty-making with Indians over 100 years ago and in 1924 all Indians became citizens of the United States and of the states in which they resided. "The citizenship relationship with one's government and the treaty relationship are mutually exclusive; a government makes treaties with foreign nations, not with its own citizens."

The Trail reply to the above maintained that the 1924 Indian Citizenship Act preserved the right to tribal citizenship, and quoted the following:

> BE IT ENACTED BY THE SENATE AND THE HOUSE OF REPRESENTATIVES OF THE UNITED STATES OF AMERICA IN CONGRESS ASSEMBLED, That all non-citizen Indians born within the territorial limits of the United States be, and they are hereby, declared to be citizens of the United States: PROVIDED, That the granting of such citizenship shall not in any manner impair or otherwise affect the right of any Indian to tribal or other property. Approved, June 2, 1924, 68th Congress, Session 1, Chapter 233.

The Trail response continued:

> The right to maintain tribal property in common is a citizenship right of a tribal member (*Choate v. Trapp*), and for the Task Force to maintain that a treaty relationship is incompatible with citizenship is legally incorrect since treaties are signed with Indian tribes, not Indian individuals. The point made by the Trail of Broken Treaties is that treaty-making should be restored to Indian tribes, not to extend it to Indian individuals. [46]

The reader can make up his or her mind on this point.

Reactions from other Indians varied. Mrs. Genevieve Hooper, Secretary of the Yakima Tribal Council, representing the tribal chairmen, made the following points on November 6: The Administration is "reacting and responding to self-styled Indian leaders who have no license to speak for reservation people. . . . We have overwhelming evidence that reservation Indians do not now approve, condone, or support the present disruption which has been caused by the caravan. . . ." Mrs. Hooper continued: "Right now, there are front page negotiations going on, but significantly without the participation of elected reservation leaders." She continued: ". . .BIA has literally been destroyed in three years" under Commissioner Louis Bruce and the emphasis is on non-reservation militant Indians who "generally do not make responsible demands and they concern themselves mainly with the hysteria of unrest, militancy, etc."[47]

Charles E. Trimble, executive director of the National Congress of American Indians (NCAI) on November 10, 1972, stated in part: "The National Congress of American Indians has never encouraged, condoned, or participated in tactics of disruption or destruction. . . ." Trimble particularly expressed his constituency's abhorrence at the "destruction and loss of the valuable, irreplaceable records relating to reservation economic development, enrollment of tribal members, land protection. . . ." However, Trimble then went on to praise the objectives of the Caravan (Trail group) and indicated that NCAI had attempted to "enlist the cooperation of the Indian organizations and the government agencies. . ." but that these attempts failed "largely due to the apathy of the government agencies. . . ." Trimble charged that "in the most sinister atmosphere imaginable, the Interior Department, the Bureau of Land Management, in conjunction with the Vice President's own National Council on Indian Opportunity, is working clandestinely to muster tribal leaders for the defense of the administration."[48]

On November 10, only five hours after Trimble's statement, Webster Two Hawk, president of the National Tribal Chairmen's Association (NTCA), made a statement. Following are some of the highlights: The Board of Directors of the National Tribal Chairmen's Association (NTCA) recognized that many who participated in the Caravan (Trail group) did so in good faith but were betrayed by their leaders, who were described as "ruthless, self-seeking, self-appointed," and who turned the Caravan into an "orgy of wanton, senseless destruction."

NTCA believed that "had affirmative and timely steps been taken" the "initial occupation" and "subsequent senseless destruction and theft of valuable tribal records" could have been avoided. The NTCA board "strongly rejects the recognition and support of this and other dissident groups who claim to represent reservation people and Federally recognized tribes by leaders of the Bureau of Indian Affairs and calls for the immediate dismissal. of those who recognize and support such groups." Federal negotiations should be carried out with responsible elected tribal leadership.

NCTA further demanded "immediate investigation. . .of all sources of funding, whether Indian or non-Indian for Indian groups that use intimidation and threat of violence." Contracts with such groups should be terminated. "During the course of the invasion of the Bureau of Indian Affairs building, the lives and safety of some of the tribal leaders were threatened by members of the dissident group. The use of force and duress must not be condoned. . . ." NTCA stressed that the "very appearance of any such condonation would have serious repercussions for elected tribal leaders in the peaceful and orderly path to progress. . . ."

The NTCA statement concluded:

> Finally, the Board wishes to make it clearly understood that it recognizes the problems that exist in achieving progress and bringing to Indian peoples the fruits of American society enjoyed by other American citizens. We are working for that goal and will continue in our programs and operations. There have been many injustices in the past. The Indians have suffered much. Many of the problems mentioned by the dissident group do exist. We recognized those problems and are working toward their solutions. However, senseless, near treasonable acts of destruction and violence will not serve to accomplish any good end. It is our desire to work peacefully with the United States Government and the various segments of American society in order that together we might bring peace and prosperity not only to the Indian peoples, but to all Americans.[49]

The White House's main concern was to avoid the temptation to engage in an upward spiral of violence or to overreact, as the Ohio guardsmen had done at Kent State 30 months before. Direct, positive, and high level attention was being given to Indian matters as followup to President Nixon's Indian message to the Congress on July 8, 1970. Bradley Patterson's analysis of the irony of the Trail of Broken Treaties is presented in Appendix D.

The BIA closedown probably would not have occurred if the event had not taken place just before the 1972 presidential election. Any attempt to evict the AIM group by force after November 2 would almost certainly have resulted in bloodshed. Since the White House indicated it would not use force on November 2, the Indian militants seized their opportunity and dug in. Some Interior and National Tribal Chairmen's Association officials believed that a firm position the afternoon of November 2 would have persuaded the Indians to leave and thus have avoided the takeover of the BIA building.

The media had a field day. The Indians called on church groups and others for food donations, press interviews were held, TV screens throughout the nation flashed pictures of a small band of Indians holding the U.S. Government at bay.

Wounded Knee

On February 27, 1973, approximately 200 armed men, members and supporters of the American Indian Movement, broke into buildings, including private homes, took hostages, destroyed property, committed armed assault and stole property, according to a court of claims opinion.[50] Many of the leaders of the Trail of Broken Treaties were involved in this seizure of Wounded Knee, a small town of about 400 persons on the Pine Ridge Reservation in South Dakota. Although some of the occupying Indians were residents of the Pine Ridge Indian Reservation or members of the Oglala Sioux Tribe, many were not and came from various tribes. According to Wilcomb Washburn this was a "planned, artificially staged, media event. xxxThe ringing name of Wounded Knee evoked memories of a historical tragedy—the massacre of 200 Indians in 1890 by the U.S. Cavalry. . . . The site—complete with a steepled white church sitting on a bare ridge—provided a ready-made Hollywood set for television reporters who flocked to cover the event."[51]

The Federal government reacted promptly and assigned some 300 U.S. marshals, FBI agents, and BIA police to circle the hamlet and contain the disorder. "A decision was made by the Federal officers to attempt to end the occupation through peaceful negotiations with the occupiers. This decision was both humanitarian and reasonable, as an armed assault by the Federal officers would undoubtedly have resulted in casualties among the innocent victims of the occupation, as well as among the assaulting force and the armed men unlawfully occupying Wounded Knee."[52] Negotiations were finally successful and the occupation ended 71 days after it began.

D'Arcy McNickle interprets the Trail of Broken Treaties and Wounded Knee episodes as the result of the Indian frustration with their lot due to two centuries of Indian policy that almost destroyed them as a people. He says "The anger that exploded in Washington and at Wounded Knee had its kindling point in the acts of the Eighty-third Congress (1953-54), by which two major tribes and several lesser Indian communities were destroyed."[53] McNickle was referring to Menominee and Klamath as the major tribes. However, Menominee was not destroyed. It became a Wisconsin county, and is now, again, a Federally recognized tribe. Klamath, as well as Menominee, had voted for termination. The Klamaths, terminated from trust and other special

>

Federal services by an act passed in 1954, had had a choice of continuing under a private trust or selling their assets and taking their pro rata shares in cash. Twenty-two percent did not sell their assets, but did vote to do so 10 years later.

These decisions by the Indians themselves can hardly be laid at the feet of the American people and government policy as McNickle does. The first sale resulted in a pro rata share of about $45,000. The second sale 10 years later more than doubled that amount per individual. [54] The Commissioner of the Court of Claims stated: "According to the evidence in the record, the occupation of Wounded Knee cannot reasonably be attributed to anything that the Federal Government did which it ought not to have done, or to anything that the Federal Government failed to do which it should have done." The Commissioner continued: "The innocent victims of the occupation of Wounded Knee are in the same category as thousands of other persons in the country who each year, unfortunately and sometimes tragically, suffer personal injuries or property damages as the result of the criminal activities of lawless persons."[55]

McNickle was closer to the mark when he analyzed Wounded Knee in relation to the factional conflict within the Oglala Sioux Tribe at Pine Ridge. The Indian Reorganization Act (IRA) constitution adopted in 1935 was opposed by traditionalists. McNickle states that the IRA government placed "Control of tribal affairs in the hands of members who were in part assimilated to the white political system, were often of mixed blood, and were not at home in the Sioux language." In 1973 impeachment proceedings initiated by the opposition failed to oust the then tribal chairman and the traditionalists called upon the American Indian Movement (AIM) for help. [56]

This description of the differences between traditionalists, generally a minority as in the case of Pine Ridge, and the majority, some of whom are mixed blood, raises a question about the thesis of continuing tribalism as put forth by McNickle. Who constitutes the tribe? Who expresses genuine tribalism? Is tribalism in fact, breaking down through miscegenation, impact of white culture, and loss of utility for many persons with some Indian blood?

Wilcomb E. Washburn of the Smithsonian Institution also interprets Wounded Knee as in part a result of the struggle between the "ins" and "outs" and suggests that it symbolized the emergence of an Indian voice which "celebrated separatism instead of integration, political activism instead of dignified acquiescence, repudiation of white goals and values, and rejection of existing tribal organizations." This, says Washburn, has forced a reconsideration of the governments elected under the IRA policies adopted in the 1930s. [57]

McNickle and Washburn may not have given sufficient attention to the largely urban background of many of the AIM leaders. AIM had a cause with which the vast American public appeared sympathetic and thus the group may have gotten away with a great deal of illegal activity and trespassing on the rights of other Indians under the cloak of "helping the Indians."

Wilcomb Washburn has raised the question of the possible destruction of tribal government by Indian radicals and white backlash. Indian radicals attack tribal governments, saying that elected leaders are unrepresentative. As Washburn puts it, "what these spokesmen mean is that they do not like what the majority wants."[58]

The Longest Walk

The Longest Walk was described in a Methodist leaflet:

On February 11, 1978, some 180 Native Americans set out from San Francisco to walk across the continent to Washington, D.C. . . . It grew out of the concern of Indian people for anti-Indian legislation currently before the Congress . . . . If enacted, these bills will take away the responsibility to control their own lives, their own children and their own communities. . . . The Longest Walk is . . . a walk to commemorate all the forced walks the Indian people have made in the past—the Trail of Tears, the many forced removals and marches of Eastern tribes to Oklahoma resulting in the death of 4,000 native people, the Walks of Chief Joseph, the Navajo people, and many, many more tribes that were forceably removed from their lands. . . .[59]

There are two relevant facts not mentioned in the above:

(1)   The leaders of the Longest Walk included prominent American Indian Movement (AIM) leaders, such as Dennis Banks and Vernon Bellecourt, who led the Trail of Broken Treaties and its sacking of the BIA building in 1972, and many of whom had participated in the takeover of Wounded Knee in 1973.

(2)   It included no elected tribal leaders.

The allegations concerning the effect of the proposed legislation were somewhat overdrawn. One of the bills proposed the abrogation of treaties; another proposed limiting tribal jurisdiction to Indians; a third proposed quantification of Indian water rights; another would prohibit Indian fishing of steelhead trout to sell; a fifth gave the state of Washington complete control over Indian hunting and fishing off of reservations; the sixth was one of the bills to abrogate aboriginal land claims of the Maine Indians; the seventh proposed extinguishment of Indian aboriginal land claims in the state of New York; the eight and ninth were resolutions proposing the limiting of off reservation fishing in Oregon and Washington, and giving the states control of off-reservation hunting and fishing; and finally the proposed Criminal Code Reform Act of 1977, which aimed at codifying the U.S. Criminal Code.[60]

Some of the subjects of these bills dealt with the complicated jurisdictional situation in many parts of Indian country and others were concerned with off-reservation fishing and hunting in part stimulated by the Boldt fishing decision in the state of Washington, discussed below in this chapter. It is difficult to find in these bills language that threatens taking away "the responsibility to control their own lives, their own children, and their own communities," or that indicated that non-Indians wanted "to decide where Indians should live and in what manner they should live" as claimed by Walk leaders and the Methodist leaflet.

Like the Trail of Broken Treaties affair, there were preliminary plans for housing and feeding. Churches in the Washington area were visited by three advance persons seeking volunteer shelter and feeding arrangements. A flyer issued by Walk leaders indicated that monetary contributions should be made payable to the Board of Church and Society of the Methodist Church, 100 Maryland, N.E., Washington, D.C. The Methodist Church sponsored the Walk and furnished headquarters space in the District of Columbia.

The Federal government, of course, was aware of its previous experience. Some 5,000 to 10,000 Walk people were estimated to arrive on July 15. When the middle of June arrived, volunteer housing and feeding had not yet materialized. If the Federal government had not provided Greenbelt Park and the Army tents and kitchens, there would have been potential for another "media event"—the TV image of these "leaders" of "Indian nations" and the followers without food, sanitation, or money, being "callously neglected" by the capital of the greatest country in the world. Would mention be made of the fact that the "leaders" urged their followers to come without arranging for adequate housing, food and meeting places, and transportation home?

In Harrisburg, Pennsylvania, Mayor Paul Doutrich had given the Indians permission to stay at an unused firehouse, according to the *Washington Post*. He said the Indians stole $1000 worth of firemen's boots, other personal articles and 14 cots, and left piles of gift clothing at the firehouse.

Walk leader Ernie Peters responded, "The FBI and the CIA have gotten the mayor to tell these falsehoods, and we are not going to leave until he apologizes." Another leader said, "The people of Harrisburg emptied their attics to give us junk." The mayor said, "I'm disgusted and disillusioned. We gave you a warm welcome and all the help we could." He did not apologize and the Indians finally left.[61]

The Friends Committee on National Legislation (FCNL) in its *Washington Newsletter* of July 1978 cited the publicity of the Walk and indicated that several Friends Meetings had been active in arrangements in communities visited. "FCNL joins with those on The Longest Walk in hoping that their journey will stir the conscience of the American public to the plight of Indian nations and remind them of the unique historical and legal obligations the United States has to Indians."

Articles supporting the Walk appeared in many newspapers and publications including the *Saturday Review* on November 25, 1978 and *Fellowship*, the publication of the Fellowship of Reconciliation, in its September 1978 issue. These articles presented only the Walk point of view.

The financing of The Longest Walk involved many people but the principal private financial backer was the United Methodist Church.[62] Many of the Walk participants had no money to get home. Reverend John Adams, head of the Methodist's Department of Law, Justice and Community Relations, was deeply involved in helping find necessary funds.[63]

The Interior Department's estimate of costs to the government of The Longest Walk was about $250,000 for (1) overtime pay to U.S. Park police; (2) reimbursement to the Department of Army for use of field kitchens, tents, water tanks and other logistical support in Greenbelt Park, and (3) charter fees for buses to bring Indian demonstrators into the city each day.[64] Apparently only 2,800 Indians were at the Park at its peak, instead of the hoped for five to ten thousand.

Richard Hite of the Interior Department "said the government had adopted a policy of accommodating the Indians and underwriting the cost of much of their stay here to avoid the kind of violent confrontation that occurred in 1972. . ." (Trail of Broken Treaties).[65]

Summary

These three episodes, the Trail of Broken Treaties, Wounded Knee II, and The Longest Walk, are examples of how small groups of militants have recently pre-empted the limelight. For most casual observers these incidents probably were regarded as representing Indians in general, but these groups were not representing the major portion of Indian people on reservations. Their efforts in the Trail episode may have helped speed up or slow down action on the Indian Self-Determination Act in 1975. No one knows for certain.

These events portray the power of small organized Indian groups to command center stage in the mass media from which most of us get our information on current events and policy issues. One can admire the expert way in which these Indian leaders maximize the impact of the media. Those who may have wished to call attention to some other aspects of the issues aired were not nearly as effective in getting the media's attention.

The political aspect of the general public's view of Indian matters undoubtedly was a major factor in the government's decision not to prosecute the perpetrators of the forcible occupancy and destruction in the BIA building in 1972 and the decision to underwrite the expenses for the Walk in 1978.

The impact of public opinion or "shared images" in the execution of policy is demonstrated by these three examples.

TREATY FISHING RIGHTS (WESTERN WASHINGTON)

In the Pacific Northwest fishing is a major economic activity. As District Court Judge George H. Boldt stated in 1974:

> More than a century of frequent and often violent controversy between Indians and non-Indians over treaty right fishing has resulted in a deep distrust and animosity on both sides. This has been inflamed by provocative, sometimes illegal, conduct of extremists on both sides and by irresponsible demonstrations instigated by non-resident opportunists.[66]

Boldt Decision and Background (Phase I)

In this situation the 1974 decision by Judge George H. Boldt was like throwing a match into a barrel of gunpowder. The Court held that in addition to catching all of the fish they wanted on their own reservation, Indians in the state of Washington could catch fish off reservation at their traditional and accustomed sites for religious and subsistence purposes. In addition, they were entitled to 50 percent of the remainder of the fish for commercial purposes, leaving the other 50 percent for non-Indian fishermen.

> Few court decisions have aroused such bitterness . . . nowhere in the treaties involved were the words 50 percent used. . . . The decision and its 50 percent clause, which in effect allocated 60, 70 and even more than 90 percent of some runs to about one percent of the population, has been a disaster for non-Indian fishermen in Washington State. Coupled with the pressure of declining fish runs and an overcrowded commercial fishing fleet, it has driven many commercial fisherman to financial ruin. . . . But possibly more important than the present effects of the Boldt decision is its significance as a precedent for future cases, both in the Pacific Northwest and across the nation.[67]

Herb Williams and Walt Neubrech state further that non-Indian commercial fishermen with their catch about to be cut in half "staged their own fish-in, putting their nets in illegal waters ..." but where Indian gillnetters were allowed to fish. In 1976 for conservation purposes the state closed Puget Sound to the non-Indians but left parts open to Indians. "The tempers of the non-Indian gillnetters boiled ..." and they began fishing in defiance of the state order. One night "angry gillnetters rammed six fisheries patrol boats" and later one gillnetter was shot in the head. When asked why they were engaging in such a vain protest one gillnetter answered:

> That's the way the Indians got all those court rulings giving them most of the fish. They broke the law. They got arrested. They got court rulings. We're doing the same damn thing. We think the state is acting illegally. [68]

A petition to impeach Judge Boldt garnered 80,000 signatures.

Judge Boldt based his finding on Indian treaties, the key language of which provided that Indians could fish at "their usual and accustomed places in common with other citizens of the territory." The treaties were negotiated in 1854 and 1855 by Isaac Stevens, the first appointed governor of the Washington Territory and Superintendent of Indian Affairs. "Stevens named numerous chiefs and sub-chiefs to existing tribes as well as to tribes he himself created for the purpose of delegating responsibilities and facilitating the signing of the treaties."[69] Stevens recognized the importance of fish in the culture of the tribes and as their most important food source. Since his assignment was to negotiate the extinguishment of Indian claims to lands west of the Cascade Mountain Range, the Indians were concerned about their continued ability to carry on their fishing activities. A clause similar to the following was included in each of the treaties:

> The right of taking fish, at all usual and accustomed grounds and stations, is further secured to said Indians, in common with all citizens of the Territory, and of erecting temporary houses for the purpose of curing, together with the privilege of hunting, gathering roots and berries, and pasturing their horses on open and unclaimed land: *Provided, however*, that they shall not take shell fish from any beds staked or executed by citizens. [70]

The negotiations were carried out in "Chinook jargon" which had only a 300 word vocabulary but Judge Boldt believed the Indians understood that they would be able to fish in the manner to which they were accustomed in all off reservation treaty sites. They probably did not understand fully the phrase "in common with all citizens of the territory." There is no record of this phrase being discussed in the treaty negotiations.[71] The Boldt decision held that the fishing right was reserved by the Indians in the treaties and could not be qualified by the state, except for the police power to regulate off reservation fishing to the extent "reasonable and necessary for the conservation of the resource."[72]

Both Indians and non-Indians fished freely after the treaties. There was no problem as there were fewer Indians and non-Indians in the frontier society than at present. It was only with the rapid increase in non-Indians and economic development including large scale commercial fishing that problems emerged. The magnitude of this development, of course, could not have been foreseen by the Indians or Stevens.

Judge Boldt went on to say: "To this court the evidence clearly shows that, in the past, root causes of treaty right dissention have been an almost total lack of meaningful communication on problems of treaty right fishing between state, commercial and sport fishing officials and non-Indian fishermen on one side and tribal representatives and members on the other side. . . ."[73]

The Court then stressed: ". . .high priority should be given to further improvement in communication and in attitude of every Indian and non-Indian who is a fisherman or in any capacity has responsibility for treaty right fishing practices or regulation. Hopefully that will be expedited by some of the measures required by this decision."[74]

The Court then prescribed basic procedures to be followed by all parties. Some BIA officials believe the Court's forcing of procedures was necessary for survival of the fishery resource. The state was ordered to estimate the numer of harvestable fish that may be taken in advance of every fishing season, based on the best technical information available. The state was authorized to:

> . . .request treaty tribes to submit to the Departments of Fisheries or Game reasonable accurate estimates of (1) the type, location and amount of fishing gear expected to be used. . .; the number. . .of fish they. . .expect to take at their usual and accustomed fishing grounds for traditional ceremonial needs and for consumption by tribal members and their families; (3) the number. . .of fish they. . .expect to take on their reservations; and (4) reports of catches of fish by tribal members as to both on and off reservation treaty fishery for the purpose of establishing escapement goals and other purposes which are reasonable and necessary conservation purposes.[75]

The state was required to: ". . .make available to a treaty tribe upon its request. . ., such raw or processed data as they have available from time to time relative to the expected size, timing and condition of fish runs. . . and the current level of harvest and escapement."[76]

These court requirements resulted in the present procedure of weekly tally sheets to the state by tribes and non-Indian fishermen so that control can be exercised over the number of fish taken. Thus if it were estimated by the state that a certain stream would have a run of 700 harvestable fish, the allowable catch for Indians might be projected as 250, for non-Indians as 250, and 200 allowed to go upstream to spawn to renew the supply. If the tribal and non-Indian weekly reports indicate that the estimate was too high or too low the state would make adjustments by increasing or decreasing the allowable catch, or in some cases by closing the fishery for a period to allow enough fish escapement for spawning.

Tribes were required to issue identification cards to members fishing in off-reservation sites so that state game officials could operate intelligently under the court order. If tribes developed the appropriate tribal structure and procedures they were to police tribal fishing in off-reservation sites.

This development in policy for Indian fishing rights and rights of non-Indians involved several actors. The tribes, their attorneys, the BIA, and the Department of Justice developed the case and presented the Indian-Federal Government view to the Court. The state and various non-Indian fishing groups presented their opposing views to the Court. Some thought the contestants were of unequal fire power. Williams and Neubrech report that the Federal Government spent a million dollars through the Northwest Fisheries Advisory Service prior to the trial, had five attorneys, eight tribes had attorneys, and in addition the Federal Government hired a "top-flight private attorney," Stuart F. Pierson, and an anthropologist, Dr. Barbara Lane. The state had one attorney assisted by an attorney representing the Reefnetters Association, and an anthropologist, Dr. Carroll Riley.[77]

During the period of immediate economic impact and intense feeling after the Boldt decision a citizens' committee, Citizens United for Resource Emergencies (CURE), "gathered 156,000 signatures in a three-month period asking the state's Congressional delegation to take the lead in introducing legislation to correct the inequities in the Boldt decision."[78]

The Washington State Department of Game, responsible for sport fisheries including steelhead, took the position that "Indian treaties do not grant to any Indian citizen or tribe any privileges or immunities greater than those which the Department recognized as being held by non-Indian citizens. . . ." The Game department maintained that: ". . .under the Constitution and laws of the United States and of the State of Washington, the Department was required to regulate Indian fishing activities outside Federal and Indian reservations to the same extent and in the same manner as it regulated fishing activity by all other classes of citizens."[79]

The courts, including the Supreme Court, support special provisions for today's citizens that were the result of treaties made with at least semi-independent groups who were not citizens of the United States, who happen to be the ancestors of certain present U.S. and state citizens. The courts will take the treaties literally as applying to Indian descendants. If Congress wants to change a treaty the courts say it has the authority to do so. The state also maintained that the phrase "in common with other citizens of the territory" meant that both had equal rights and "if it was necessary to regulate fishing in the interests of conservation, the state had that right."[80]

Going into trial, the State Fisheries Department took a different view than the Game Department, providing some recognition of special Indian treaty rights and offered Indians 30 percent of the commercial catch of salmon, which was recognized as a commercial fish and outnumbered steelhead 30 to 1.[81]

Orrick Decision: Analysis of Impact (Phase II)

Up to this point the discussion has covered Phase I of the court action initiated by the Boldt decision in 1974 which was affirmed by the U.S. Supreme Court in 1979. The Supreme Court upheld Boldt but modified his decision to provide that subsistence and ceremonial needs were to be counted in the Indians' 50 percent share. Phase II concerned whether the treaty rights entitled the tribes to have the fishery resource and related habitat protected, and whether hatchery fish were subject to allocation under the findings of Phase I.

Concerning hatchery fish U.S. District Judge William Orrick held that they were like other fish and subject to allocation under the formula.[82] There were 35 hatcheries in the area being adjudicated and supported by state, Federal, and local funds. Sixty percent of the steelhead and 17 percent of the salmon available for harvest in tribal fishing areas were artificially produced.

The environmental issue concerning protection of the fish has the greatest potential economic impact. The court held: ". . .that the treaties 'implicitly reserve to Tribes the right to a sufficient quantity of fish to provide a moderate living subject to a maximum 50 percent of the harvestable anadromous fish.'" The court also decreed: ". . .that the tribes 'have an implicitly incorporated right under the fishing clauses of the Stevens Treaties not to have the fishery habitat degraded. . .resulting in such a reduction of available harvestable fish that the moderate living standard. . .cannot be met.'"[83]

This means that "if a non-Indian activity other than fishing—such as logging or dam building—reduces the number of fish available to Indians, then that activity must give way to the superior treaty-secured rights of the tribes."[84] The state, the United States and other third parties were "to refrain from degrading the fish habitat to an extent that would deprive the tribes of their moderate living needs."[85] A detailed discussion in the Court opinion defines "moderate living needs." If the tribes no longer relied on fish, this requirement would close. However, the Court stated that as long as the tribal allocation is 50 percent "there is a presumption that the moderate living needs of the tribes are not being satisfied." Third parties threatening fish habitat have the burden of showing that actions challenged by the tribes "will not impair the Tribes' moderate living needs." It will be the duty of the appropriate government agency "to fashion a remedy."[86] If there is a threat of unavoidable harm to the fishery a project may have to be abandoned. Cases coming under review to date are:

(1) Reduction of stream flow due to storage of water for an irrigation project that destroyed salmon eggs. The Court ruled that the water level had to be maintained at a level to preserve the eggs even though it would threaten adequate water storage for the project; ". . .this decision did not turn on a balancing of the tribe's interest in the fish with the interests of the water users."[87]

(2) Pending in April 1981:

(a) In *NO OILPORT v. Carter*, the issue is whether the proposed Northern Tier Pipeline, which would stretch from Port Angeles, Washington, to Clearbrook, Minnesota, will cause a reduction in fish runs subject to the treaties. The matter has been set for an evidentiary hearing, at which the tribes will attempt to meet their burden of showing that the project will adversely impact the fishery. If the tribes meet that burden, the question of what constitutes appropriate relief in a case involving a project of the size and importance of the Northern Tier Pipeline will certainly not be easy to resolve.

(b) In *Skokomish Indian Tribe v. Beaubien*, the tribe is seeking to enjoin the U.S. Forest Service from proceeding with management and planning concerning a unit of forest land. The tribe participated in administrative proceedings on management of the unit in question, alleging that the Service's management plan would have adverse impacts on fish and game resources reserved to the tribes by treaty. The Forest Service apparently did not respond to the concerns raised by the tribe, nor, apparently, did it demonstrate compliance with its trust and treaty obligations to the tribe. That failure prompted the tribe to initiate the lawsuit to compel such compliance.[88]

The impact of the environmental aspects of the Orrick Phase II decision is obvious. How serious it will be is yet to be seen. Unless the Indians and the various governments and private interests concerned can work out agreements by negotiation, Blumm and Johnson predict a great volume of litigation.

The policy position developing out of Indian treaties negotiated over 100 years ago is having great impact. It results from the courts' interpretation of treaty rights when suits are brought by the government and the lack of action by Congress to make any changes in the treaties. Although large segments of the public in the Pacific Northwest have been unhappy with the court decisions, their Congressional representatives have not been able to persuade their colleagues to modify the treaties through Federal statutes. The mere introduction of such proposals alarms some Indians (see Trail of Broken Treaties and The Longest Walk) and the general public in the country seems to support decisions favorable to the Indians.

Attempts have been made through the legislative route to help relieve the economic impact of the Boldt decision. Federal funds have been made available for hatcheries to increase the supply of fish and to purchase superfluous fishing boats. Unsuccessful attempts have been made to limit steelhead to sport fishing and to give state control of all off-reservation fishing by Indians.

The Boldt decision has also added to the strain on the relationships between the Department of Interior and the Commerce Department's National Oceanic and Atmospheric Administration (NOAA) which controls off-shore fishing of anadromous species. The Indians and Interior believe the ocean catch is decreasing the fish available in state waters, thus reducing the quantity of fish available to both the non-Indians and the Indians under the 50 percent rule.

Since other nations fish on the high seas, Indian rights as stated by the Boldt decision also affect international fishery negotiations and regulations.

Summary of Interrelationships[89]

Tribal representatives in negotiating sessions are in a difficult situation. Experience indicates that delegating responsibility to tribal negotiators has often resulting in disadvantages to the tribe, thus reinforcing the concept of consensus decision making. Tribal representatives often have little authority of make binding agreements. Any negotiation is regarded by a tribal leader as a high risk since it may subject him to the charge of "selling out the tribe's treaty rights." The safest and most effective procedure seems to be to have basic policy set and approved in advance and leave negotiation primarily for the development of implementing procedures. Tribes have also found that negotiation and compromise failed to work more often than it succeeded, whereas confrontation would often lead to tangible gains for the tribe in the State of Washington.

The fishing issue is important to tribes in the State of Washington for the following reasons: (1) it is the traditional economic pursuit; (2) it is a good educational and developmental experience for the young; (3) it is still an important source of income if adequate runs can be maintained; and (4) protecting fishing rights and administering tribal fish regulations provide central tribal responsibilities in some tribes. Tribal leaders may perceive that without this responsibility tribal members might not believe there was a great a need for tribal officials and supporting staff.

The state has problems, too. When the state fisheries department negotiated an agreement with the tribes it often found its efforts nullified by the legislative or the state attorney general's office. This undermined the credibility of the fisheries department with the Indians. Even if the state officials come into agreement, the actions of country and city officials may disrupt the agreement by contrary land use planning or permit approvals.

At the Federal level the following are involved: Forest Service (USDA); Pacific Marine Fisheries Council and NOAA (Department of Commerce); BIA, Bureau of Reclamation and Fish and Wildlife (Interior); Corps of Engineers (Defense); the Bonneville Power Administration; Environmental Protection Agency; Council on Environmental Quality; Office of Management and Budget; and the White House.

The power to address the complicated fisheries problem is fragmented among three levels of government plus the tribal governments, and within each level throughout many agencies or tribes. Each has its own constituency which may or may not cooperate in developing a solution to the fishery problem or go along with it after development. There is no central point of leadership and the climate for resolution is poor.

James C. Waldo, a consultant for the Northwest Water Resources Committee, outlined four alternative courses of action: judicial, Congressional, comprehensive framework for negotiated settlement, and status quo (one case at a time as raised by tribes). These were presented to the Northwest Water Resources Committee for review in 1981.

THE SIOUX AND THE BLACK HILLS

History and Background

The Black Hills award of over $105 million dollars for the Sioux Indians, approved June 30, 1980, by the Supreme Court resulted from continuous pressure by the Indians and effective work by their attorneys.

Under the Fort Laramie Treaty of 1868, the United States pledged that the Great Sioux Reservation, including the Black Hills, would be "set apart for the absolute and undisturbed use and occupation" of the Sioux Nation (Sioux), and that no treaty for the cession of any part of the reservation would be valid as against the Sioux unless executed and signed by at least three-fourths of the adult male Sioux population. The treaty also reserved the Sioux' right to hunt in certain unceded territories. Subsequently in 1876, an "agreement" presented to the Sioux by a special Commission but signed by only 10% of the adult male Sioux population, provided that the Sioux would relinquish their rights to the Black Hills and to hunt in the unceded territories, in exchange for subsistence rations for as long as they would be needed.[90]

The impetus for the 1876 "agreement" was the discovery of gold in paying quantities in the Black Hills by Lt. Col. George Custer in 1874. In spite of efforts by U.S. military to prevent it, large numbers of prospectors, miners, and settlers entered the area "without the consent of the Indians." Public pressure "to open the Black Hills developed and increased."[91] In 1876 General Custer was defeated at the Little Big Horn while attempting to get the Sioux to return to their reservation. Congress cut off rations for the Sioux until they ceded the Black Hills to the United States. The president appointed the 1876 Commission which negotiated an agreement with the chiefs and head men of the Sioux tribes.[92] Less than 10 percent of the male Sioux population approved the agreement, so Congress enacted the agreement as a law on February 28, 1877.[93] The Sioux ever since have regarded this law as a breach of the treaty. In 1920 a special jurisdiction act was passed and the Sioux took the case to the Court of Claims which decided against the Sioux in 1942. Upon enactment of the Indian Claims Commission Act in 1946 the Sioux submitted their claim to the Commission, which held the Sioux were entitled to just compensation. On appeal by the government to the Court of Claims, the Court agreed with the Commission on the entitlement, but said that the merits had been decided in 1942 and the claim was thus barred.

The attorneys for the Sioux went into action and persuaded Congress to pass an act authorizing the Court of Claims to review the case on its merits without regard to previous decisions.[94] The attorneys also obtained an Act to prevent the government from deducting offsets such as food subsidies and other services to the Indians which would have totaled more than the claim.[95] The final result was the 1980 award which was based on the $17.5 million value at the time of the taking and 5 percent interest since 1877.

In awarding the three Sioux attorneys, Arthur Lazarus, Marvin J. Sonosky, and William Payne, a $10.5 million fee Judge Daniel M. Friedman, for a unanimous Court of Claims opinion, wrote that the attorneys' success in the case was a "remarkable achievement" and stated that "the odds against success when the lawyers entered the litigation in 1956 were overwhelming."[96]

This award process shows the forces at work in arriving at public policy in connection with the Sioux Black Hills claim. The Sioux were persistent and kept presenting their case. The pressures of the miners and settlers in the Black Hills forced the government to do something to legalize their presence and activity. It was probably impossible to physically obtain the signatures of three-fourths of the adult Sioux as required by the 1868 treaty. The headmen and 10 percent agreed to the 1876 agreement and Congress enacted the agreement into law. Part of the public attitude at the time was a reaction to the sudden end of Custer and his men at the hands of the Indians. The subsequent events were shaped by general public policy, such as the establishment of the Indian Claims Commission to hear all Indian claims of which the Sioux took advantage.

The executive, the Congress, the courts, the Claims Commission, the Sioux, their attorneys, General Custer, and the miners and settlers in the Black Hills following the 1874 discovery of gold all influenced policy at various stages in this case.

After the Claims Award

On July 23, 1980, $105 million was transferred from the Treasury Department to the Department of the Interior and invested for the Indians pending legislative decision on the method of payment and distribution of the award. The interest accumulated may amount to a considerable sum before this happens. There are two obstacles. One is that the Sioux are far from unanimity on whether to accept the award. Many say they want the land, not money. The other obstacle is BIA's administrative task of determining who the eligible Indians might be, estimated to take several years at least.

BIA does research to determine beneficiaries of awards, processes plans for use of judgement funds in compliance with the Indian Judgement Funds Distribution Act (1973), prepares descendancy rolls of judgement award beneficiaries and performs requisite actions on individual enrollment appeals.

In the Black Hills claims award (Docket 74-B, CC 148-78) the award of $105,994,431 was appropriated on July 23, 1980, and the funds transferred to the United States Treasury. The Oglala Sioux Tribe of the Pine Ridge Reservation rejected this award and filed suit in the U.S. District Court seeking among other things restoration of the Black Hills and damages in terms of billions of dollars. The U.S. and the attorney for the tribe agreed that research on beneficiaries would be limited until the appeal was decided. The court later held that it lacked jurisdiction and on January 18, 1982, the U.S. Supreme Court denied a writ of certiorari. The BIA has asked for an opinion from Interior Department Solicitor as to whether research can proceed as the Oglala Sioux promise further litigation.

Once the "go ahead" is received BIA must determine whether the eight plaintiff "Black Hills Tribes" are legitimate beneficiaries. The tribal groups involved are: Oglala (18,000 approx.), Rosebud (9,700), Standing Rock (8,200), Cheyenne River (4,600), Crow Creek (2,400), Lower Brule (1,000), Ft. Peck Sioux (5,000), Santee Sioux (3,700). There may be approximately 50,000 beneficiaries.

BIA's research will identify the beneficiary tribes and their ties to the Great Sioux Reservation of 1868 which contained the Black Hills. This research will also provide the necessary information to develop a formula for the division of funds among the tribes. The next step will be to prepare tribal rolls of members eligible for the award. Existing tribal rolls cannot be used as they are because of the diversity in enrollment criteria. The Bureau will examine the 1934-1935 censuses in depth for clues on enrollment eligibility for purposes of the award. Also the dates of present rolls vary—the Oglala and Rosebud rolls have not been revised since April 1, 1935, except for two corrections by the Oglala Sioux in 1941.

Because of the size of the award and the amount of publicity it has received there may be over 100,000 applications for tribal membership filed. A large percentage of the rejected applicants may appeal. Even though the constitution or ordinances of only one of the tribes provides for final determination of eligibility by the Secretary of the Interior, this is a requirement for rolls used for distributing trust assets.

A draft of a proposed bill will accompany the final research report but it will not contain provisions for actual utilization of the shares until after tribal proposals have been received. [97]

The Sioux attitudes include those of beneficiaries who wish to reject the award, others who suggest the money should be accepted and used to buy land, and almost all Sioux who object that the award is too small in any event. BIA's position (1981) is that the Sioux lost the Black Hills in 1877 by Congressional action. The courts cannot award land to the Indians, only Congress can make such awards. The Interior Department states that compensatory payment for the taking of the Black Hills was made on July 23, 1980 when funds were withdrawn from the U.S. Treasury for this purpose.

The Sioux view is long standing. In 1875 the Sioux offered to sell the Black Hills for $70 million and the 1875 Allison Commission offered $6 million, or $400,000 a year for the right to mine, cultivate, and graze livestock, and $500,000 (paid over a ten-year period) for surrender of the Sioux' off reservation hunting rights. No agreement was reached. The new 1876 Commission took the actions previously mentioned leading to the 1877 Congressional Act.

In 1979 a United Sioux Meeting was held at Pierre, South Dakota, for three days, August 28-30. This was after the Court of Claims decision but before its confirmation by the Supreme Court. The issue was misstated by the Indians as an offer by the government to "buy" the Black Hills for $105 million and whether the Sioux wanted to "sell." Some refused to understand or accept that the land was taken. The issue is compensation for the taking.

> The meetings had little structure and it was felt by many present that Russell Means had kept the talk centered on the Black Hills. He continually insisted that the Sioux would not sell the Black Hills and appealed to an International Tribunal (i.e. the United Nations) to settle the issue. The media present played into his hands because they did not or would not understand the issues, and with spot news coverage, directed most responses to the spurious question of whether the Sioux would sell the Black Hills."[98]

The BIA representative at the meeting noted that the disunity of the Sioux was obvious. Solidarity proved impossible becasue of the pressure from extremists and their domination of the newspaper publicity. "The non-Indian population of South Dakota, also misinformed as to the issues, is nervous about continued talk about selling the Black Hills. They are influenced to some extent by what they assume occurred in the State of Maine."[99]

The Oglala Sioux Tribe of Pine Ridge has appealed the Supreme Court decision and the Interior Department cannot pay the Sioux award until court appeals are settled. A resolution adopted in March 1981, by the Sioux Nation Treaty Council (traditionalist non-IRA groups) requested a meeting with the President of the United States. The text follows

---

Whereas, the contents of the 1868 Treaty cannot be changed unless there are three-fourths (3/4) Adult male signatures on any signed documents, and

Whereas, the original contents of the 1868 Treaty is and shall be upheld by the Sioux Nation, and

Whereas, any treaties and/or agreements that were signed and issued after 1868 are NULL and VOID, and

Whereas, the position of the Sioux Nation shall not be changed, and

Therefore be it resolved that the Sioux Nation is requesting a meeting with the PRESIDENT of the UNITED STATES as soon as possible, and

Be it further resolved that this meeting is very important, it concerns the problems arising from the Federal Regulations, Public Laws, the separate Indian groups among other problems which are the main issues constituting poverty, lack of livelihood, lack of jobs for the Indian people, alcoholism, poor health of the Indian people, and that the traditional government be recognized and

Be it further resolved that the Federal Court has no authority on the Sioux Nation, and

Further resolved, the Sioux Nation also request that the presence of a foreign treaty commissioner at this meeting.

CERTIFICATION

I, the undersigned, as Secretary of the BLACK HILLS SIOUX NATION COUNCIL hereby certify that the above-mentioned was adopted by a vote of *27* for, *0* against; and *0* not voting, representing eight (8) Sioux Reservations at the meeting held at Digman Hall, St. Francis, South Dakota on the 14 day of March, 1981.

Secretary, Black Hills Sioux Nation Council

This resolution was signed by Reginald Cedar Face, the secretary, and Oliver Red Cloud, the chairman of the Black Hills Sioux Nation Council.

The elected tribal governments operating under constitutions in Sioux country are having their difficulties. Traditionalists do not recognize them, and although the traditionalists are a minority, they make it difficult to come to a resolution on emotional issues.

Even though the Sioux attorneys in the Black Hills case achieved a result most impartial observers thought was almost impossible, some Indians attacked them. The non-IRA or traditional group members of the Black Hills Sioux Nation Council sought in 1980 to say that attorneys appointed by the councils did not represent the Sioux as the IRA councils had not been established in 1868. Therefore they wanted the attorneys taken off the case.[100]

Anyone who differs with the traditionalist view is liable to be taken to task. Vine Deloria, Jr., a Standing Rock Sioux, author and former executive director of the National Congress of American Indians, suggested that the Sioux use the over $100 million to buy land.[101]

A letter to the editor in *The Dakota Sun* (Fort Yates, ND August 14, 1980) read as follows:

This is a response to a signed article in *The Dakota Sun*, on July 12, 1980, entitled: "Vine Deloria, Jr., Says Sioux Should Try To Buy Back Black Hills."

The Hunkpapa Treaty Council and the Yanktonai Bands realize the literary successes and the prestige he has acclaimed, but when Mr. Deloria proclaims that we, the rightful owners of the Black Hills, should sell, then we have something to say and about Mr. Deloria.

First, the Lakotahs and Dakotahs have never relinquished the Title to Sacred Black Hills which belongs to the Lakotahs/Dakotahs from time immemorial.

Second, Mr. Deloria is advocating the acceptance of the funds from the ridiculous offer of funds from the United States government for the re-purchase of the land which is already ours to begin with.

Third, Mr. Deloria accepts the derogatory brand of 'Sioux'—a term meaning 'cut throat'—condoning the cultural genocidal policies being practiced by the United States government on Lakotah/Dakotah peoples.

Fourth, attorneys Sonosky, Payne, Lazarus, and Case are employed by the Indian Reorganization Act (IRA) Tribal Councils to negotiate a financial settlement on their behalf without consultation with the Traditional Bands or Treaty Councils who are in complete agreement for the return of the lands being addressed in Dockets No. 74 and 74-B. These attorneys have not made any attempts to seek return of the lands—only financial benefit as each firm will receive 10 percent off the top. Mr. Deloria would best serve the Lakotah/Dakotah peoples by pursuing the return of the lands, be it judicially or legislatively.

Fifth, Mr. Deloria has lost direct contact with the district peoples, especially on the reservation, on which he is barely enrolled; nor does he represent in any circle the Hunkpapas or the Yanktonais. He does not or is not experiencing the direct governmental genocidal policies, as he has left the reservation on his own accord and is now profiting financially and otherwise as an 'Indian expert.'

Sixth, Mr. Vine Deloria, Jr., has sold out!

Furthermore, we, the Traditional Bands and Treaty Councils, are experiencing a gross misconception about the proposed financial settlement on the Black Hills, We wish the 'outside' world to understand that the Tribal Councils, created under the Wheeler-Howard Act of 1934, do not represent, nor are they authorized to represent, under the Fort Laramie Treaty of April 29, 1868, the hearts and minds of the traditional peoples of our Bands!

We, the Traditional Bands and Treaty Councils, do not recognize the 'Claims Attorneys' as employed by the Tribal Councils, who advocate the acceptance of the monetary settlement. We are also not consulted in the discussion and passing of Tribal Council Resolution No. 323-79, passed on November 7, 1979, when the power of attorney was passed to the Tribal Claims attorneys to sign and execute any writing or document that would be appropriate or necessary to carry out the settlement of this case.

We have spoken! ! !

Reginald Bird Horse
Thomas Iron Cloud
Joseph A. Walker
Milo Iron Road

The Dakota Indian Movement is attempting to return to the Black Hills,[102] has set up Yellow Thunder camp, and has secured the support of the American Friends Service Committee.[103] Indians favoring the elected tribal governments have opposed the camp. Sioux divisions and pressures are still resulting in increased polarization of both Indians and non-Indians in South Dakota.

The *Washington Star* in the July 5, 1980 editorial section provided a summary of the policy issues involved.

On Settling Indian Claims

. . . . What winners do to losers in struggles for prizes as desirable as the lands of the American West is never attractive. There is a natural impulse in any person of good will to see the problem as one of righting old wrongs.

However, even if the settlers, miners, land speculators, government officials and soldiers who came to the Dakotas in the late 19th century had all conducted themselves with greater ethical scrupulousness than they did, there is little reason to suppose the Indian's cultural trauma could have been avoided. The only examples history offers of primitive peoples surviving encounters with more sophisticated societies are those in which barbarians conquer nations where civilization has grown too complacent to push its frontiers. That hadn't happened in the restless, footloose America that was, in General Custer's day, trying to rebuild a polity after the physical and spiritual devastations of civil war.

More disquieting considerations stem from the impossibility of undoing history. The question is not only how far back retroactive justice can go, but how just it can hope to be. . . . .

The Sioux settlement, like the other Indian land claims settlements that have been made in recent years, in Maine and elsewhere, is pegged to what might have happened had the presumed fair value of the disputed land been prudently invested in subsequent years. This leaves out a good many historically plausible contingencies, such as the Indians dissipating their resources the way non-Indians so often do. In fact, it places the settlements in a category dominated by moral fantasy and contemporary political power rather than by incontrovertible legal rights.

. . . .The lineage tests for deciding who is and isn't an Indian can be both far-fetched and arbitrary. Will one great-grandparent do?

To make culture rather than race the criterion of Indianness is no help. Such are the compulsions of modernity that the spirit has generally gone out of the old customs if they survive at all, even with federal funds to pay for professionals to teach crafts and rituals once transmitted by tradition.

. . . . It will undoubtedly soothe sore consciences and please the people who get the money. It is also likely to encourage more litigation and more dubious separatism among those who, on whatever grounds, are labeled Indians.

What it is unlikely to do is to solve the dilemmas posed by the reality of their situation in the here and now. Caught between old ways that have lost their authority and new ways they find both compelling and hard to assimilate, today's Indians are prey to paralyzing ambivalences. Among the tragedies of their plight is their vulnerability to the vices of modernity — not just drink and welfare inertia but ideological grievance politics and a guerrilla theater approach to participation in the civic process. It is for this perhaps more than for anything that happened at Wounded Knee that they challenge our understanding and merit our compassion.

Washington Star

SUMMARY: INVOLVEMENT IN DEMOCRATIC PROCESS

In all of the examples we have discussed, the Indians were major participants, often with the assistance from their attorneys, the government, and various interest groups. The states were deeply involved in most cases. State citizens and business interests have a large stake in fishing, land claims, and other Federal-Indian policies. State governments were not seen as monolithic but somewhat fractured by functions and problems of coordination.

The Federal government has many different departments and agencies concerned with Indian policy. Orchestrating these various parts into an integrated policy objective is a major challenge. Each agency has its unique clientele, special mission, and agency view. The coordination of various programs within the BIA is difficult. Harnessing the activities of all Federal agencies to contribute to a central Indian policy is a monumental task. In addition, Federal entities such as the Interior and Justice Departments are sometimes in a conflict of interest situation—that of promoting Indian rights while also protecting the interests of the general public from extreme claims by Indians.

Bureaus of the Interior Department such as BIA and Land Management are often assigned the job of carrying out policy decisions. The working out of details for implementing the Alaska and Maine land transactions fell heavily on BIA and the Bureau of Land Management for the following: designating acreage, recording titles, and making exchanges. Supervising and enforcing the subsistence preference for rural residents (mostly Native) in Alaska will involve frequent negotiation among Natives, BIA, and the public land managers in the Fish and Wildlife Service, National Park Service, and the Bureau of Land Management. Carrying out the various facets of the Washington Indian treaty fishing rights involved BIA and Fish and Wildlife from Interior, Commerce, and Justice. When the courts give the go-ahead on the distribution of the Black Hills award, several years of work by BIA personnel will be required to develop rolls of Indians eligible to receive funds. After the Alaska Settlement Act, the development of rolls of eligible Natives and entities was a major task for BIA officials. The working out of details and procedures for implementing the Maine lands settlement will require BIA, state, and Indian cooperation.

As noted in the Alaska, Maine, fishing rights, and Black Hills discussions, the judicial system has played a prominent role. In the Washington fishing case the courts in effect "legislated" policy and also maintained supervision over the "execution" of that policy.

The impact of the perceived views of the general public on major policy issues is also evident. The action decisions in the Trail of Broken Treaties were obviously influenced by public attitudes and official assessment of possible public reaction. Attempts on the part of Congressmen from the Pacific Northwest to override Judge Boldt's fishing decisions by statute did not succeed as their colleagues' constituents did not have the same views as the petition signers in the State of Washington. Outside of Alaska and Maine, the general public's sentiment seemed to favor the type of results that evolved. The Executive Branch and the Congress were concerned about the Indian and general public reaction to any action less favorable to the Indians. It seems reasonable to conclude that the perceived views of the public provide both a stimulus to and restraint of public officials, depending on the circumstances. The general public view expressed in many ways and through various channels does determine the perimeter of governmental action—the limits within which government officials must act.

This discussion has concentrated on areas of perhaps unusual magnitude. However, the cases tend to illustrate the nature of policy changes over time. All of the above examples underline the importance of the interaction of various elements in our society and government in the formation of policy. In essence they illustrate the democratic process under our form of government. They also indicate that Indian policy is not only of historical interest. It is of great importance to many citizens today—both Indian and non-Indian.

Footnotes

[1]Some of these issues are treated in Theodore W. Taylor, *The Bureau of Indian Affairs: Public Policies Toward Indian Citizens*, to be published by Westview Press, 1983.

[2]Robert D. Arnold, *et al.*, *Alaska Native Land Claims* (Anchorage, Alaska: Alaska Native Foundation, 1978), revised ed., pp. 82-83. Hereafter cited as Arnold.

[3]Arnold, pp. 106-108, outlines the pros and cons of each of these options.

[4]Arnold, p. 111.

[5]Arnold, p. 126.

[6]Arnold, pp. 139-140.

[7]Federal Field Committee for Development Planning in Alaska *Alaska Natives and the Land*, (Anchorage, Alaska, October 1968). Distributed by the U.S. Government Printing Office.

[8]Arnold, p. 141.

[9]85 Stat. 688.

[10]Maps of the boundaries of the regional corporations and many other details can be found in Arnold.

[11]89 Stat. 1145, June 2, 1976.

[12]90 Stat. 1934.

[13]91 Stat. 1369.

[14]94 Stat. 2371.

[15]Arnold, pp. 135-136.

[16]Arnold, p. 279

[17]Arnold, p. 86.

[18]Arnold, p. 88.

[19]Arnold, p. 120.

[20]Arnold, p. 85.

[21]Arnold, p. 141.

[22]Arnold, p. xix.

[23]Omnibus Act of 1976, sec. 4, 80 Stat. 1145.

[24]4 Stat. 730.

[25]388 F. Supp. 649, 667 (D. Me. 1975). See also, O'Toole and Tureen, *State Power and the Passamaquoddy Tribe: "A Gross National Hypocrisy,"* 23 Me. F. Rev. 1 (1971).

[26]Joint Tribal Councils of Passamaquoddy Tribe v. Morton, 528 F. 2nd 370 (1975).

[27]Richard S. Jones, "Land Claims by Eastern Tribes," Congressional Research Service, Library of Congress, Issue Brief Number 1B 77040, January 15, 1981, p. 5.

[28]Recommendation to President Carter, under letterhead Kilpatrick, Cody, Rogers, McClatchey, and Regenstein, Atlanta, Georgia, July 15, 1977, signed by William B. Gunter.

[29]Congressional Record, U.S. House of Representatives, March 1, 1977, H1533.

[30]AIPRC, *Report*, May 17, 1977, pp. 608, 609, Minority Report by Congressman Meeds.

[31]Act of August 13, 1946, 60 Stat. 1949.

[32]AIPRC *Report*, p. 609.

[33]Timothy A. Vollmann, "A Survey of Eastern Land Claims: 1970-1979," Maine Law Review, Vol. 31:5, pp. 14-15. Hereafter cited as Vollman.

[34]348 U.S. 272, 1955. Vollmann, p. 15; see also AIPRC *Report*, pp. 606-609.

[35]Note from Peter Taylor, Special Counsel, Select Committee on Indian Affairs, received in April, 1982.

[36]Press release, The White House, October 10, 1980.

[37]Vollman, p. 15.

[38]See Appendix C for the status of other aboriginal land claims cases based on alleged violation of the Trade and Intercourse Act, referred to in recent court cases as the Nonintercourse Act.

[39]*Legislative Review*, August 1972, p. 33. Published by the Indian Legal Information Development Service, Washington, D.C. Hereafter cited as *ILIDS Legislative Review*.

[40]Based on a release by the national office of the American Indian Movement (AIM) reported in *ILIDS Legislative Review*, August 1972, pp. 32-33.

[41]Conversation with Bradley H. Patterson, February 26, 1982.

[42]Statement received along with letter from Bradley H. Patterson, February 3, 1982.

[43]*ILIDS Legislative Review*, November, 1972, pp. 23-24.

[44]*Ibid.*

[45]*ILIDS Legislative Review*, December/January 1973, p. 19.

[46]*ILIDS Legislative Review*, December/January, 1973, pp. 22-23.

[47]*ILIDS Legislative Review*, November 1972, pp. 22-23.

[48]*ILIDS Legislative Review*, November 1972, pp. 28-29.

[49]*ILIDS Legislative Review*, November 1972, p. 30. For further detail see the November 1972 and the December/January 1973 issues of the *ILIDS Legislative Review*. Quotes of Caravan leaders, other Indians and government officials are presented along with commentary by editors Laura Wittstock and Richard La Course. D'Arcy McNickel's preface in his book *Native American Tribalism* (New York: Oxford University Press, 1973) gives his view of the Caravan.

[50]*The Innocent Victims of the Occupation of Wounded Knee v. the United States*, before the Chief Commissioner of the U.S. Court of Claims, Opinion filed June 10, 1981, in Congressional Reference Case No. 4-76, pp. 16, 17. Hereafter cited as *Court of Claims Wounded Knee Report*. Victims at Wounded Knee were the subject of a proposed bill, S. 2907, to pay them in full settlement of their claims against the United States. Senate Resolution No. 378, 99th Cong., 2nd Sess., referred the bill to the chief Commissioner of the Court of Claims who was requested to file report as to the facts and months of the claimant.

[51]Wilcomb E. Washburn, *The Indian in America,* The New American Nation Series, ed. by Henry Steele Commager and Richard B. Morris (New York: Harper Torchbooks, 1975), p. 250.

[52]*Court of Claims Wounded Knee Report.*

[53]D'Arcy McNickle, *Native American Tribalism: Indian Survivals and Renewals* (New York: Oxford University Press, 1973), pp. vi and vii. Hereafter cited as McNickle.

[54]William T. Hagan, *American Indians* (Chicago: University of Chicago Press, 1979), p. 164.

[55]*Court of Claims Wounded Knee Report.*

[56]McNickle, pp. x and xi.

[57]Washburn, *The Indian in America,* pp. 250-251.

[58]Wilcomb E. Washburn, "Can Tribal Government Survive?", *C.T.C.A. Newsletter* (California Tribal Chairmen's Association), Vol. 2, No. 1, March, April 1979, p. 1.

[59]"The Longest Walk," a leaflet produced by the Board of Church and Society of the United Methodist Church, no date, but soon after February 11, 1981. Hereafter cited as Methodist leaflet.

[60]The list of bills is given in the Methodist leaflet.

[61]*Washington Post*, July 7, 1978, p. A-7.

[62]Paul W. Valentine, *Washington Post,* July 27, 1978, p. C-1.

[63]Mary McGrory, *The Washington Star*, July 31, 1978, p. A-3.

[64]Alice Bonner and Paul Valentine, *Washington Post*, July 28, 1978, p. A-5.

[65]*Ibid.*

[66]U.S. v. State of Washington, 384 F. Supp. 329 (1974); George H. Boldt, District Court Judge. Hereafter cited as Boldt.

[67]C. Herb Williams and Walt Neubrech, *Indian Treaties, American Nightmare*, (Seattle, Washington: Outdoor Empire Publishing, Inc., 1976), pp. 7, 8. Hereafter cited as Williams and Neubrech.

[68]Williams and Neubrech, pp. 8-10.

[69]Michael Blumm and Brad Johnson, "Indian Treaty Fishing Rights and Protection of the Environment," *Anadromous Fish Law Memo*, Natural Resources Law Institute, Lewis and Clark Law School, Portland, Oregon, April 1981, p. 2. Hereafter cited as Blumm and Johnson.

[70]Treaty of Medicine Creek, 10 Stat. 1133 (1855).

[71]Blumm and Johnson, p. 3.

[72]Boldt, p. 333.

[73]Boldt, p. 329.

[74]Boldt, p. 329.

[75]Boldt, p. 417.

[76]Boldt, p. 417.

[77]Williams and Neubrech, p. 8.

[78]Williams and Neubrech, p. 8.

[79]Boldt, p. 394.

[80]Williams and Neubrech, p. 9.

[81]Williams and Neubrech, p. 9.

[82]U.S. v. Washington, No. 9213-II, slip op. at 20, W.D. Wash., September 26, 1980. Hereafter cited as Orrick.

[83]U.S. v. Washington, No. 9213-II, Amended Judgment, 2 at 2 and 3, W.D. Wash., January 16, 1981, cited in Blumm and Johnson, p. 16.

[84]Blumm and Johnson, p. 17.

[85]Blumm and Johnson, pp. 20-22.

[86]Blumm and Johnson, pp. 24-25.

[87]Blumm and Johnson, p. 27.

[88]Blumm and Johnson, p. 27.

[89]Material for this summary is based on: James C. Waldo, *U.S. v. Washington, Phase II: Analysis and Recommendations*, Study for Northwest Water Resources Committee (Gordon, Thomas, Honeywell, Malanca, Peterson and O'Hern), September 1981.

[90]U.S. v. Sioux Nation of Indians, No. 79-639, June 30, 1980, Supreme Court of the United States.

[91]Sioux Nation of Indians v. U.S., U.S. Court of Claims, No. 148-78, June 13, 1979, pp. 4-5. Hereafter cited as *Court of Claims 1979*.

[92]*Court of Claims 1979*.

93 19 Stat. 254.

94 92 Stat. 153.

95 88 Stat. 1499 (1974).

96 Scout J. Paltrow, The Washington Star, May 27, 1981.

97 Interviews with staff of the Office of Indian Services and review of file materials, April 1982.

98 Memo to Acting Deputy Commissioner from Robert Pennington, Chief, Branch of Tribal Services, September 6, 1979.

99 Robert Pennington, notes, September 7, 1979.

100 The Dakota Sun (Fort Yates, ND), July 31, 1980.

101 The Dakota Sun (Fort Yates, ND), July 24, 1980.

102 Oyate Wichao, publication of the Dakota American Indian Movement, February-May 1981.

103 *Ibid.*

CHAPTER 3
FEDERAL GOVERNMENT SERVICES
TO INDIANS

INTRODUCTION

Indian tribes were strong, independent groups at the beginning of this nation. They were avidly sought as allies by both the British and the Colonists during the Revolutionary War. The young American nation dealt with tribes as independent groups and utilized representatives with ambassadorial functions to negotiate agreements. The President and the Congress were often involved in Indian relations and policy, and the Federal Government was designated as having the major responsibility for Indian relations by Article I, Sec. 8, of the Constitution which vested power in the Congress to regulate commerce with Indian tribes.

Henry Knox, Secretary of War under George Washington, was assigned administrative duties related to agreements with Indians, such as the paper work and funding involved in annuity payments provided for in treaties. These administrative functions became the nucleus of the Bureau of Indian Affairs established by statute in 1832. Military officers were often used as negotiators, sometimes as Indian agents, and, when necessary, as leaders of military units to control Indians or non-Indians when events got out of hand. The War Department played a prominent role in Indian matters through most of the 19th century.

Territorial governors often served as Indian agents as well as carrying out their other governmental functions and reported to the War Department on Indian matters and to the State Department on other territorial affairs. William Henry Harrison when Governor of Indiana Territory was the lead negotiator in fifteen treaties between 1800 and 1812 which secured land for most of what today is Illinois, Indiana, and portions of Ohio, Michigan and Wisconsin.

In 1849 the Bureau of Indian Affairs (often referred to as the Office of Indian Affairs) was transferred to the new Interior Department. Since religious organizations had been active in educational and other "civilizing" activities for Indians, President Ulysses S. Grant appointed many superintendents nominated by religious groups and in 1871, 67 of the 74 agencies were headed by such nominees. This practice was abandoned in the 1880s.

A Board of Indian Commissioners was appointed by the President in 1869 to have joint control with the Secretary of the Interior over the disbursement of appropriations. The Board was abandoned in 1933.

The cessation of treaty-making with Indians in 1871, the passage of the Allotment Act in 1887, the confinement of Indians to reservations, and the inability of many Indians, especially traditional hunting groups, to support themselves resulted in the assumption of many aspects of tribal government by Indian agents. The number of Bureau of Indian Affairs employees was greatly increased to administer the assignment of allotments of land, disbursement of rations, maintenance of law and order, and other duties related to the governing of Indian communities.

Toward the end of the 19th and the first quarter of the 20th century, the Bureau of Indian Affairs was the preeminent agency for Indian matters. In 1921 the Snyder Act indicated that the BIA was to provide for the general support and civilization of the Indians through programs for education, welfare, health, industrial assistance, improvement of irrigation, and administration of land. To carry out these programs the Commissioner was to employ superintendents, matrons, farmers, physicians, Indian police, Indian judges, and other employees and provide buildings, grounds and other incidental services for the administration of Indian affairs.

Thus the Bureau of Indian Affairs was a composite of Federal, state and local government for reservation Indians, plus being trustee for Indian land and resources, normally a private sector function. It was a government in miniature responsible for all activities normally provided by three levels of government for other citizens.

Citizenship for Indians had been conferred by treaty provisions as early as 1817. The Allotment Act of 1887 provided that Indians receiving allotments of land would become citizens of the United States, but was amended to provide that citizenship would accrue upon termination of the BIA's trust responsibility for the land. As a result of the fine showing of Indian troops in World War I, the interdependence of Indian groups with the larger society, and the policy aim of integrating Indians into American society, the Congress in 1924 conferred citizenship on all Indians, not already citizens, born within the territorial limits of the United States.

Studies by Laurence F. Schmeckebier (1927) and Lewis Meriam and Associates (1928) further described BIA organization and functions and made recommendations for improvement including the goal of transferring responsibility for Indian services to the Indians themselves and to the state and local governments so that the same governments would be involved as for other citizens.

An early indicator of the movement toward assumption of Indian functions by other Federal agencies was the Social Security Act of 1935 which resulted in the administration of various categorical grants, such as Aid to Families with Dependent Children (AFDC), directly from the Social Security Administration through the states to citizens—Indian citizens as well as other citizens. This was a forerunner of what was to happen many times in the next forty years as the Federal government assumed new functions serving all citizens.

Another impetus for transfer of BIA responsibilities to other Federal entities was the centrifugal force of specialties seeking their own habitat. The leaders of Indian education and Indian health in BIA had long sought independence from lay supervision by generalists such as the Commissioner, area directors, and agency superintendents. Indian health was considered for transfer to the Public Health Service as early as 1936 and the transfer actually occurred in 1955. This moved 3500 employees (25 percent of the BIA staff) and a key function out of BIA. In contrast to normally accepted bureaucratic mythology, Interior sought the transfer and the Department of Health, Education and Welfare, supported by the Bureau of the Budget, opposed it.

Interior's main arguments for the transfer were:

1. The Public Health Service is a specialized health agency and could do a better job than an Interior Department Bureau.

2. The Department of Health, Education and Welfare had many grant-in-aid programs financed in part with Federal funds, and could better determine the extent the Indian is receiving services available to him as a citizen.

3. In any event, the Bureau had become more dependent on the Public Health Servcie for medical personnel.

4. The fragmentation of Indian services with the need for Indians to work out problems and services with another agency through normal community and agency facilities would be worth any administrative difficulty that might be encountered.

In the Senate hearings on the transfer (83rd Cong., 2d Sess., May 28 and 29, 1954) the Interior spokesman recognized that its position would also logically support the transfer of other functions for similar reasons, such as education, welfare and law and order. However, if other transfers were to be made they should be done later as moving too much at one time would be too big an adjustment for the Indians as well as for the states and communities involved.

Interior's position in pushing for the transfer of Indian Health to the Public Health Service would not have made much sense in the 1920s when the Indian agency superintendent and his staff were "the government" on many reservations. However, the reservation situation was changing. In 1934

Commissioner John Collier succeeded in persuading Congress to enact the Indian Reorganization Act which reordered policy by declaring the Federal goal to be the development and strengthening of tribal governments so that they could move toward the administration of their own affairs. Thus, in point 4 above, it was argued that if these tribal governments or other Indian groups had to work with different government agencies in the same manner as other communities it would help them gain experience and increase their ability to become more nearly self-sufficient.

In opposition to Interior the Department of Health, Education and Welfare argued:

1. The fragmentation of functional responsibilities for Indian affairs at the Federal level would cause confusion of policy, duplication of effort, and lack of coordination.

2. The Public Health Service was already largely staffing the Bureau's medical service and this would not be materially changed.

3. The transfer of responsibility in itself could not be expected to solve problems of geography, economic status, and cultural, social, and education levels.

4. The Public Health Service did not know the legislative, historic, and cultural background of the Indians; the Bureau did.

5. There would be administrative difficulties, such as using the same common utility services, duplication of administrative structure, and ·unnecessary expense.

6. Because of the above, the transfer would tend to increase the difficulties of pursuing the policy of integrating the Indian into the general pattern of community and state service.

The transfer of the health function was based in part on a "plan to dismantle the Bureau of Indian Affairs by tranferring its separate functions to the executive departments which handled that specific area."[1] For example, in addition to the transfer of health to the U.S. Public Health Service, education would be transferred to the Office of Education and law and order to the Department of Justice.

This program did not develop as envisioned.

The BIA did succeed in involving the Federal Extension Service of the Department of Agriculture in leadership and assistance in Indian extension work since the BIA was contracting with state extension services to help Indian farmers. A memorandum of understanding with the Federal Extension Service became effective in 1956.[2]

The turbulent 60s brought many changes to American society including social legislation of the Kennedy and Johnson presidencies such as civil rights, aid to education, war on poverty, housing, manpower training, and economic development. Philleo Nash, Commissioner of Indian Affairs in the early 1960s, wanted to utilize the total resources of the Federal government for Indian communities.[3] He stimulated arrangements with the Department of Labor to apply the provisions of the Manpower Development and Training Act to Indians. He persuaded Congress to approve the eligibility of Indian reservations for War on Poverty funds and encouraged tribal leaders to apply for and utilize Federal grants. The Office of Economic Opportunity (OEO) established a Community Action Project for Indian reservations and Commissioner Nash strongly endorsed this program. To carry out the Indian program OEO established an "Indian Desk" and other departments often adopted this same practice. In contrast to the philosophy of Commissioner Glenn Emmons, in whose administration the health function was transferred from BIA, Nash looked to Indian Desks to act as technical advisers to the Bureau rather than as recipients of BIA functions. However, the agencies with funds for Indians often dealt directly with tribes and individual Indians.

Examples illustrate what took place in the 60s: (1) Public school districts were authorized to count Indians in the formula for reimbursement under the impact aid program. (2) Prior to 1960 the BIA had not had a housing program as such. The establishment of the Department of Housing and Urban Development resulted in a vigorous Indian housing program with HUD providing most of the funds and with sanitation and water supply funds coming from the Indian Health Service. BIA worked closely with these two agencies and helped tribes apply for and administer funds. In 1966 there were 19,000 units of standard housing on Indian reservations, in 1970 this number had increased to 30,560, and by 1980 to 76,000 standard units of housing.[4] (3) OEO Indian projects were funded at $27 million in 1971 and the Economic Development Administration (EDA) from the mid 1960s to 1971 spent $100 million for Indian commercial and industrial endeavors. (4) Various provisions of the Elementary and Secondary Education Act, as amended, helped public and Indian schools fund programs to meet special Indian student needs.

These examples illustrate the success since the 1960s of Indian advocates who sought special provisions for Indians in legislation which provided services or grants to the general public. These advocates not only included BIA but the staffs of the House and Senate committees dealing with Indian affairs, Washington-wise Indian lobbies, aggressive tribal leaders and Washington representatives retained by individual tribes (see chapter 5).

By 1970 the BIA was responsible for only 50 percent of Federal funding for Indians. The approximately $600 million for Indian programs in 1970 was distributed to the following departments and activities: Agriculture, $22 million; Commerce, $22 million; Defense, $2 million; Office of Economic Opportunity, $33.5 million; Health, Education and Welfare (HEW), $170 million; Housing and Urban Development (HUD), $22.5 million; Interior, $314 million; Labor, $6.5 million; and the Small Business Administration, $4.5 million.[5] BIA accounted for $309 million of the Interior figure.

In 1980 BIA spent only one-third of the $3 billion available for Indian programs from the Federal government. As is obvious from the totals for 1970 and 1980, funds for Indians had increased five-fold in the decade. A summary of funding for current Indian programs is provided in Tables 3-1 and 3-2 and Figure 3-1 is a organization chart of Federal government agencies. Tables 3-1 and 3-2 do not include funds spent on Indians in many programs generally available to all citizens such as Social Security, food stamps, unemployment compensation, home energy assistance, AFDC, and Supplemental Security Income (SSI).

TABLE 3-1

INDIAN FUNDING BY AGENCY ($ IN MILLIONS)

Agency	1980 Actual	1981 Est.	Carter 1982 Est.	Reagan 1982 Est.
Interior	1023	1048	1079	1004
Housing and Urban Development (HUD)	884	843	740	34
Health and Human Services (HHS)	655	717	806	663
Education	231	276	284	256
Labor	198	157	203	102
Agriculture (USDA)	36	45	53	53
Commerce	26	19	26	0
Treasury (Revenue Sharing)	10	11	11	11
Total	3063	3116	3202	2123

Source: From a fact sheet prepared by the Office of Management and Budget, dated March 20, 1981. Included as attachment 3 in a Memorandum to Tribal Leaders, March 31, 1981, from James F. Canan, Acting Deputy Assistant Secretary, Indian Affairs, Interior Department. Fact sheet does not include Indian participation in Federal programs generally available to all U. S. citizens, and therefore, excludes funding for such items as Social Security, Food Stamps, Unemployment Compensation, Home Energy Assistance, Aid to Families with Dependent Children, and Supplemental Security Income.

TABLE 3-2

INDIAN FUNDING BY PROGRAM AND AGENCY ($ IN MILLIONS)

	1980 Actual	1981 Estimate	1982 Carter Budget	1982 Reagan Budget
Education	484	528	536	492
Interior	(270)	(274)	(282)	(266)
Education	(214)	(254)	(254)	(226)
Health Services/Nutrition	583	652	708	680
HHS	(547)	(607)	(655)	(627)
USDA	(36)	(45)	(53)	(53)
Housing	867	829	727	18
Interior	(19)	(23)	(24)	(18)
HUD	(848)	(806)	(703)	(0)
Social Services	121	124	130	118
Interior	(87)	(90)	(96)	(90)
HHS	(34)	(34)	(34)	(28)
Employment	250	203	249	136
Interior	(52)	(46)	(46)	(34)
Labor	(198)	(157)	(203)	(102)
Economic Development .	88	84	92	62
Interior	(26)	(28)	(29)	(28)
Commerce	(26)	(19)	(26)	(0)
HUD	(36)	(37)	(37)	(34)
Natural Resources	74	87	87	86
Interior	(74)	(87)	(87)	(86)
Trust Activities	51	45	48	48
Interior	(51)	(45)	(48)	(48)
Management & Facilities .	131	141	151	151
Interior	(131)	(141)	(151)	(151)
Construction	251	247	319	194
Interior	(160)	(149)	(172)	(156)
HHS	(74)	(76)	(117)	(8)
Education.........	(17)	(22)	(30)	(30)
Other Interior Funds ...	153	165	144	127
Revenue Sharing	10	11	11	11
Total Federal Funds	3,063	3,116	3,202	2,123
Interior Trust Funds ...	969	511	465	465
Total Federal/Trust	4,032	3,627	3,667	2,588
Est. Federal funds per capita	$4,400	$4,450	$4,600	$3,000

Source: From a fact sheet prepared by the Office of Management and Budget, dated March 20, 1981.

FIGURE 3.1. THE GOVERNMENT OF THE UNITED STATES

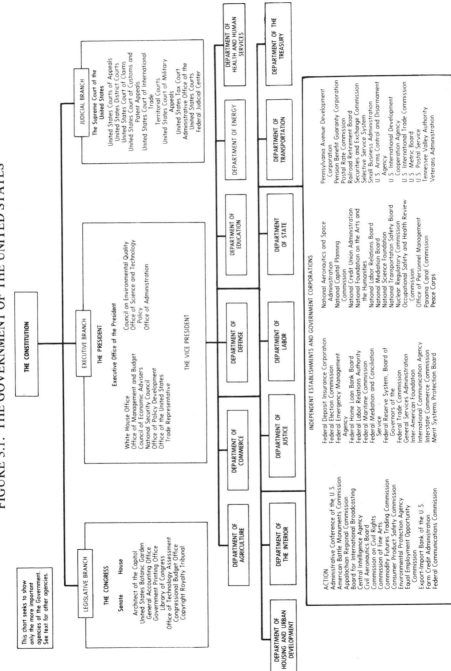

The history of Federal government agencies dealing with Indians indicates that in the early days all pertinent parts of the Federal government were involved—the Executive Branch including the President and the State and War departments, the Congress, and the Courts. Gradually most Federal executive activities related to Indians were concentrated in the Bureau of Indian Affairs (1870-1930). Then with the advent of the Indian Reorganization Act and the encouragement of tribal government, the U.S. citizenship of Indians, the desire of specialists to work with their own kind, and national policies resulting in the assumption of many new responsibilities by the Federal government for all citizens, the pendulum began to swing back toward increased fragmentation of Federal services for Indians.

Federal Agency responsibilities outlined in the following pages portray the wide scope of services and funds provided to Indian communities as the result of the trends and events briefly described above. The Reagan administration is reducing funding for some of these programs.

DEPARTMENT OF THE INTERIOR

Since 1849 when the Bureau of Indian Affairs was transferred from the Department of War to the Department of Interior, Interior has had the primary responsibility for carrying out Federal functions for Indians. Although Indian functions are now dispersed throughout the Federal structure, the Bureau of Indian Affairs remains the primary agency.

Bureau of Indian Affairs

The Bureau of Indian Affairs (BIA) is directed by an Assistant Secretary of Interior who discharges the authority and responsibility of the secretary for Indians. (See Fig. 3-2) He has one deputy (1983) who administers the BIA in lieu of a commissioner. The principle objectives of the Bureau are to encourage and train Indian and Alaska native peoples to manage their own affairs, to promote full development of Indian human and resource potential, to make available public and private aids to Indians and to utilize Indians in the direction and management of programs for their benefit.

BIA works with the Indian people, their governments and other interested groups to help provide adequate educational opportunities, social and community development, economic advancement and effective use of Indian-owned natural resources consistent with resource conservation. The BIA is trustee for Indian lands and monies held in trust by the United States. To carry out its responsibilities the Bureau has the organizational entities and programs shown in Table 3-3, BIA F. Y. 1983 Budget Request.

FIGURE 3.2. DEPARTMENT OF THE INTERIOR

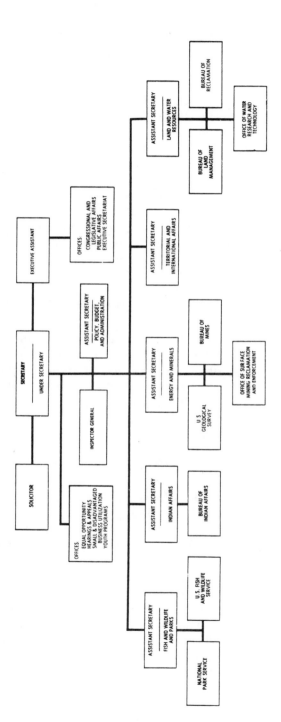

DEPARTMENT OF THE INTERIOR

TABLE 3-3

BIA F.Y. 1984 BUDGET REQUEST AND F.Y. 1983 EXPENDITURES
($ IN THOUSANDS)

	FY 1983 Approp. to date	FY 1983[2] Budget Estimate	FY 1984 Budget Estimate
School Operations	177,075	179,556	174,947
Johnson O'Malley Education Assistance	35,579[1]	35,579[1]	26,000
Continuing Education	51,451	51,658	48,121
EDUCATION	264,105	266,793	249,068
Tribal Government Services	25,473	25,609	23,534
Social Services	100,187	100,187	98,609
Law Enforcement	35,697	35,972	34,521
Housing	23,233	23,298	22,068
Self-Determination Services	52,822	52,876	60,198
Navajo-Hopi Settlement Program	3,899	3,923	3,951
INDIAN SERVICES	241,126	241,865	242,881
Employment Development	27,429	27,554	27,641
Business Enterprise Development	10,854	10,966	15,543
Road Maintenance	21,037	21,301	22,351
ECONOMIC DEVELOPMENT AND EMPLOYMENT PROGRAMS	59,320	59,821	65,535
Forestry and Agriculture	69,360	70,236	73,402
Minerals, Mining, Irrigation and Power	14,981	15,005	15,881
NATURAL RESOURCES DEVELOPMENT	84,341	85,241	89,283
Indian Rights Protection	17,634	17,723	16,323
Real Estate and Financial Trust Services	28,405	28,877	27,732
TRUST RESPONSIBILITIES	46,039	46,600	44,055
FACILITIES MANAGEMENT	88,900	89,872	88,910
Management and Administration	47,854	48,826	49,434
Employee Compensation Payments	4,582	4,582	6,829
Program Management	7,241	7,377	5,520
GENERAL ADMINISTRATION	59,677	60,785	61,783
1983 PROPOSED SUPPLEMENTALS			
Fire Suppression		14,000	-0-
Federal Employee Pay Cost (distrib. in column 2)		(7,469)	-0-
OPERATION OF INDIAN PROGRAMS (Total)	843,508	864,977	841,515
Irrigation Systems	18,900	18,900	5,325
Building and Utilities	48,350	48,350	50,550
Land Acquisition	-0-	-0-	-0-
CONSTRUCTION (Total)	67,250	67,250	55,875
ROAD CONSTRUCTION (Total)	43,585[3]	43,585[3]	4,000[3]
TOTAL, FEDERAL APPROPRIATIONS	954,343	975,812	901,390

[1]Includes $9,350 for Alaska school transfers, to remain available until expended.

[2]Program amounts include actual appropriations and pending supplemental requests.

[3]Does not include construction project funds which will be provided through contract authority from the Highway Trust Fund as part of the Federal Lands Highway Program of the Department of Transportation (1983=$75.0 million; 1984=$100.0 million).

Source: *Indian News Notes*, Vol. 7, No. 4, Bureau of Indian Affairs, Office of Public Information, Jan. 28, 1983.

Education: Education is the largest BIA program in terms of funds and personnel. BIA operates schools for approximately 30,000 students, funds contract schools with tribes for 8,000 students and supervises supplemental funds for approximately 180,000 Indian students in state public schools. Twenty to twenty-five percent of reservation Indian children are educated in BIA schools and two percent in tribal schools funded by BIA. Many Indians serve on local public school boards in school districts serving Indian children. College scholarships for 20,000 Indian students were provided in 1980 and some tribally operated post-secondary schools and adult education programs were supported. Education is viewed by many as an important process for helping Indians achieve economic, social and political self-sufficiency.

Services to Tribal Governments: Funds and assistance are provided to tribal governments to improve governmental operations including judicial capacities and managerial functions. BIA negotiates "self-determination" contracts for tribal operation of their own programs using BIA funds. Welfare assistance is available from BIA when state services are not adequate. BIA supports law enforcement services either through its own employees or by contract with the tribes in those instances in which state law and order jurisdiction is not applicable to particular reservations. BIA assists tribes and individuals in obtaining new and rehabilitated housing, including HUD programs which have provided the bulk of new housing on reservations in recent years. Housing funds have been severely reduced.

Economic Development and Employment: Adult vocational training, job placement, work experience and on-the-job training are available to promote Indian economic self-sufficiency skills. BIA also encourages and helps with commercial, business, industry and tourism enterprises. Credit and financing is provided by BIA and other agencies. Roads are important to the reservation economy and about 18,000 miles of road are maintained by BIA.

Natural Resources Development: Indian agencies assist Indian land owners in improving agriculture, range, irrigation and electric power, forestry, fish, wildlife, recreation and environmental quality. Water entitlements are supported. Some tribes possess energy-producing minerals and BIA helps them maximize income from these resources. Irrigation is important in parts of the West and BIA subsidizes Indians engaged in irrigated farming.

Trust Responsibility: The BIA is trustee for Indian land and thus is responsible for working with Indians to obtain the greatest possible return from land use while at the same time preserving or conserving the resource through such activities as sustained yield management of forest and range, and wise drilling and control procedures for oil and gas. There are 52 million acres of Indian land in trust. BIA protects Indian resources such as water, hunting and fishing rights.

For income from tribal resources and claims awards, BIA has certain responsibilities, e.g., to see that interest income is obtained and that funds are used for appropriate purposes.

Administrative Support: Construction and maintenance of school and other buildings, hiring and supervising personnel, preparation of budgets, accounting, purchase of materials and supplies, payroll and other services are major activities in an organization the size of the Bureau with 12,000 permanent employees (75 to 80 percent have some Indian blood). Most buildings, facilities and employees are located on Indian reservations throughout the country.

Summary: The Bureau of Indian Affairs combines the tremendous variety of many local and state functions with Federal functions. It has added duties of trustee normally found only in the private sector. Involved are direct service operations, technical assistance, training, monitoring of work contracted out and surveillance of reimbursable work done by other Interior bureaus. Complicating the situation are racial and cultural factors as well as an estimated 5000 statutes, many treaties, and thousands of court decisions on Indian policy and procedure.[6]

Other Interior Bureaus

Although the BIA is the central organization for Indian affairs in the Department of the Interior, other Interior bureaus are also involved. Indian activities in these bureaus are funded in two ways: reimbursement primarily by the BIA or tribe, or directly from the relevant bureau's own appropriation.

The U.S. *Fish and Wildlife Service* provides fishery technical assistance to tribes in the preparation of fish management plans and in the implementation of such plans; fish hatchery operations and fish stocking for Indian reservations; predatory animal and prairie dog control; and wildlife management planning, including inventories and management plans for deer and other big game.

The U.S. *Geological Survey* (USGS) conducts inspections, reviews permits or lease plans, and makes environmental assessments for oil and gas, coal and other energy programs on Indian reservations. This includes help in monitoring royalty accounting for the Indian share of income from oil and gas production. The USGS also carries out field geologic and geophysical investigations of the mineral potential of Indian reservations, water resource investigations including quantitative and qualitative studies and preparation of aerial topographic and other maps for Indian reservations.

Cadastral (boundary) surveys and issuance of land patents for transferring land to Alaska Natives under the Alaska Native Claims Settlement Act, in

Maine, and other land transfers are performed by the *Bureau of Land Management*.

The *Bureau of Mines* helps determine the mineral potential on Indian reservations. The Office of Surface Mining worked with the Navajo and Crow tribes on land recovery plans related to surface mining in 1981.

Archeological investigations by the *U.S. Park Service* help BIA and the tribes. The Park Service advises on facilities such as the Navajo fairgrounds and the Yakima cultural center, tribal park and recreation facilities and rehabilitation of Hopi villages. It also has investigated approximately 4,000 Native historic sites and cemeteries under the provisions of the Alaska Native Claims Settlement Act. The Service also provides technical assistance to tribes on ranger, park, and museum activities.

The *Bureau of Reclamation* is constructing the waterworks for the Navajo Irrigation Project with reimbursable funds from BIA. With its own appropriated funds, Reclamation worked with approximately 15 tribes in 1981 on various stages of irrigation and water projects including, in some instances, impacts on fishery and wildlife resources. Many of these projects may help support Indian claims to water rights.

In addition to the Assistant Secretary for Indians, the *Office of the Secretary of Interior* includes the *Office of Hearings and Appeals* and the *Office of the Solicitor*. The Office of Hearings and Appeals is in charge of Indian probate hearings, claims under the Alaska Native Claims Settlement Act, and administrative appeals on Indian matters. The Office of the Solicitor provides legal advice and counsel regarding Indian affairs.

The Secretary of the Interior appoints the five commissioners of the *Indian Arts and Crafts Board* who serve without compensation and employ a professional staff to promote the development of Native American arts and crafts and to operate three regional Indian museums. Annual sales of Native American arts and handicrafts total several hundred million dollars, but Native American interests control only a small proportion of this market. The Board assists in expanding Native participation through over 150 Native craft marketing enterprises and other promotional and informational efforts. The Board also helps Natives counteract misrepresentation of imitation arts by working with consumer protection officials, newspapers, and private marketing organizations. Funds for this activity are carried in the BIA appropriation for convenience. The 1982 amount was $856,000.

Table 3-4 presents a summary of Indian services by the U.S. Department of Interior bureaus and offices, other than BIA, for fiscal year 1981.

In addition to the specific programs described above, the special expertise and organizational capability of the various activities in the U.S. Interior Department are utilized for services to Indians when appropriate. This does not mean that the various bureau programs are always in harmony with BIA objectives.

TABLE 3-4

SERVICES FOR INDIANS, INTERIOR ACTITIVITIES
OTHER THAN BUREAU OF INDIAN AFFAIRS,
1981 ($ IN THOUSANDS)

Bureau, Service or Activity	Reimbursable	Non-Reimbursable
Fish and Wildlife Service		
Fish and game activities on various reservations	$ 1634.4	$ 3121.6
Geological Survey		
Conservation, geologic, water resource and mapping services; technical assistance for oil, gas, coal etc. on Indian reservations	4315.6	3075.8
Bureau of Land Management		
Realty conveyances, realty records and cadastral surveys on Indian land	1300.0	7960.0
Bureau of Mines		
Assessment of mineral potential on Indian reservations	1547.0	—
Office of Surface Mining		
Abandoned mine land restoration programs	—	520.9
National Park Service		
Archeological, cultural and recreational assistance to Indian groups	897.6	1160.1
Bureau of Reclamation		
Navajo irrigation construction	11480.0	—
Construction, operation and maintenance of various Indian projects	—	31546.0
Office of the Secretary		
Board of Indian Appeals	—	236.0
Indian Probate	—	1118.0
Office of Solicitor - work on Indian matters	40.0	3500.0
Total	$21214.6	$52238.4

Source: Information from bureaus and activities in response to a memorandum dated November 20, 1981, from the Director, Office of Budget, Interior Department, requesting programs and funds for Indians for fiscal year 1981.

DEPARTMENT OF HOUSING AND
URBAN DEVELOPMENT (HUD)

The principle agency concerned with housing needs, fair housing opportunities and improving the nation's communities is the Department of Housing and Urban Development (HUD). It has been a major factor in new and improved housing for Indians. The Office of the Secretary of HUD has staff offices with department wide coordinating responsibilities in functional areas and one of these is the Office of Indian and Alaska Native Programs.

Indian Housing Program

HUD works through Indian Housing Authorities (IHAs) established by tribal governments or under state law. HUD funds and assistance have been providing about 70 percent of the additional housing in Indian areas.[7] Technical assistance and funds are in the form of (1) preliminary loans for survey and planning, (2) development loans during construction and (3) debt service annual contributions to pay interest and principal on the obligations issued to provide the permanent financing. Some of the projects are rental, but most are mutual-help home ownership opportunity projects in which the participating families make a contribution of land or labor for which they are given credit toward acquiring home ownership.

Modernization for Indian Housing Authorities (IHAs)

This program provides funds to IHAs for needed physical and management improvements in existing rental projects and to finance selected physical improvements in existing home ownership projects. The improvements are financed over a 20-year period.

Operating Subsidies

Subsidies as required are provided to IHAs to help maintain and operate projects, retain minimum operating reserves and offset certain operating deficits.

For Indian mutual help homeownership projects, an operating subsidy will be paid only to reimburse an IHA for: (1) HUD-approved costs of Independent Public Accountant audits; (2) administrative charges for vacant units; (3) collection losses due to payment deliquencies on the part of homebuyer families whose mutual help and occupancy agreements have been terminated and who have vacated the home, and the actual cost of any maintenance (including repairs and replacements) necessary to put the vacant home in a suitable condition for a substitute homebuyer family; (4) the cost of

HUD-approved homebuyer counseling but not in duplication of such counseling funded under a development cost budget; (5) HUD-approved costs for training of IHA staff and commissioners; and (6) other unusual operating costs as determined by HUD, justifying payment of operating subsidy.

For mutual help projects, no operating subsidy is paid for utilities, maintenance or other items for which the homebuyer is responsible under the mutual help and occupancy agreement.

Community Development Block Grants

Grants to Indian tribes and Alaskan villages can be for a single activity or for several activities. Eligible for funding are such activities as housing rehabilitation programs, construction or rehabilitation of recreational facilities, property acquisition, senior centers, tribal facilities, water and sewer improvements, and commercial and industrial facilities. Only 20 percent of a grant can be used for planning and administration.

Comprehensive Planning Assistance (701 Program)

The purpose of this program for Indian tribes is to improve the capacity of tribes to plan and manage their program goals and activities. Grants may be made for as much as two-thirds of the estimated cost of a planning project and can be used only to carry out planning and related activities.

Urban Development Action Grants (UDAG)

A 1980 amendment authorized consideration of Indian tribes for these grants for distressed communities. Assistance may be made available for economic revitalization in communities with out-migration and declining tax base, and for reclamation of neighborhoods with high housing abandonment or deterioration. There were no Indian funds specified for 1981.

DEPARTMENT OF HEALTH AND HUMAN SERVICES (HHS)

The Department of Health and Human Services (HHS) is concerned with people and touches the lives of more Americans than any other Federal agency. Its functions range from social security to improving health services and from serving newborn infants to elderly citizens.[8] Many of the HHS programs are available to Native Americans as citizens when they meet program eligibility requirements.

Indian Health Service (IHS)

Of those programs that specifically relate to Indians, the most important is the Indian Health Service (IHS) which is a bureau within the Health Services Administration of the Public Health Service.

> The Indian Health Service operates a program of comprehensive health services for eligible American Indians and Alaska Natives; provides hospital and medical care services and preventive and rehabilitative health services; develops innovative health services delivery systems; conducts tuberculosis and other communicable disease control activities; promotes self-determination of Indian people through community development and participation in program operation and administration; encourages and assists in the development of water supply and waste disposal systems; and provides training for health personnel. [9]

The Indian Self-Determination and Education Assistance Act of 1975 (P.L. 93-638) provided a mechanism for Indian tribes to determine and operate through contract their own health programs. The Indian Health Care Improvement Act, enacted in 1976 [10] authorized resources to carry out the objectives of Indian self-determination, established national goals for programs providing health services to Indian people, and required the Secretary of HHS to report to the Congress on additional authorities needed during the last four years of the act, FYs 1981-1984. In response, the Secretary in April 1980, submitted a national plan based on 250 tribal and 41 urban Indian health plans to guide program development and resource allocations.

Some tribes choose to operate major portions of the health care system directly. For example, fully functioning health programs are being operated (1981) by the Seneca Nation of New York, the Menominee Tribe of Wisconsin, the Norton Sound Health Corporation, and the Bristol Bay Area Health Corporation of Alaska. Hospitals are being operated by the Creek Nation in Oklahoma, the Navajo Health Foundation in Arizona, and the Norton Sound and Bristol Bay organizations cited above. [11]

During FYs 1976-1979, IHS funded 22 tribal feasibility projects, 475 tribal development projects, and 1,082 tribal operations contracts for tribal health programs. Tribes and other Indian organizations operate 252 health clinics and health stations. Tribally operated health delivery systems during FY 1980 included 13,793 in-patient days and approximately 575,000 clinic outpatient visits; 38,600 hospital outpatient visits; mental health, alcoholism, and nutrition counseling, and assistance to the aging. More than 5,000 tribal employees in 1980 engaged in providing health services directly or by contract with other health facilities. [12]

IHS also emphasizes identification of Indians with a potential for education and training in the health professions and encourages and assists them in enrolling in health or allied health professional schools. In support of this effort IHS provides scholarship grants to Indians for pre-professional education to enable Indians to qualify for a health profession school. Also available are scholarship grants to Indians and others for completion of health professional education, with an obligation of service payback. The Secretary of HHS may make one grant to an individual who has completed his obligated service and who agrees to engage in private full-time clinical practice in a health manpower shortage area for at least one year. This grant is to assist in meeting the costs of beginning a private practice, such as acquiring equipment or renovating facilities, hiring nurses and other personnel to assist in providing health services. [13]

Health Facilities. IHS-operated health facilities in FY 1982 included 48 hospitals, 99 health centers, and 300 smaller health stations and satellite clinics.

In addition to the IHS and tribal health delivery systems, the IHS operates a contract health care system for services not available in IHS or tribal facilities.

Environmental Health. IHS offers technical assistance, services and training for all aspects of environmental health including rabies control, plague control, water supply and waste disposal, safety, injury control, radiation hazards, and disease vector control.

Sanitation Facilities. IHS also coordinates the program to provide essential water and sanitation facilities for Indian homes and communities on reservations. This activity is under an interdepartmental agreement among the Department of Housing and Urban Development (HUD), the Bureau of Indian Affairs (BIA) and the Indian Health Service (IHS). With the completion of projects authorized through 1980, more than 900 of the 1,500 Indian and Alaska Native communities will have been provided community water and/or sewer systems, serving about 127,000 Indian and Alaska Native homes. Half of these homes were built or renovated under Indian housing programs.

Emergency Medical Services (EMS). Until recently, ambulance and emergency services were almost non-existent in many isolated reservation settings. By 1979 there were 47 tribal ambulance services. IHS makes every effort to support the continued operation of these programs. Emergency care in IHS hospitals and health centers has always been provided, but it is being upgraded to meet national standards.

IHS-State Cooperative Program. Maximum utilization of health resources for Indians is achieved through many direct and indirect cooperative programs between IHS, the tribes and various state agencies. Examples are:

Improved pregnancy outcome funds from the Arizona State Health Department (funds from HHS) to the Kayenta Health Corporation were utilized with assistance from the Nurse-Midwifery Branch of the IHS facility at Window Rock, Arizona.

A grant from the Arizona State Health Department to the Phoenix IHS office was administered by IHS to reduce infant mortality on the San Carlos Apache reservation.

New Mexico's laboratories for identifying communicable disease organisms are available for the IHS vector control program for diseases such as plague, rabies, and encephalitis.

Community Health Representatives. Services include community outreach and health services. This program is operated by tribal organizations funded by IHS. It is a paraprofessional cadre of indigenous people and often a crucial element in health care in remote portions of reservations.

Mental Health. This program provides mental health services in crisis intervention, and out-patient visits and post hospitalization follow-ups. It endeavors to maintain children in their home community because removal often is detrimental to mental health. An attempt is made to identify "at risk populations" and to provide needed intervention services. IHS funds 62 tribal mental health programs.

Family Planning. In view of the joblessness and poverty of many reservations accompanied by a high birth rate, the author asked BIA and IHS whether there were any family planning programs available to Indians. There is no family planning program in either agency. If asked, BIA social workers may refer Indian clients to the IHS for medical advice but no policy or guidelines exist. IHS will provide information on birth control methods when appropriate as a part of its medical services so that Indians wishing to regulate the size of their families may do so. There is no official goal to reduce the size of families. This is a private matter for Indian families. Live births per 1,000 population in 1978 were: 31.5 for Indians and 15.3 for the population at large.[14]

Program Management. The headquarters organization provides program direction by establishing goals and priorities, coordinates IHS activities within the program and with other governmental programs, prepares and justifies the budget, gathers and analyzes statistics, carries out research and development, and performs legislative and regulative activities.

The eight area and three program offices provide program direction and administrative support to each of the 49 hospitals, 102 health centers and several hundred other clinics.

The Medicare/Medicaid reimbursement to IHS for services to Indians eligible for Medicare or Medicaid was estimated to reach up to $20 million annually for fiscal years 1981 and 1982.

Program Results. The results of IHS programs are reduced infant deaths, and deaths due to influenza, pneumonia, accidents, cirrhosis of the liver, homicide and suicide, diabetes mellitus, and tuberculosis. Since 1955 the 3-year average infant mortality rate has been reduced by 74 percent and the maternal mortality rate has been reduced by 90 percent. Tuberculosis dropped from 57.9 deaths per 100,000 population in 1955 to 5.1 deaths per 100,000 in 1978, a reduction of approximately 91 percent.

Indians are still behind the U.S. general population, however, by various measures of health.[15] IHS is intensifying programs for preventive medicine and santitation in cooperation with the states and tribes to continue to reduce this gap.

Administration for Native Americans (ANA)

The Office of Human Development Services (HHS) has programs servicing the general public with some specific provisions for Indians. The purpose of the Administration for Native Americans is to promote economic and social self-sufficiency for American Indians, Native Hawaiians, and Alaskan Natives. Grants are made to governing bodies of Indian tribes, Alaskan Native villages and regional corporations, and other public or private non-profit agencies. Excluding Navajo, grants in 1980 averaged $125,000 for tribes, and $87,000 for urban groups. Navajo, the largest tribe, received a grant of $4.8 million.[16]

More recently, ANA has moved away from financial assistance projects which fill in service gaps or provide for a basic administrative structure. In fiscal years 1980 and 1981, ANA funded 30 reservation and off-reservation grantees to develop and carry out local strategies for social and economic development. In fiscal year 1982, all refunding applications were reviewed and funded on the basis of this developmental approach to gain self-sufficiency.

ANA is the offspring of the Indian grants program of the Office of Economic Opportunity (OEO) and the Health, Education and Welfare's (HEW) Office of Indian Affairs which were merged in HEW in 1973. The Native American Programs Act of 1974[17] extended the program and included Native Hawaiians. The statute recognizes that the broad purposes of the Act could lead to duplication with other Indian programs and provides that the Secretary must satisfy himself that funded activities "will be in addition to, and not substitution for, comparable activities."

Examples of activities are:

—The Leech Lake Reservation is a part of the Minnesota Chippewa Tribe. The ANA states that in earlier years, the reservation used its ANA funding to help develop a strong economic foundation for the community. In 1981 the reservation owned and operated 11 businesses, including logging and construction operations, a rice paddy, and a $2.5 million-a-year restaurant-grocery-service station operation. ANA funding has been used to strengthen personnel functions for 375 employees.

—The Creek Nation used its ANA grant to enhance an agricultural co-op, which includes a dairy, feed lots, forage and grain storage facilities and a large machinery and shop building. In 1976, nine persons were employed; in 1981 fifty people were employed.

—The Pueblo of Acoma has identified and analyzed both organizational and community problems, developed a land use data bank and developed a manual for administration operations. ANA funds for FY 1981 were used by the Council for comprehensive planning using demographic data and a natural resource inventory.

—ANA has joined with other organizations, public and private, in funding the Council of Energy Resource Tribes (CERT) which was created by 25 tribes with energy resources.

—ANA reports that one of its most successful interagency undertakings is a 4-year-old Indian employment initiative which has resulted in the establishment of Tribal Employment Rights Offices (TEROs) on reservations. A Tribal Employment Rights Planning Committee funded by ANA and the Department of Labor supports the TEROs with know-how, training, and the dissemination of information. The TERO project helps tribes use their authority to enforce Indian preference on the reservation and to take steps to end discrimination in public and private hiring near the reservation. ANA states that employment of Indian people on reservations has at least doubled and in some places tripled as a result of TERO negotiations with contractors and other employers. In 1981 there were 39 TEROs.

In addition to these activities with Federally-recognized tribes, ANA also provides support to off-reservation Indian communities.[18] Examples are funding for Oklahomans for Indian Opportunity and the Institute for Development of Indian law.

Other Health and Human Services (HHS) Offices

Other HHS offices with Indian programs are:[19] (1) *Alcohol, Drug Abuse, and Mental Health Administration* carries out preventive and rehabilitative measures although the description does not specifically mention Indians; (2) the *National Institutes of Health* broadens opportunities for ethnic minorities, including Indians, for biomedical research; (3) the *Health Resources Administration*, Bureau of Health Facilities, promotes energy conservation for all health facilities; (4) the *Office of Family Assistance* in the Social Security Administration provides assistance to Indian tribes and organizations to offset the rising costs of energy; (5) the *Administration for Children, Youth and Families* in the Office of Human Development Services funds Head Start for Indians as well as others and is authorized to fund assistance to Indian tribal organizations within any state which has a plan for child welfare services under the Indian Child Welfare Act of 1978;[20] and (6) the *Administration on Aging* has a program to promote the delivery of services provided other citizens under the Older Americans Act of 1965. In 1982, HHS combined some of the above programs into block grants.

The HHS *Intra-Departmental Council on Indian Affairs*, chaired by the ANA commissioner, includes the assistant secretaries, officials of major programs and the heads of all Indian programs in the Department. The council coordinates activities within the Department, with other Federal agencies, and with major private Indian organizations.

DEPARTMENT OF EDUCATION (DOE)

The Department of Education (DOE) coordinates Federal assistance to education. Most DOE programs for Indians are under the jurisdiction of the Assistant Secretary for Elementary and Secondary Education. This assistant secretary is responsible for policy, direction and coordination of activities relating to pre-school, elementary and secondary education of the Department, including grants to state agencies and local school districts for Indian education.[21]

Indian Education

The Office of Indian Education Programs administers grants to local educational agencies (K-12) to meet special educational needs and culturally related academic needs of Indian children, as well as grants "to improve educational opportunities for adult Indians." This office also is responsible for programs designed to prepare individuals for teaching or administering programs for Indian children and for awarding fellowships to Indian students in graduate and professional programs. It also coordinates other efforts to improve educational opportunities for Indians at all educational levels.[22]

Grants and Fellowships

Grants are made to local educational agencies not on Indian reservations which have at least 10 Indian children or in which Indians constitute at least 50 percent of the total enrollment.[23] Schools located on or near an Indian reservation are eligible, as well as any schools in Alaska, California, and Oklahoma. Certain Indian tribes or tribal organizations operating a school for the children of the tribe are deemed to be local educational agencies eligible for grants.

Grant funds may be used for the establishment, maintenance, and operation of educational programs; for projects to improve the educational opportunities of Indian children; for Indian adult programs to decrease illiteracy, provide skill training, help adults earn high school equivalency diplomas; and to encourage Indian culture and heritage.

Fellowships are provided for Indians to pursue studies for careers in medicine, law, engineering, natural resources, business administration, education and related fields. These fellowships may include individual stipends, dependency allowances, tuition and fees, book allowances, and, in some cases, research expenses. The appropriation for these fellowships in 1981 totaled $1.5 million.

Vocational programs carried out by tribes under the Indian Self-Determination and Education Assistance Act of 1975 or under the Johnson-O'Malley Act (JOM)[24] may be funded by the Office of Vocational and Adult Education of the DOE.

Indians are eligible for post secondary education grants, bilingual education programs and other DOE programs on the same basis as non-Indians.

Particularly noteworthy is that the DOE considers as eligible Indians other than those recognized by the Bureau of Indian Affairs for many of its programs, as does the Administration for Native Americans in HHS. Since most (80 percent) of the Indian children on reservations are educated in public schools as well as most Indian children living off the reservation, it is obvious that the DOE programs are important. BIA's JOM funds are coordinated with DOE funds by regular meetings between BIA and DOE staffs in which they exchange information on who is receiving funds, to avoid duplication.[25]

DEPARTMENT OF LABOR (DOL)

The Department of Labor fosters, promotes and develops the welfare of wage earners in the United States. One of its responsibilities is to sponsor training programs and help workers find jobs.

Indian Employment and Training

Under the Employment and Training Administration headed by an assistant secretary, there is an Office of National Programs, which in turn has a *Division of Indian and Native American Programs* with a small central staff and five regional offices. This division provides employment and training to Native Americans who are unemployed, underemployed, or economically disadvantaged, using funding authorized by the Comprehensive Employment and Training Act (CETA) of 1978. Eligible grantees are state and Federal tribes or organizations, Alaska Native villages, Native Hawaiians, and non-reservation Indian groups in all 50 states.[26]

Each grantee designs its own program, emphasizing employment and training goals to support local economic development and the creation of unsubsidized employment opportunities.

In 1981, $177,616,768 was allocated to Native Americans. CETA Title III funds are based on the number of unemployed and low income persons in an area through a formula approach. Funds from other Titles are based on the number of unemployed only. Economic development activities under Title VII are allocated on a competitive basis. Other Titles provide funds for youth programs.

A grantee must be a Native American entity with a governing body capable of administering a program and must have a service population of at least 1,000 persons.[27] CETA funds go direct to grantees with no deductions for administrative costs, which are funded from other Department appropriations.

Examples of past grantees are: Creek Nation East of the Mississippi, Alaska Federation of Natives, American Indian Center of Arkansas, Indian Center of San Jose, Colorado Division of Labor and Employment Training Services, Georgia State Commission on Indian Affairs, Indiana Indians Consortium Organization, Baltimore Mayor's Office of Manpower Resources, North American Indian Association of Detroit, New Jersey Department of Labor and Industry, American Indian Community House in New York City, North Carolina Commission on Indian Affairs, Ohio's Office of Manpower Development, Manpower Services Council of Virginia, and, of course, the governing bodies of many Federally recognized tribes.[28]

From fiscal year 1975 through fiscal year 1981 the Indian and Native American Employment and Training Program granted over $1 billion.[29]

DEPARTMENT OF AGRICULTURE (USDA)

The Department of Agriculture (USDA) works to improve farm income, expand markets for agricultural products, curb hunger and malnutrition, enhance the environment, and maintain and improve soil, water, forest and other natural resources. The department provides rural credit and sponsors conservation, conducts agricultural research and education, and safeguards and assures standards of quality in the daily food supply.[30]

All of the above activities are available to all qualifying individuals, including Indians.

There are two specific programs for Indians, however.

Indian Acute Distress Donation Program

Under this program administered by the Agricultural Stabilization and Conservation Service, feed grains owned by the Commodity Credit Corporation may be donated to Indian tribes for livestock feeding. This may occur in conditions of "chronic acute distress of the needy members of an Indian tribe due to severe drought, flood, or other catastrophes."[31]

This same program is generally available to all citizens under the Emergency Livestock Feed Program of USDA.

Indian Land Acquisition Loan Program

These funds may be used to "buy lands or interest in lands within an Indian reservation or Alaskan community. Funds may also be used to pay expenses incidental to the land purchase including the cost of appraisal, title and legal services, surveys, and loan closing."[32]

General programs available to Indians as citizens.

Loan Programs. The *Agricultural Stabilization and Conservation Service* provides cost sharing to small private forest landowners for transplanting and timber stand improvement. Indian tribes or other native groups may participate if they meet eligibility requirements. Individual Indians on tribal land are not eligible.[33]

The *Farmers Home Administration* (FmHA) assists eligible Indian farmers and ranchers to become owner-operators of family farms. Loan funds may be used to buy or enlarge family farms, to construct or repair modest farm dwellings and service buildings, to develop domestic water and sewage systems, to provide land and water development, to fund pollution control and energy saving practices, to establish approved forestry practices, and to refinance debts. Farm ownership loans are secured on the borrower's land. Loans to Indians secured by land in trust must be reviewed by the Bureau of Indian Affairs. FmHA credit is for those in rural America unable to obtain reasonable credit from other sources.

Grazing assistance loans are provided to Indians on reservations who organize grazing associations and qualify for assistance. Irrigation and drainage loans are to assist, among others, eligible Indian groups in making the best use of land and water resources. Rental and cooperative housing loans also may be made to Indians. If secured by trust, the mortgage is subject to applicable tribal or BIA regulations. Rural housing loans may be made to low and moderate-income Indian families lacking adequate housing who will become the owner occupant of a home. Rural housing site development loans are available to Indian applicants who own or will own the site, even though in restricted status. Recreation loans are available to Indians, among others, to convert all or a portion of their property to outdoor income-producing recreation enterprises. An applicant must be engaged in farming at the time he applies for a loan.

Community facility loans are available to Indian tribes for such facilities as fire and rescue services, transportation, traffic control, and community social, cultural, health and recreation activities. Also eligible are industrial park sites, access ways and utility extensions. Indian tribes are also eligible for financing of industrial sites in rural areas—including land, buildings, and utilities—to facilitate the development of private business enterprises when other financing is not available. Financing for water and waste disposal systems for Indian tribes, among others, is available under certain conditions to help assure orderly growth in rural areas.

The *Food and Nutrition Service:* (1) administers the food distribution program on Federal Indian reservations, (2) provides supplemental foods for mothers and young children (WIC) and other supplements, and (3) administers other programs which are used by Indians such as food stamps, child nutrition (school lunch), and special milk programs. These programs are to help meet the nutritional needs of low income families as well as help expand markets for food that American farmers produce. Twenty-nine tribes had WIC programs for fiscal year 1981.

In addition the Food and Nutrition Service participates with HHS in providing nutritious meals for elderly people—once a day, five days a week. In fiscal year 1981, 85 Indian tribal groups were participating in this program.[34] Jones lists tribes by state that are participating in the Food and Nutrition Service's food distribution program.[35]

Business, Soil and Other Programs. Agriculture's *Office of Small and Disadvantaged Business Utilization* helps Indian businessmen and women with reference to procurement preference programs and grants and loan activities.

Soil Conservation Service (CSC) programs are available to Indians; however, none of its programs is specifically or exclusively for Indians. These programs are to protect and develop soil, water and related resources on nonfederal lands. SCS makes and publishes results of soil surveys, collects data on water and wind erosion, flood-prone areas, water content of snow pack, and encourages use of conservation plants which reduce erosion and sedimentation. SCS administers watershed projects and participates in river basin studies.

Other programs in the USDA not mentioned above are available to all citizens, including Indians.

DEPARTMENT OF COMMERCE

Economic Development Administration (EDA)

The Department of Commerce encourages, serves and promotes the nation's economic development and technological advancement. The domestic economic development activities are primarily the responsibility of the Assistant Secretary for Economic Development who supervises the Economic Development Administration (EDA).

Until September 30, 1981, the Assistant Secretary for Economic Development had a Special Assistant for Indian Affairs performing staff duties related to the use of EDA's programs for the benefit of Indians. All program managers and regional directors were directed to coordinate their Indian activities closely with the Indian desk and seek the advice and assistance of its staff in making decisions on Indian matters.[36] The Office of Special Assistant for Indian Affairs was not funded for 1982.

The line responsibility for aiding areas with severe unemployment and low family income rests with the offices of business development, public works, technical assistance, development organization, economic research, planning and program support, and the directors of EDA's six regional offices responsible for carrying out these programs.

Indian reservations having a need for economic development are eligible along with other groups for grants to help create full time permanent jobs for the unemployed and the underemployed. These grants may be for planning activities to assure effective utilization of resources [fiscal year 1980; $33,752,000; Indian—$3,752,000); public works to provide immediate useful work to the unemployed (fiscal year 1980: $228,500,000; Indian—$4,159,000); grants and loans for construction of public facilities for long term economic growth (fiscal year 1980: $228,500,000; Indian—$16,141,000); loans and loan guarantees to help business expand or develop plants in depressed areas including Indian reservations (fiscal year 1980: $116,430,000; Indian—$0); technical assistance through feasibility studies, marketing analysis, and training (fiscal year 1980: $30,976,000; Indian—$623,000); and special adjustment assistance for severe economic dislocation (fiscal year 1980: $86,929,000; Indian—$750,000)[37]

Minority Business Development Agency (MBDA)

The Department of Commerce eliminated the Indian Desk in EDA for fiscal year 1982 but is in the process of strengthening its Indian business development programs through the Minority Business Development Agency (MBDA).[38] The purpose of this agency is to overcome the social and economic disadvantages of minorities in the business world.

MBDA provides national policies and leadership in forming and strengthening a partnership of business, industry, and government with the nation's minority businesses. Management and technical assistance is provided minority firms on request, primarily through a network of local business development organizations which the agency funds. Organizations performing this service for Indians are:

Atlanta Region—Eastern Band of Cherokee Indians, Cherokee, North Carolina.

Chicago Region—Minnesota Chippewa Tribes, Cass Lake, Minnesota.

Dallas Region—All Indian Development Association, Albuquerque, New Mexico; Oklahomans for Indian Opportunity, Norman, Oklahoma.

San Francisco Region—Alaska Federation of Natives, Inc., Anchorage, Alaska; Indian Enterprise Development Corporation, Phoenix, Arizona; Navajo Small Business Development Corporation, Fort Defiance, Arizona; United Indian Development Association, Los Angeles, California.

Washington National (Indian Office)—American Indian Consultants, Scottsdale, Arizona.

MBDA conducts its activities through its six regional offices and 39 district offices. Obligations incurred for the support of MBDA activities for fiscal year 1980 totaled $44,400,000 of which $1,648,300 was allocated to service for Indians.[39]

National Oceanic and Atmospheric Administration (NOAA)

Grants for fisheries are made to treaty tribes in the state of Washington for the purpose of conserving, developing, and enhancing anadromous fisheries resources. These grants are on a 50-percent basis; matching funds may be provided by the tribes or BIA. Obligations for fiscal year 1980 were $37,000.

NOAA also is responsible for conserving fur seal herds on the Pribilof Islands. Fiscal year 1980 obligations were $5,105,600. Medical facilities are provided by the Department of Health and Human Services and education and social services by BIA for the approximately 650 Aleuts on the islands.[40]

DEPARTMENT OF JUSTICE

The Department of Justice has several activities of importance to Indians.[41] The Civil Rights Division enforces the civil rights of American Indians including prohibition of discriminatory conduct in voting, employment, public education, housing, public accommodations and facilities, rights of prisoners and mental patients. An Indian who believes his civil rights have been violated may write or call the Special Litigation Council, Department of Justice, Washington, D.C. 20503. Cooperation with the BIA, Indian Health Service, Administration of Native American Programs, National Congress of American Indians, the National Tribal Chairmans' Association, the National American Court Judges Association, and other Indian groups with offices in Washington results in alleged infractions being reported to Justice and appropriate investigations and actions. Close contacts also exist with U.S. attorneys, local legal aid offices (eg. California Indian Legal Service), tribal councils, state officials, and other interested groups (eg. Native American Rights Fund, All Indian Pueblo Council, National Youth Council) in states in which investigations or lawsuits are being conducted. The Office of Revenue Sharing and the Equal Employment Opportunity Commission refer cases for investigation and possible litigation. Reports of the U.S. Commission on Civil Rights are also available.

In 1973 the Office of Indian Rights (OIR) was established within the Civil Rights Division in order to allow the development of expertise in Indian civil rights. This office had 12 positions in 1980, but was not funded in 1981. In response to Indian expressions of concern, the department appointed the former director of OIR as Acting Special Counsel for Indian litigation. Also the Acting Deputy Assistant General for Policy and Planning was designated as the liaison with Indian rights organizations.[42]

Since the Justice Department is the government's trial lawyer, the Indian Resources Section in the Land and Natural Resources Division supervises the litigation of civil suits in which the U.S. seeks to protect the tribal assets and jurisdiction. Litigation for individual and tribal rights to property, hunting, fishing, and water are also this section's responsibility. This section supervises litigation involving alleged infringement by states of tribal rights in taxation, liquor control, law enforcement, reservation boundaries and other related matters. Approximately 540 cases were in process as of January 31, 1981.[43] The Indian Resources Section initiates litigation only when requested by the Department of Interior.

The Community Relations Service (CRS) of the Department of Justice helps resolve problems causing tension and conflicts with the voluntary cooperation of the disputants. Although education, administration of justice, and economic matters are the most frequent problems, CRS has assisted

Indian groups in conflict situations involving treaty rights, hunting and fishing rights, and intratribal conflicts such as at Wounded Knee in the early 1970s. Training in conflict management and community relations techniques is provided tribal officials, Indian police, and education agencies.[44]

The ambivalence of Justice's posture is illustrated in that it not only litigates for Indians as described above, but it also has the responsibility for defending the United States against claims by Indians before the Court of Claims. Active cases in January, 1981 totaled 107.[45]

In 1968 Congress established the Law Enforcement Assistance Administration (LEAA) within the Justice Department to provide financial and technical assistance for a comprehensive national crime control program. Recently an Indian Justice Section was established but it was phased out at the end of fiscal year 1981. Programs for Indian tribes since 1970 included construction of 65 criminal justice facilities; training of tribal police; development, training for, and expansion of tribal courts; improvement and expansion of correction facilities and staff; research and the development of new codes; attacking local juvenile crime problems, and working on the establishment of full faith and credit between tribal courts and state courts. A key problem recognized by the Indian Justice Section was the determination of jurisdiction between Indian tribes and states and lack of law and order coverage in some areas because of uncertainties and lack of funds.[46] Funding for Indian LEAA projects was: $200,000 in 1978; $1,400,000 in 1979; and $600,000 in 1980. No funds were available in 1981 and none were requested in 1982.

Federal Bureau of Investigation

Federal Bureau of Investigation (FBI) jurisdiction on Indian reservations covers investigation of major crimes, application of other Federal laws, enforcement responsibility for protection of hunting and fishing rights, and investigation of possible fraud or embezzlement by tribal officials.[47]

The House Committee on the Judiciary noted that there were three law enforcement agencies operating on Indian reservations: the BIA and the tribes have day-to-day police functions, unless this responsibility has been transferred to the state; the FBI has no day-to-day police functions. The FBI's main responsibility is to investigate violations of Federal law. The committee recommended actions that would help avoid poor law enforcement and duplication.[48]

SMALLER PROGRAMS IN OTHER AGENCIES

Department of the Treasury

In addition to being the depository for all agency appropriations, Treasury maintains and accounts for certain Indian-owned trust funds. The Office of Revenue Sharing administers the general revenue sharing program. In fiscal year 1981 the entitlement for 347 eligible Indian and Alaskan Native governments was $11.1 million.[49] No funds were provided in the administration's budget for fiscal year 1982.

Commission on Civil Rights

The U.S. Commission on Civil Rights has neither enforcement nor funding authority, but does have authority to make findings and recommendations concerning discrimination to the president and Congress. The Commission has reported on a variety of issues related to American Indians, including the issuance of an Indian Civil Rights Handbook and a report entitled "Indian Tribes: A Continuing Quest for Survival" published in June, 1981.[50]

Department of Defense

The Department of Defense has three activities relating to Indians.[51]

The Corps of Engineers often has projects benefitting Indians. Examples for fiscal year 1980 are: Federal breakwater and shoreline revetment at Neah Bay, Washington, incidentally benefitting the Makah Indian Reservation (the Corps spent in 1978: $52,511; 1979: $507,943; 1980: $1,122,245; 1981: $6,000); boat basin and ocean shore revetment incidentally benefitting the Quileute Indian Reservation at La Push; Swinomish channel near La Conner, Washington, incidentally benefitting the Swinomish Indian Reservation; Metlakatla small boat harbor on the Indian reserve on Annette Island (total cost over several years—$3,970,000); approval under certain conditions for construction on Federal land at Ceasar Creek Lake, Ohio, of an Amerind Center to serve the general public and Indians in promoting Indian traditions, religion and culture—agreement between UNITE (Union of Native Indian Tribes for Education) and the state of Ohio provides for construction, maintenance and operation of the center by UNITE, but the state will assume responsibility if UNITE defaults; and emergency flood protection and aid in 1979 along a stretch of the Rio Grande River which affected the pueblos of Isleta, Santa Ana, Santo Domingo, Sandia, and San Felipe.

The National Guard Bureau has developed a special program supported by a handbook to encourage the recruitment of Indians. The handbook has sections on "What It Means to Be an Indian" and "American Indian Program Activities," and an appendix with data about Indians and tribes.

The Navy emphasizes employment of Indians in their summer youth program. Navy and Marine Corps activities in areas with high concentrations of Indians are requested to allocate a "meaningful share" of summer employment to Indians and engage in positive recruitment.

Department of Energy

The Department of Energy created an Office of Indian Affairs in the Secretary's Office in October 1977, but in 1981 these responsibilities were transferred to the Undersecretary. Projects are funded through the Council of Energy Resource Tribes (CERT) for energy research development and management.[52]

Department of Transportation (DOT)

Through the National Highway Traffic Safety Administration (NHTSA) the Department of Transportation assists Indian tribes in reducing the number of traffic accidents. Funds may be provided for periodic vehicle inspection, motorcycle safety, driver education, alcohol and highway safety, identification and surveillance of accident locations, traffic courts, traffic records, traffic engineering services, pedestrian safety, police traffic services, and pupil transportation safety. Funds can also be used for purchase of ambulances, emergency medical equipment, radar speed guns, driver training simulators and alcohol breath and blood testing equipment. The program is administered by BIA and coordinated with the National Highway Traffic Safety Administration.[53] Other related programs are CETA in DOL, National Institute on Alcohol Abuse and Alcoholism and the Indian Health Service in HHS, and, formerly, LEAA in the Department of Justice.

NHSTA published a pamphlet "American Indian Highway Safety Program," in 1979. It gives the history of the program, data on Indian traffic safety, and points out Indian safety needs.

Anyone seeing the roads on or near most reservations the condition of the vehicles driven by Indians, and the amount of alcohol consumed by Indians can only conclude that the combination presents a formidable problem.

Nationally our data show at least half the motor vehicle fatalities are due in some measure to alcohol. In comparison, leaders of two larger Indian Nations, one in the midwest, the other in the southwest estimate that 90 percent or more of their tribes' deaths in traffic accidents involve excessive drinking.

In addition, traffic problems of the Indians are further complicated by the fact that many reservations, and the areas surrounding them lack adequate police surveillance or emergency medical service.[54]

Since funds for highway safety are limited, the Indian situation was analyzed to determine how best to concentrate limited resources for maximum benefit. NHTSA found that there were 496 native groups recognized by BIA, that they were scattered in 27 states and included 218 Alaskan villages. Of the 496 groups, 326 had populations of less than 300 and 82.9 percent had populations of less than 1,000 members. The tribes were found to have varying degrees of autonomy which created complex traffic safety relationships with towns, counties, states, and the Federal government. NHTSA has directed its programs to 11 tribes: Colville, Choctaw, Flathead, Fort Peck, Fort Belknap, Mescalero, Navajo, Papago, Pine Ridge, Rosebud, and Yakima.[55] Funds channeled through the Interior Department were increased from an annual amount of $381,204 in 1974 to $973,698 in 1979, for a total during the six years of $3,996,280.

Environmental Protection Agency (EPA)

The Environmental Protection Agency (EPA) works with state and local governments and Indian tribes to identify, control, and reduce water pollution sources. Tribes have received funds directly from EPA and also through contracts with statewide planning agencies.[56]

Along with other citizens, Indians are eligible for air pollution control fellowships and manpower training grants. Indian tribes may participate, as well as states, in regulating pesticide use. Grants are available for certification, training, and enforcement activities.

Solid waste and hazardous waste problems are helped by technical assistance, training and funds. Indian groups are eligible along with others.

Equal Employment Opportunity Commission

Any tribe with a tribal employment rights office may apply for funds to help assure Indian preference for work on the reservation.[57]

National Endowment for the Arts

In promoting the arts, the National Endowment has funded Indian projects among others. In 1980 the Solaris Lakota Sioux Indian project received $15,000 which included dancers' salaries. Media arts were aided by grants. Examples are: a $5,000 grant to the National Congress of American Indians (NCAI) for screening films about American Indians, and $8,000 to the Zuni Communications Authority for collecting and editing a radio series of traditional stories in the Zuni language. Museum funds have gone to such projects as the Akwesasne Library and Cultural Center, Mohawk Reservation, New York (1981: $6,660); Cherokee National Historical Society, Tahlequah,

Oklahoma (1980: $5,000); and the Heye Foundation Museum of the American Indian, New York, N.Y. (1980: $30,000; 1981: $75,000).[58]

National Science Foundation

The National Science Foundation (NSF) sponsors graduate fellowships for minority individuals (including Indians) who demonstrate ability for advanced training in the sciences. Minority scientists may receive funds to begin independent research careers through provision of scientific equipment, release time and help in establishing research collaboration between themselves and small colleges and universities. Those educational institutions with more than 50 percent Indian or other minority groups may receive necessary instrumentation and other resources to initiate a program of research, increase quality of research, and encourage greater collaboration between scientists at major research universities and scientists at primarily minority institutions. [59]

Office of Personnel Management (OPM)

Indian tribal governments are eligible for assistance under the Intergovernmental Personnel Act. OPM has agreements with BIA and ANA to offer technical assistance to tribes in improving their personnel systems including management and training, and to administer personnel management intern programs for tribal employees. Twenty grants for fiscal year 1978 and nineteen for fiscal year 1979 benefitted tribes in thirteen states. Twenty-five tribal projects in fourteen states received $397,000 in fiscal year 1980.

Tribal governments are eligible to participate with OPM in cooperative recruitment and examining of potential candidates, as well as engaging in temporary assignment of personnel among Federal agencies, state and local governments, Indian tribes or tribal organizations and institutions of higher education. Indian governing bodies that perform substantial governmental functions are eligible for grants for personnel administration improvements.[60]

Small Business Administration (SBA)

Although the Small Business Administration (SBA) has no specific program for Indians, it has programs that are available to all qualifying individuals without regard to their ethnic background. Several programs are oriented toward helping socially and economically disadvantaged individuals. SBA has a Native American Affairs Officer to assist such groups in receiving help.

Opportunity loans provide up to $100,000 to small businesses owned by low-income or socially or economically disadvantaged persons.

Procurement assistance is given businesses that are owned or controlled by disadvantaged persons to insure participation in Federal contracting. Management and technical assistance is provided to existing or potential businesses which are disadvantaged.

Small Business Investment Companies (SBIC) are helped so that they can provide management and financial assistance to eligible small business concerns. Debentures issued by SBICs are guaranteed by SBA. SBA will guarantee surety bonds so that such bonds will be available to small contractors unable to obtain a bond without a guarantee.

Small minority businesses capable of supplying goods and services to major corporations are helped by SBA to overcome deficiencies as identified by the major corporation. Concerns owned or controlled by American Indians, Eskimos or Aleuts are specifically identified, along with other minorities, as being eligible.[61]

Smithsonian Institution

The Smithsonian Institution provides assistance to Native American groups interested in establishing and operating museums as follows: offering approximately twenty internships of two to twelve weeks at accredited museums, organizing four regional workshops with funding for 70 participants per year, providing conservation services for Native American museum collections, and helping with technical assistance. A Coordinator for the Native American Museum Program supervises this work. Funding in fiscal year 1980 was $35,619 plus $149,893 from a Department of Labor contract; for fiscal year 1981: $54,816.[62]

SUMMARY

Because of the special relationship of Indians to the Federal government and the trust status of their land, specific provisions for serving Indians are found in many statutes and are carried out through numerous agencies. One-third of the Federal funds specifically for Indians is channeled through the Department of the Interior and the other two-thirds through the other agencies described in this chapter.

Indians not on a Federal reservation or not residing on or owning trust land are eligible for services from the local, state, and Federal governments in the same manner as other citizens. They also have the same responsibilities.

There has been a tendency to establish special Indian services, offices, or coordinators in numerous agencies although some are being phased out. If reductions in Federal domestic expenditures continue, special programs and services for Indians in the various agencies are likely to decrease.

FOOTNOTES

[1]*The Annals of the Americam Academy of Political and Social Science*, 436 (March 1978): p. 53. Raymond Butler "The Bureau of Indian Affairs Since 1945," Hereafter cited as *The Annals*.

[2]Theodore W. Taylor, *The Regional Organization of the Bureau of Indian Affairs* (Cambridge, Harvard University: PhD Thesis, 1959), p. 246. Hereafter cited as Taylor, *Thesis*.

[3]*The Annals*, p. 55.

[4]Theodore W. Taylor, *The States and Their Indian Citizens* (Washington: U.S. Department of the Interior, Bureau of Indian Affairs, 1972), p. 108. Hereafter cited as Taylor, *States*. See also Theodore W. Taylor, *The Bureau of Indian Affairs: Public Policies Toward Indian Citizens* (to be published by Westview Press, Boulder, Colo., in 1983). Hereafter cited as Taylor, *The Bureau of Indian Affairs*.

[5]Taylor, *States,* p. 66, footnote.

[6]For a fuller treatment of the Bureau of Indian Affiars see Taylor, *The Bureau of Indian Affairs*.

[7]Richard S. Jones, *Federal Programs of Assistance to American Indians*, A Report prepared for the Select Committee on Indian Affairs, U.S. Senate, by the Congressional Research Service, Committee Print, GPO, June 1981, pp. 141-152. Hereafter cited as Jones.

[8]*The United States Government Manual 1982/83*, Office of the Federal Register, National Archives and Records Service, General Services Administration (Washington: Government Printing Office, revised July 1, 1982), p. 257. Hereafter cited as *U.S. Government Manual 1982/83*.

[9]Ibid. p. 267.

[10]25 USC 1601; P. L. 94-437.

[11]HHS Budget Justification for FY 1982, pp. 110-111.

[12]Ibid. pp. 11-12.

[13]Jones, pp. 118-121.

[14]Dr. R.C. Kreuzburg, Indian Health Service, telephone conversation May 13, 1982.

[15]Age Adjusted Mortality Rates and Ratios, IHS Budget Justification FY 1982, p. 22.

[16]Jones, pp. 133-135 and telephone conversation with ANA.

[17]88 Stat. 2324.

[18]Statement by A. David Lester, Commissioner, Administration for Native Americans, before the Select Committee on Indian Affairs, U.S. Senate, June 23, 1981.

[19]Jones, pp. 121-132.

[20]P.L. 95-608. As of October 1981 no funds had been received by any tribe under this authority.

[21]*U.S. Government Manual 1982/83*, pp. 233-234.

[22]40 Federal Register 5807, 2/7/75.

[23]Jones, pp. 84-104.

[24]April 16, 1934 (48 Stat. 596).

[25]Telephone conversation with Elizabeth Holmgren, Office of the Director, Indian Education Programs, BIA, October 6, 1981.

[26]Jones, pp. 221-223.

[27]Code of Federal Regulations 688.10; Jones, pp. 221-223.

[28]Indians and Native American Programs, 1977-1978 Report, U.S. Department of Labor.

[29]Table, Indian and Native American Employment and Training Program Funded Under the Comprehensive Employment Training Act, received from EDA Indian Desk August 24, 1981.

[30]*U.S. Government Manual* 1982-83, p. 94.

[31]Letter to author from Stuart P. Jamieson, Coordinator, Indian Affairs, USDA, December 8, 1981.

[32]Ibid.

[33]Jones, p. 5-6.

[34]Jones, p. 31.

[35]Jones, p. 37.

[36]Economic Development Administration, Bulletin No. 92-80, November 20, 1980.

[37]Jones, pp. 44-50.

[38]Letter to author from Victor M. Rivera, Director, September 24, 1981.

[39]Jones, pp. 51-53.

[40]Jones, pp. 52-53; BIA information from telephone conversation with Raymond Butler, Division of Social Services, October 6, 1981.

[41]Jones, pp. 215-220.

[42]Department of Justice Appropriation Authorization Act, FY 1982, 97th Cong., 1st sess., House Committee on the Judiciary, Report No. 97-105, May 19, 1981, pp. 4 and 5.

[43]*Legal Activities*, 1981, U.S. Department of Justice, p. 15.

[44]Jones, pp. 219-220.

[45]*Legal Activities*, 1981, U.S. Department of Justice, p. 15.

[46]LEAA Indian Program Brief, U.S. Department of Justice, DOJ-1981-08.

[47]18 USC 1152, which extends Federal enclave laws to Indian reservations; the Assimilative Crimes Act, 18 USC 13, assimilates state law into Federal enclaves where there exists no Federally defined offense; and the Major Crimes Act, 18 USC 1153, grants Federal jurisdiction over thirteen major felonies.

[48]House Committee on Judiciary, Report No. 97-105, May 19, 1981, pp. 5-8.

[49]Jones, pp. 263-266.

[50]Jones, p. 5.

[51]Jones, pp. 54-83.

[52]Telephone conversation with Rachael Wing, December 9, 1981.

[53]Jones, p. 224.

[54]Page 3 of the Manual, reprinted in Jones, pp. 226-259.

[55]Jones, pp. 232-235.

[56]Jones, pp. 266-301.

[57]Jones, p. 302.

[58]Jones, pp. 303-306.

[59]Jones, pp. 307-311.

[60]Jones, pp. 311-325.

[61]Jones, pp. 326-337.

[62]Jones, pp. 339-341.

CHAPTER 4
STATE AND LOCAL GOVERNMENT
SERVICES TO INDIANS
INTRODUCTION

State and local governments provide an estimated 80-85 percent of government services received by Indians.[1] The heavy involvement of states in services to their Indian citizens is not very well known by either the special publics interested in Indian matters or by the general public. Indians, BIA, and Indian interest groups play down state services and emphasize the Federal relationship. Even the states tend to emphasize the Federal relationship because it relieves their tax burden when the Federal government assumes responsibility.

The American Indian Policy Review Commission (AIPRC) Report reflects little emphasis on state services except that such services should be severely limited. Members and staff of the Senate Select Committee on Indian Affairs have been a part of the Indian subsystem and have pushed for a separate Indian status and direct Federal relationship with Indian tribes. However, the Committee did recommend that state and county governments sit down with tribal governments in an attempt to resolve their jurisdictional conflicts.[2]

Although the role of the states is currently minimized, it does not alter the fact of the importance of that role. This current attitude also is a reflection of the historical tendency to swing from one Indian policy emphasis to another over time.

During the colonial period the colonies and, under the Articles of Confederation, the states had a considerable influence on affairs within their borders.[3] Since that time state and local governments have been involved with Indians continuously, even though jurisdiction over Indian tribes was placed in the Federal government under the constitution.

Many Indians are not on reservations and not all Indians are active members of tribes. These Indians are served by state and local governments. In the 1950s the objective of BIA and the Federal government was to add to these groups by transferring BIA functions to the Indians themselves or to the states.

Commissioner John Collier indicated in 1943 that post-war programs for reservations should consider what functions could be transferred to the tribes as well as to the state, county or municipal governments, such as law and order, health and education. In 1951 Commissioner Dillon S. Myer reaffirmed the objective of a step-by-step transfer of Bureau functions to the Indians themselves or to the appropriate agencies of the local, state, or Federal government. Assistant Secretary of the Interior Orme Lewis stated in 1953 "that Federal responsibility for administering the affairs of individual Indian tribes should be terminated as rapidly as the circumstances of each tribe will permit" by tranfer of functions to appropriate public bodies and the tranfer of the trust responsibility for Indian properties to the Indians themselves. This was followed by House Concurrent Resolution 108 in August 1953 which declared it to be the policy of Congress "to make the Indians . . . subject to the same laws . . . as are applicable to other citizens of the United States . . . ." [4]

During the 1950s education, social services, roads, and law and order were transferred from BIA to states and counties in varying degrees. In California, for example, in the 1950s the California Indians, the governor and the legislature endorsed the transfer of Federal responsibilities to the state and counties or to the Indians. By the end of the decade California had assumed responsibility for Indian education, welfare, and law and order in the same manner as for its other citizens. This was progress toward the then pronounced Congressional and BIA goal of BIA working itself out of a job. But in the 1960s California and its Indian citizens reversed their views and sought reinstatement of BIA and IHS services.

Education is the most prominent example of the many state services in effect today for Federally recognized tribes and their members as well as for all other Indians. Education of the young is one of the most important functions of a society or cultural group. In contrast to the situation in the 1920's a much higher percentage of Indian children of reservation residents today are being educated by the larger U.S. society through state public school systems. Approximately 80 percent of the students with Indian parents who are members of Federally recognized tribes and live on or near the reservation attend state public schools. Almost all other Indian students (not on or near a reservation) are in public schools. So 90 to 95 percent of all Indian students are in state public schools. Only about 2 percent of reservation students are in tribally operated schools funded through contracts with BIA, and approximately 18 percent of reservation students are in BIA operated schools. As citizens of their county and state, Indians serve on county school boards often along with their non-Indian neighbors. BIA also has funds to help public schools provide special help and curricula for the Indian students. These funds (Johnson-O'Malley funds) [5] must be expended under the direction of a school board of which a majority of the members are Indian, or with the approval of an Indian parent advisory committee.

Law and order is another important state responsibility for many reservation Indians as well as for those living off the reservation. The mixed situation in police and court responsibilities among the BIA, the tribes, the states, and the Department of Justice (FBI and U.S. district attorneys) results in many complications. No specific statistics are available, but of the 1,421,400 Indians in 1980, the vast majority are under state law and order jurisdiction. Even those who reside on reservations with tribal or BIA law and order systems are citizens of the state and subject to state law and order when not on the reservation. Both tribal and Federal courts use state statutes for police and judicial guidance concerning matters not covered by Federal statutes or tribal ordinances.

The Allotment Act provided that in the event of the death of the allottee the United States would hold land in trust for his heirs "according to the laws of the state or territory where such land is located." At the end of the trust period a non-trust title would be issued to the allottee or his heirs. [6]

States have long provided social welfare services to Indians. The Social Security Act of 1935 provided for Aid to the Blind, Aid to Families with Dependent Children, Old Age Assistance and Aid to the Permanently and Totally Disabled. All of these programs were administered for Indians through the states. In 1971, 17 percent of the reservation residents were receiving categorical aid assistance through the states. In 1982, 20 percent were receiving this same type of assistance through the states although some of the programs had different names.

The Supplemental Security Income (SSI) program has replaced Aid to the Blind, Old Age Assistance and Aid to the Permanently and Totally Disabled and is funded and administered directly to recipients by the Federal government. The states are not involved. Medicare is exclusively a Federal insurance program. Medicaid is jointly funded by the Federal and state governments and administered by the states. Food stamps are funded 100 percent by the Federal government and generally administered through the states. In 1977 Congress authorized tribes either to continue under the state or take over administration of food stamps. Some of the larger tribes such as Navajo and Yankton have opted to administer their food stamp programs. President Ronald Reagan's 1982 State of the Union address proposed some rearrangements in funding and responsibility aimed at increasing the role of the states for services to their citizens.

In 1971 BIA provided foster home care for Indian children on reservations in 12 states. Between 1971 and 1982, Colorado and Maine have been added so there are now 14 states in which BIA is involved with foster home care. In the other states in 1971 foster home care was provided to Indian children, whether on or off the reservation, by state welfare departments on the same basis as for non-Indian children. The Indian Child Welfare Act of 1978 has mandated a reversal of this trend, by requiring that foster care for Indian children be provided through tribal court procedures, where there are such courts and that children be placed with Indian families whenever feasible whether the case is handled by a tribal or state court. In 1971 BIA policy was that insofar as possible Indians should have the same relationship to public welfare agencies as non-Indians. The policy remained the same in 1982. When the tax-exempt status of Indian land affected the financial ability of the states to provide services or when special Indian needs had to be met, the BIA undertook to provide the necessary assistance.

Many reservations are dependent on the state and Federal governments for certain institutional services such as college level education, mental hospitals, nursing and group homes, prisons and jails. Some tribal junior colleges are now available and some reservations have adequate jail facilities. These tribal institutions do not begin to meet the need. If IHS were not funding Indian hospital care, then this, too, would have to be largely a state service. The tribes for the most part do not have the size and resources to support such institutions.

Since many reservations are small and a limited number of people live on them, their economic viability often depends on cooperation with the surrounding non-Indian society and government. Some of the larger reservations too have found cooperation with non-Indian neighbors profitable. On the Yakima reservation in the state of Washington there are approximately 8,000 Indians, 8,000 Chicanos and 21,000 Anglos. These varied residents work together in the cultivation of apples, sugar beets and hops. The tribe has invested in a sugar plant in Toppenish and has cooperative activities with both the towns of Toppenish and Yakima. The public schools serving the reservation area, Toppenish and Wapato, have worked cooperatively with the Yakima Tribe in offering an Indian cultural education program. Both Indians and non-Indians can take the course for credit. The tribe has purchased the Yakima Flying Service which charters planes and also sells small planes.[7] Good relationships between tribal, local, and state governments facilitate economic, social, and political progress for the areas concerned. As in the case of Yakima and Suquamish, non-Indians sometimes outnumber Indians within the reservation boundaries. Furthermore reservations are islands in the midst of the larger non-Indian society.

STATES WITH SPECIAL STATE ORGANIZATIONS FOR INDIANS

State governments serve Indians mainly through the same divisions of government serving other citizens as illustrated in the educational function. However, some states have established Indian commissions or offices to assist the regular state governmental departments in working with Indian citizens. This seems to be the general practice for most states with Federal reservations where the problems of mixed civil and criminal jurisdiction, child custody, hunting and fishing rights, tax jurisdiction and similar matters provide a major challenge to tribal and state governments as well as to BIA and other agencies at the Federal level.

The following 17 states have Indian commissions or the equivalent but do not have state Indian reservations. Seventeen are considered here and three in the following section. The purposes of these Indian commissions vary with the several states but most have the general objectives of: gathering information on Indian needs and the adequacy of serving them; working with Indian, local, state, and Federal governments to help coordinate actions to provide desired services: acting as liaison between Indians and state when regular state services seem not to fit or serve a particular need; working with tribes when requested to help develop effective relationships between state service agencies and Indian citizens; and advising and recommending policies and legislation to the governor, legislature, and the state's Congressional delegation on Indian matters.

Specific instances and examples of commission activity are cited in *The States and Their Indian Citizens* published in 1972.[8] Many of these same arrangements were in effect in 1982. Some of the same problems exist, and, in some cases, have been exacerbated as in the Pacific Northwest. Some problems have peaked and seem to have been resolved as in the land claims cases of Alaska and Maine.

Many states responded generously with information to acting Deputy Assistant Secretary for Indian Affairs Kenneth L. Payton's letter of October 16, 1981 to all state governors asking for information on state programs.[9] This information is summarized below.

Arizona

The Arizona Commission of Indian Affairs supplements service to Indian citizens through state agencies. Seven Indians, two non-Indians, and four ex officio members—governor, attorney general, superintendent of public instruction, and director of health services—serve on the commission which had a budget of $117,000 for 1981.

The state has nearly 100 intergovernmental agreements with the 20 Indian reservations, ranging from rights-of-way to the provision of services or sharing of salaries for technical services. For example the Arizona Division of Weights and Measures has a written agreement with Navajo to test weights and measuring devices in cooperation with Navajo tribal staff.

However, there are problems and the Commission helps to focus on them and suggest solutions. At a meeting of the Joint Select Committee on Indian Affairs of the Arizona legislature (July 18, 1979) the Chairman of the Commission stated:

". . .based on increases in intergovernmental conflicts, state-Indian relationships appear to be heading toward a decline. Nevertheless, in aiming for appropriate protocol between the tribes and the state government and recognition of inherent tribal governmental powers, the commission will continue to check into conditions which may lead to disruptive influences in intergovernmental relations, so that in turn cordial relations already established at the local level between Arizona Indians and their non-Indian neighbors are not alienated or severed. . . .our Commission will assist state agencies in their work with Arizona Indian people. . .our own state policies toward Indian people should reflect current Congressional legislation which upholds strong tribal self-government and protection against assertions of state jurisdiction."[10]

At the same meeting the chairman of the commission pointed out that in the area of civil and criminal jurisdiction in 1977 the attorney general's office "furnished a list of approximately 50 items which needed to be resolved between the state and the various tribes. . . .we recommend that. . .the number of cross-deputizations of peace officers on-and-off reservations be increased substantially. . . ." For law and order, social welfare, and health care the chairman said that ". . .conflicts can be prevented if more opportunities for negotiated contracts and/or agreements for state services were encouraged and extended to Indian tribes."

California

California abolished its former Indian Commissioner and in May 1976 the Governor established the Office of American Indian Coordinator, which is located in the Governor's office.

The coordinator (1) maintains liaison with Indian groups and state and Federal officials concerned with Indian services, (2) reviews and evaluates such services and Indian needs, and (3) assists in policy and program development by clarifying relationships between the state government and land-based as well as non-land-based Indians: advising the governor and cabinet on needed state programs and policies to improve the social and economic conditions of California Indians, drafting legislative proposals to initiate new programs, reviewing Federal policies which adversely affect California Indians and recommending revisions. The coordinator is also responsible for disseminating information on Indian legislation, programs and cultural events.[11]

Colorado

The Colorado Commission on Indian Affairs was established by statute in

1976. The Commission consists of the lieutenant governor as chairperson, the chairpersons of the two Ute tribes and two other Indian members, four directors of important state departments, and two members at large. The annual funds for the commission approximate $31,000. The paid staff includes an executive director and a part-time assistant.

The Commission is concerned with both the reservation Indian and the urban Indian. . . .there are about 18,000 Native Americans living in Colorado with approximately 10,000 dwelling off the reservations. As Federal assistance continues to decline, this number will rapidly increase in a short period of time and many will be seeking employment and living facilities in the inner-city and the surrounding areas. The Commission is working to provide solutions to the potential problems which this may create before the fact.[12]

Some of the recent accomplishments of the commission were: the Family/Child Resource Center to help train parents who desire to get back children placed in foster homes; the Towaoc Pottery Industry; and the Indian Child Welfare Act Agreements with the two tribes.

Discussion among the Commission, state agencies, the private sector, the two Ute tribes, and urban Indians developed the following:

1. The tribes have needs which state government should be directly involved in solving.

2. State government is a valuable resource for all Colorado citizens.

3. The Ute people and urban Indians are Colorado citizens.

4. State government is willing and sincere in facilitating the tribes as they strive to better their lives.[13]

Maryland

The Maryland Commission on Indian Affairs was created in 1976 and is responsible for initiating, directing and coordinating projects which further the understanding of Indian history and culture. The Commission assists Maryland tribes in seeking recognition from the Federal government and studies the economic and social needs of the 8,000 Indians in Maryland.[14]

Michigan

Michigan's Committee on Indian Affairs, established in 1965, has nine members and an executive director who, in addition to functions assigned many other commissions, is also authorized to apply for and accept grants from governmental or private sources.[15]

Minnesota

In Minnesota the Indian community is fluid. "Indians receive benefits similar to non-Indians when they reside in the Twin Cities."[16] The Governor has a special assistant for Indian affairs. The state funds several Indian programs including about $500,000 for Red Lake welfare.

The Indian Affairs Intertribal Board is the lineal descendent of the Indian Affairs Commission established in 1963. The voting board consists of the elected chairman of each of the eleven reservation governments and two at-large members elected from their own ranks by Minnesota Indians enrolled in Federally-recognized tribes outside the borders of the state. Five non-voting Urban Advisory Council members are appointed by the Board. The Governor and commissioners (directors) of various departments administering Indian programs, three members of the senate and three members of the House of Representatives serve as ex-officio members. The Board is served by an executive director, an administrative assistant, two Indian affairs representatives and two clerk typists.

The 1980-1981 state funds available to the Board totaled $196,000 and expenditures totaled $189,000.

The objective of the original Commission and the current Board was and is to provide for "the Indian voice in state government." The state regards its Indian residents as members of political entities which have "functioning governments traceable to tribal councils which governed before Minnesota existed." As stated in the Board's 1981 Report "this relationship between Indian people (through their tribal governments) and the state government. . . is the key to the existence of a State Indian Affairs Office."

During 1981 the Board and the advisory council were concerned with housing programs, relations between Indian communities and the police departments in Minneapolis and St. Paul, a flood plain problem on the Upper Sioux Reservation near Granite Falls, and a problem which developed between the City of Prior Lake and the Shakopee-Mdewakanton Reservation regarding a burning site on Indian land.[17]

Montana

Montana has a State Coordinator of Indian Affairs initiated in 1982 with a small staff and a budget of $87,000. The Coordinator is located in the governor's office and is responsible for working with the tribes and urban

Indians and for advising the state legislature, the governor, and the state's Congressional representatives on Indian matters.

As in other states the various departments provide many services to Indians. Although Indians comprised only 4.7 percent of the state's population in 1980, in 1981 Indians constituted 19 percent of the corrections population. Nineteen percent of those in alcohol treatment programs, 18.3 percent of participants in Aid to Families with Dependent Children (AFDC), and 24.2 percent of those receiving food stamps were Indian. Of applicants placed in jobs by the department of labor and industry, 4.7 percent were Indian.[18]

In 1979 the Montana legislature established the Reserved Water Rights Compact Commission to negotiate water rights of the state and its non-Indian citizens and the Indian tribes. In early 1982 negotiations were in process with four Montana tribes. The state preferred negotiation to litigation.[19]

Nebraska

Nebraska has a 15-member Nebraska Indian Commission with an executive director assisted by five staff members. It was created in 1970 and is attached to the state's department of economic development. There has been a great deal of friction between Indians and non-Indians in communities near the South Dakota border and some of the purposes of the Commission reflect this. They are: to promote beneficial legislation at both the state and Federal levels; coordinate existing programs such as health, housing, education, welfare, law and order, and economic development; develop new programs to meet specific needs; keep the Governor's office and public informed of the situation in Indian communities; and encourage local involvement by Indian people for the benefit of the Indian community. The Commission's budget for 1981 was $168,000. In addition, the state allocated $37,692 to the Commission for contracting with the Omaha, Sante Sioux, and Winnebago tribal councils for alcohol treatment programs. The Nebraska Division of Alcoholism and Drug Abuse has an "Indian Desk," and allocated an additional $79,658 direct to tribes in 1981. This division also sponsors an Indian advisory board and funded the Lincoln Indian Center Alcohol Program in the amount of $56,000 in 1981.

For law and order, the Nebraska State Legislature appropriated $75,385 to replace the depleted tax base of counties which provide police protection to those reservations subject to state jurisdiction and $85,600 to Indian law and order boards in two isolated villages. A full-time Indian Religious Coordinator is employed to work with inmates in the state prison and a reformatory.

Reservation schools participate in the state education programs, based on criteria that do not include being an Indian as a factor. To the statement in the letter to the governors that the Federal government "reimburses most state and local expenditures for Indian children living on tax-exempt land," the Executive Director of the Commission, Marvin Buzzard, stated this perception was incorrect. "The Federal government does not reimburse any costs at the local and state level. It is true Impact Aid supplements those efforts but it does not replace or reimburse local and state expenditures."[20]

Nevada

The Nevada Indian Commission has five members—three Indians and two members from the general public appointed by the Governor—and is served by a staff of three, headed by an executive director. The Commission is charged to ". . .study matters affecting the social and economic welfare and well-being of American Indians residing in Nevada." Of the approximately 13,000 Indian citizens in Nevada a little more than half reside on 23 reservations.[21]

Commission expenditures were $58,000 in 1980. During 1979-1980 biennium the Commission studied the impact of the proposed MX Missile System on Indian sacred and burial sites, tribal Bureau of Land Management grazing areas and the future economic development of the tribes. The Commission worked on health care with the tribes and with the Indian Health Service. Problems in acquisition of food stamps and commodities and the receipt of benefits from the Social Security Administration were addressed. The proposed closure of Stewart school by BIA was opposed.

The Commission introduced and the legislature passed a bill which provided for county conveyance to tribes of undivided interests in Indian allotted land upon which taxes were delinquent.

During the biennium the Commission distributed $50,000 worth of state surplus road equipment to tribes. The Washoe Tribe was assisted in its efforts to develop a Tribal Game Management Board. The Commission strove to increase the cooperation of Indian tribes with state, local, and Federal agencies.[22]

New Mexico

The New Mexico Office of Indian Affairs helps coordinate state functions with tribal officials. The commission has published a pamphlet "Four Winds" which describes the background, location, and basic facts about each of the Indian groups in the state which is helpful to non-Indians working with Indians as well as to the considerable number of tourists visiting New Mexico's Indians. National policies affecting New Mexico Indians are carefully monitored to determine potential impact on Indians and state programs such as Federal budget proposals and actions. The State Department of Education and other state offices provide the same basic services to their Indian citizens as to other citizens.[23]

North Carolina

North Carolina's Commission of Indian Affairs is a state advocacy agency established in 1971 by the North Carolina General Assembly. The Commission's board is composed of seven state officials, including the lieutenant governor and the speaker of the house, and fifteen Indian members, representing the state's seven Indian organizations. Commission staff receive directives from this board and from the North Carolina Department of Administration.

In 1981, the Commission's total staff numbered eighty. Approximately half of these staff members were based in the central office in Raleigh. Remaining staff were based in the Commission's eight field offices located throughout the state. Of the total commission staff, eight were supported by a state allocation of $190,000. The remaining staff positions were financed through the various Federal programs operated by the Commission. Federal funds received by the Commission in fiscal year 1981 totaled $1,810,000.

Of the 64,635 Indians of North Carolina, the approximately 6,000 members of the Eastern Band of the Cherokee are Federally recognized and, thus, receive BIA services. In addition to BIA monies, the Eastern Band of the Cherokee also received funds from the State of North Carolina: Human Resources: $2,123; Employment Security Commission: $15,540; Department of Transportation: $14,258.

The great majority of the remaining Indian citizens of North Carolina are members of the four state-recognized tribes—the Lumbee, Coharie, Haliwa-Saponi and Waccamaw-Siouan. Although the largest of the North Carolina tribes, the Lumbee, have been recognized as a tribe by the U.S. Congress, it is not eligible for BIA services.

The fifteen Indian members of the North Carolina Commission of Indian Affairs Board are representatives of seven state Indian organizations. These seven organizations are: Coharie Intra-Tribal Council, Cumberland County Association for Indian People, Guilford Native American Association, Haliwa-Saponi Indian Tribe, Lumbee Regional Development Association, Metrolina Native American Association, and the Waccamaw-Siouan Development Association. These seven Indian organizations operated a variety of Federally funded programs in 1981 including programs in the areas of employment and training, education, economic development, and social services. In 1981, the Commission and the seven Indian organizations generated $10,000,000 in Federal funds for the Indians of North Carolina.[24]

North Dakota

The North Dakota Indian Commission, with an executive director as the head of its staff, administers a North Dakota scholarship program funded by the state (1981-1983: $145,000) and helped 91 students who were attending college in 1981. The Commission also administers "seed money" through the Indian Development Fund for Indians who wish to start a business on the reservation. During 1981 the legislature appropriated $383,000 for an Indian alcohol abuse program and four reservations participated. The state channels Federal dollars to Indians for AFDC ($4 million) and foster care ($459,000). In each instance these programs are about 26 percent of the entire state load. The Indian scholarship program is available only to "resident persons of at least one-fourth degree of Indian blood or for enrolled members of tribes" residing in the state.[25]

Oregon

The Oregon Commission on Indian Services was created by statute in 1975 "to advise the Legislative Assembly and other Oregon officials and agencies on the needs of American Indian people," to make program recommendations, to serve as a liaison between the state and the tribes and to serve as a clearinghouse. The speaker of the house and the president of the senate appoint eight Indian members from nominees submitted by Indian groups and one senator and one representative also serve on the commission. In carrying out its "clearinghouse" and "information" functions the Commission publishes an Oregon Directory of American Indian Resources.[26]

Some of the specific relationships between the tribes and the state follow.

Law enforcement units and police officers on Indian reservations are subject to state police and probation standards and training unless jurisdiction is returned to the tribe. Tribal members are exempt from state income taxes if they resided on the reservation when the income was earned. Money paid to tribes for the condemnation of tribal lands is exempt from state income taxes. The director of the state department of revenue is authorized to enter into agreements with tribes on the collection of taxes on the sale of cigarettes. An agreement in 1980 with the Confederated Tribes of the Umatilla Indian Reservation provided that the tribe would continue to collect the state cigarette tax and the state would refund the amount collected from Indians within the reservation. Upon the request of a municipality, county, Indian reservation, or other planning agency, the state may assist in land use studies, surveys, and other technical services. If a scenic waterway involves Indian lands the state may enter into agreements with the appropriate tribe or tribes. State law provides for distribution of food to counties and Indian tribes. In connection with sewage treatment projects, Indian tribes are eligible along with municipalities and may act jointly with municipalities or special service districts. A special statutory provision in state laws governing fishing states "Nothing in this section is intended to affect Indian fishing rights as granted by Federal treaties." In the state mental health program, if a tribal reservation extends into two or more counties the state mental health division may contract with the tribe for the operation of a community health program "in the same manner that the division contracts with a county court or board of county commissioners." In state legislation concerning energy, the term "municipal corporation" includes an Indian tribe or tribes acting jointly in connection with a small scale local energy project.

Oregon has 12 pages of rules governing the placement of Indian children, family foster care, group residential care, adoption placement, and termination of parental rights based on the Indian Child Welfare Act of 1978. The Children's Services Division "seeks to promote the stability and well-being of Indian families and to avoid the unnecessary removal of Indian children from their families. . .and intends to cooperate fully with Indian tribes and organizations in the planning and implementation of effective programs to serve Indian children and families."[27]

Rhode Island

Rhode Island's Commission on Indian Affairs, established in the Office of the Governor in 1976, performs liaison services on Indian matters with the state and Federal governments. It is not involved in the social services area. In May 1979, the state's Indian Land Act turned over 1,800 acres to the Narraganset tribe, implementing "an agreement reached by the tribal council, the state, and Federal Justice Department and Indian affairs officials. Negotiations began after the Indians filed suit in 1975 for their ancestral land." The $3.5 million to purchase the land came from a Federal appropriation. "Rhode Island bought the last of the land from the tribe for a small sum in 1890 without Federal authorization." The state act provided for an Indian-dominated corporation to manage the land.[28] However, in February 1982 the land was still not totally under the Narragansett community's control and the commission was working to achieve that goal.

Mary Jane Banfield, former executive director of the Commission, initiated the Narragansett land claim before the Commission was established in 1976. She learned of the "justification for the claim while working at the Tomaquag Indian Museum. . . ." The Commission provided information and followed through on legislation until it was enacted.

The Commission consists of five representatives from the Narragansett Indian Tribe, two representatives from the Rhode Island Indian Council, and one representative from the community at large—all appointed by the Governor.

Rhode Island also is the home of the Rhode Island Indian Council, a chartered non-profit organization, incorporated in 1975 to serve off-reservation and urban Indian people in Rhode Island. The council has administered a statewide CETA program for Indian people. The Commission and the Council cooperate in carrying out Indian services and activities. In 1980 they held a joint meeting with the Narragansett Tribal Council to discuss mutual concerns such as the Indian Youth Conservation Corps, Indian scholarships, urban Indian funding, a statewide Indian newspaper, Indian child day care, Indian housing authority and state jobs.

The Commission during 1980 testified before a Federal task force on the "definition of an Indian" seeking to maintain eligibility for Federal funds, worked with BIA in identifying and documenting Narragansett genealogy for Federal recognition and helped the Narragansett tribe with proposals for funds. For the 1980 fiscal year the budget of the Commission was $35,000.[29]

South Dakota

The South Dakota Indian Affairs Office is set up to act as a liaison between state, Federal, tribal, and local governments. It also handles individual requests for assistance. The Indian Affairs Office staff consists of the coordinator, deputy coordinator, and an administrative assistant. Most recently the office has been instrumental in starting the South Dakota Indian Child Protection Team and stimulating its growth. The office involves itself with many organizations and has brought attention to working with the handicapped, elderly, and in areas of child abuse and neglect.[30]

Utah

Utah has a unique situation. Thirty-seven and one-half percent of the net oil and gas royalties from Navajo land in Utah is paid to the State of Utah to be expended by the state for the health, education, and general welfare of the Navajo Indians residing in San Juan county. In 1981 Utah received over $2,600,000 from the royalty and almost $765,000 from interest from the Oil Royalty Fund for a total income of approximately $3,400,000; expenditures in 1981 were approximately $1,500,000.

An Indian Affairs Commission was created in 1959 to administer the assets of the Oil Royalty Fund derived from the extension of the Navajo Indian Reservation in Utah as a result of Federal legislation in 1933.[31] In 1968 and again in 1979 the state organization was changed. The function is now located in the Department of Community and Economic Development because of emphasis on economic development activities, under the name, "Division of Indian Affairs." There is a Board of Indian Affairs consisting of seven members, all appointed by the Governor with the advice and consent of the senate. This is a policy board but it also appoints the director of the Division of Indian Affairs with the concurrence of the executive director of the department of community and economic development and the Governor. The Division of Indian Affairs administers and supervises programs developed by the Board.

Appointments to the Board are limited to two terms of four years, terms are overlapping, and not more than four can be from the same political party. One member shall be a Navajo Indian residing in San Juan County, one member a Ute Indian from Unitah or Duchesne County, one member a resident of San Juan County but not an Indian, and the remaining four members selected from the state at large. "All members shall be chosen with due regard for their knowledge of, or interest in, promoting the education, health and welfare of the Indians residing in the state."

Two corporations have been created by the Division of Indian Affairs: (1) the Utah Navajo Development Council (UNDC) with contract funds from the Division providing for social programs, and (2) Utah Navajo Industries (UNI) which promotes and provides job opportunities. Social programs include health care, educational programs, housing and other community related services, natural resource development, road construction and maintenance, etc. In 1982 UNDC was funded for over $1 million and UNI for a little over $400,000.

Utah "provides all services to Indians that it provides to everyone else. Residence on an Indian reservation makes no difference." Approximately one-third of Utah's 19,000 Indians live on reservations.[32]

Washington

In Washington and the Pacific Northwest, additional institutional arrangements have developed in an attempt to work out solutions under the Boldt fishing decision, (see Chapter 2, Treaty Fishing Rights) such as the state of Washington's use of an Indian Task Force to evaluate state services to Indians in 1971 and 1973. Two publications outlined conditions as seen by the Task Force and made recommendations especially aimed at state agencies such as the game commission. In 1978 a Governor's Advisory Council edited and approved a revised edition which will be referred to as the Task Force Report.[33]

The Advisory Council has membership from three groups: seven members from reservations, eight members from rural landless Indians, and eight Indians from urban centers. The Task Force Report protests the genocidal programs of the non-Indian society, proclaims self-determination and the necessity of a Federal subsidy to achieve it. It made recommendations for improvement, such as an Indian law and order advisory committee, funded by the Federal government to work with the state law and justice advisory council.

As a result of the Boldt decision the Northwest Indian Fisheries Commission has been established, funded by BIA with representatives from western Washington tribes. Another advance is the formation of the Columbia River Basin Fisheries Alliance with representatives from treaty tribes, commercial fishermen, sports fishermen, and packers and guides with the overriding aim of preserving the fishery resource, even though the members may strongly disagree on procedure. Communication may be the first step to developing a consensus.

Noted in the Task Force Report are requirements of the larger jurisdictions over smaller areas for such actions as siting of major industrial and energy facilities, water and air pollution control, and watershed protection.

The Task Force pointed to political goals: "It is imperative at this point to have the cooperation of state and Federal officials to accomplish two things: (1) institutionalize meritable existing programs which are now dependent on soft monies and the public mood; (2) create means to develop a continuous flow of political bargaining between Federal, state, and local government and Indian citizens."[34] The Task Force recommended (1) the formation of Indian pressure groups "in alignment with non-Indian forces and existing power structures, especially at the local level, such as the Association of Washington Counties and the Association of Washington Cities" and (2) the use of the Governor's Indian Advisory Council to have direct input into the highest level of state government.[35]

STATES WITH STATE INDIAN RESERVATIONS

Five states have state Indian reservations. Some of these also have special organizational arrangements or individuals concerned with Indian matters.

Florida

State lands are available to the Miccosukee tribe. In fact, the Miccosukee restaurant, store and service station are on state dedicated land which may be transferred to Federal trust. The Miccosukee tribal headquarters and cultural center are on U.S. Park Service land under a permit to January 4, 2014. An estimated fifty percent of the approximately 500 Miccosukees live on Park Service land along the Tamiami Trail.

In 1974 the Governor created a Florida Governor's Council on Indian

Affairs, a private not-for-profit organization, with 15 members appointed by the Governor. In 1982 the Council had membership as follows: four Seminoles, four Miccosukees, and seven at-large members (one traditional Seminole, one Creek, two attorneys, a state senator, "an old Indian friend," and one college professor). Florida state government cabinet heads negotiate directly with Indian tribes and groups. The Governor's Council provides tribal access to the state decision making process through advice to the Governor and the legislature and serves as an Indian advocate. The Council staff, headed by an executive director, had $90,000 of state appropriated funds for 1981-1982. The legislature also appropriated $154,000 for Indian education in 1982 and $40,000 for the Northwest Florida Creek Indian Council. The Governor's Council administers about $500,000 for Indian programs, mostly from Federal agencies but some from private sources.[36]

There are approximately 1,400 Seminoles on Federal trust land served by BIA's Seminole Agency. The Miccosukees also have a BIA funded agency.

New York

New York has been deeply involved with Indian affairs since colonial times. The State Department of Social Services has an Indian Services Specialist who works with the Iroquois and the Algonquin tribes.

The Iroquois Nations/Tribes that are Federally recognized are the Cayuga, Oneida, Onondaga, Seneca, St. Regis Mohawk, Tuscarora and Tonawanda Band of Senecas. The Algonquin Tribes, namely the Poospatuck and Shinnecock do not have land in Federal trust, are not recognized by the BIA but are recognized state reservations.

Of New York's 39,500 Indians only about 11,000 are eligible for BIA services. In 1980 approximately 20,500 lived in the New York City area.

Through the years New York has provided health, education and social services for Indian people. During the 1950s the BIA assumed that New York's Indians were under the jurisdiction of the state. The Bureau was of the opinion that all Federal responsibility had ceased except for a treaty annuity requirement to one of the tribes. Federal laws were enacted in 1948 and 1950 confirming state criminal and civil jurisdiction over reservation Indians.

The Maine land claims raised the question of the Trade and Intercourse Act and since reservation lands had never been transferred to New York by Federal statute, the BIA is again offering its program in a limited way.

New York allocated approximately $8.5 million to its Indian citizens on reservations in 1981: (1) Public Assistance, Foster Care, and Medical: $2 million; Education: $4.8 million; Library: $172,000; Health: $330,000; Aging: $386,000; Alcoholism: $422,000; Roads: $289,000.

Members of New York tribes have free hunting, fishing and trapping privileges.[37]

South Carolina

South Carolina has no Federally recognized Indians, although at one time the Catawba tribe was Federally recognized. In 1970 this tribe had about 400 members, 200 of whom lived on the state-recognized "Old Reservation." Among the Indian groups are the Edisto, Pee Dee and Santee. A report published in 1979 indicated the main needs: correction of substandard housing and water supplies; improvement of roads, upgrading of poor educational opportunities and facilities; and development of employment opportunities. Isolation was an important underlying factor in all of these needs.[38]

Texas

The Texas Indian Commission (1965) consists of three citizen members and has an executive director and one assistant. The Commission supervises two state Indian reservations, each with a superintendent and staff reporting to the executive director. The two groups of Indians on these reservations are the Alabama-Coushatta and the Tigua. Both are recognized as tribes by the Federal government but they have no land in Federal trust and are not eligible for services from the BIA. The goal of the Texas Indian Commission and the Indian leadership of the two tribes is economic self-sufficiency. It is hoped that the tourist complexes developed for the two reservations will lead to economic independence. For the 540 Alabama-Coushatta Indians this may be as soon as 1985.

There are approximately 25,000 urban Indians from 80 different tribes in the Dallas-Fort Worth area according to the Executive Director of the Commission. The Commission has helped obtain mutual help housing for the two reservations and indicates the need is great for urban Indians also.

Texas has about 600 Traditional Kickapoos who migrate to and from Mexico. Their status is somewhat uncertain. The state legislature passed a law recognizing the Kickapoos as a tribe and authorizing the Texas Indian Commission to serve them. However the state attorney general said the law discriminated on the basis of race which is prohibited by the Texas Constitution. This was changed by P.L. 97-429, January 8, 1983, 97th Congress, 2nd sess, federally recognizing these Kickapoos and authorizing the purchase of 100 acres in trust.

Texas funds its Indian programs as follows: Commission: $94,000; Alabama-Coushatta superintendent and staff: $133,000; and Tigua superintendent and staff: $297,000. Texas state funds for Indians are expected to approximate $1 million for the 1982-1983 biennium. [39]

Virginia

Virginia has two state reservations, one for the Pamunkeys (approximately 40 persons in 1970) and the other for the Mattaponis (approximately 60 persons). The Indians own their reservation land which is not taxed by the state. There are no Indians served by BIA in the state. As is obvious most of Virginia's 9,000 Indians are not on the two reservations.

The Pamunkey and Mattaponi tribes have received Federal funds for local projects from EDA, HUD, CETA and Revenue Sharing. An Indian Museum and Community Center was completed in 1980 for the Pamunkey Indian Tribe. The state appropriates funds for subsidized school lunch and textbook programs and for paving and road maintenance for the two reservations.[40] On March 8, 1983, the General Assembly of Virginia amended the Code of Virginia (Title 9, chapter 20.1) to provide for a ten-member Commission on Indians appointed by the Governor of which at least five members will be Indians, with responsibility to gather information on Indians, conduct studies and research, and "suggest ways in which Indians may reach their potential and make their full contribution as wage earners and citizens, to society and this Commonwealth."

ALASKA AND MAINE

The relationships of Alaska and Maine to their Native citizens is somewhat different than in other states with Federally recognized native groups.

Alaska

Alaska has the highest percentage (16 percent) of Natives to the total population of any state. As indicated in Chapter 2, the Natives traditionally have sought citizenship and participation in state affairs. The Alaska Native Claims Settlement Act provided for use of the corporate mechanism under Alaska state law for administering the land and funds awarded rather than the traditional BIA and trust approach. "The state of Alaska currently has no programs in place targeted specifically for the Indian population. State programs are designed to provide public services to all residents without regard to ancestral background." In some instances Indian villages and groups are organized as municipalities under the Alaska governmental system. Alaska provides public schooling for all children including Indian children. Metlakatla is the only Federal reservation in Alaska. [41]

Maine

Until recently Maine had the only state Department of Indian Affairs. The Indians of Maine and the BIA believed the Federal government had no special responsibility for Maine's Indians. Maine's Indian reservations were considered state reservations. All that changed in 1980. Some aspects of that change are discussed in Chapter 2. Here attention is focused on the new relationships between the state and its Indians.

The jurisdictional framework regulating the relationship between the state and the tribes is provided by Maine's P.L. 1980, Chapter 732, known as the "Maine Implementing Act" and the Federal act, P.L. 96-420, "The Maine Indian Claims Settlement Act." The two acts became effective December 12, 1980.

Generally the Passamaquoddy Tribe and the Penobscot Nation "will be functional equivalents of Maine municipalities having the same rights, powers, duties and liabilities as municipalities." These include the power to tax, to pass ordinances, to sue and to be sued, to dispense and receive services, and the general home rule powers of such municipalities under the laws of the state. Civil actions, custody and domestic relations are under tribal authority. The Penobscot court uses the Maine rule of civil procedure. "As Maine Municipalities, the tribes are eligible for State funds flowing to other municipalities."

The "tribe's eligibility for special Federal Indian programs" was also made clear by the legislation. Welfare provides an example of the interface between the tribes, the state and the BIA. Under state law the State Department of Human Services reimburses municipalities 90 percent of the general assistance costs that exceed .0003 of the municipality's valuation. This applies to tribes in their capacity as Maine municipalities. The former state appropriation to the Maine Department of Indian Affairs for welfare assistance, $450,000 in FY 1979-1980, is no longer made. As Maine municipalities, the tribes are required to provide general assistance to all eligible residents and non-residents. Since the tribes are eligible also to receive Federal funds for general assistance, the state will consider such Federal funds received by the tribe as the municipal share of the funding of welfare. If Federal funds exceed the municipal share under the state formula, the excess is credited to the state's share.

However, if there are both Indians and non-Indians living within the tribe's "municipal" jurisdiction and the Federal general assistance funds are limited to Indians, this would not qualify the tribe for state reimbursement because all legal residents must be served under state law. Insofar as funds were applied equally to all residents, the tribe would be eligible. Thus, if the Federal funds could be used only to support Indians and there were no non-Indians within the tribe's (municipality's) jurisdiction, the tribe would qualify for state reimbursement.

The non-taxable nature of Indian land under Federal trust is another area involving relationships with the state and private citizens. Non-Indians living on trust land are subject to state personal and real estate taxes and do not have the right to vote in tribal elections. However, they are entitled to receive any municipal or governmental services provided by the tribe with minor exceptions. The trust land is in so-called "Indian territory." Indian territory land is owned by the tribe and individual Indians will occupy parcels assigned to them. Creditors, of course, cannot foreclose on trust land. However, the Federal statute established a Tribal Trust Fund and creditors are entitled to be paid out of this fund. It is estimated that the annual trust fund income to each tribe will be in excess of $1,250,000 and adequate to satisfy any creditors.

In fiscal year 1979-1980 Maine funded nearly the entire cost of the education of Indian children in the amount of $770,000. In FY 1980-1981, after the legislation, BIA contributed $807,000 to the education of Maine Indian children and in effect took over the funding. Tribes create their own school committees like any other municipality and similarly operate under state education statutes.

In law enforcement, tribal police are equivalent to municipal police and within tribal territory can enforce all laws, state and tribal. Within tribal territory non-Indian violators are subject to state courts and Indian violators are subject to tribal courts. The tribes regulate fishing in tribal territory except for large ponds, rivers and streams, which are under the authority of a Tribal-State Commission. Tribal police and all state law enforcement officers enforce Tribal-State Commission regulations. All violators of Tribal-State Commission regulations, Indian and non-Indian, are tried in state courts. Tribal police are under state law requiring that they receive training applicable to local police officers.[42]

STATES WITHOUT SPECIAL STATE ORGANIZATIONS FOR INDIANS OR STATE INDIAN RESERVATIONS

Some states which do not have special governmental units for Indian affairs, do nevertheless have some official Indian relationships, such as the Native American Study Committee of the Wisconsin Legislative Council.

Iowa without Indian reservations, nevertheless has the Mesquakie Indian Settlement of the Sac and Fox of the Mississippi Tribe located in Tama County.[43] The Constitution and Bylaws of the Sac and Fox Tribe of the Mississippi in Iowa, approved by the Secretary of Interior in 1937, uses both the terms "settlement" and "reservation" in referring to the Sac and Fox in

Iowa. The constitution states: "It is hereby recognized that all the land within the Sac and Fox Reservation is tribal land, having been bought by the tribe with its common funds, and is now held in trust for the Sac and Fox Tribe in Iowa by the Secretary of the Interior." The BIA 1981 Annual Report of Indian Lands indicates 3,535 acres held in tribal trust for the Sac and Fox.

Iowa forwarded a report entitled "Race Relations in Tama County" which outlined the complete network of resources available, or not available, to the Sac and Fox settlement and the relationships of the settlement with Tama county and the Tama-Toledo area.[44] Included are the interrelationships involved in law and order, water and sewer hookups, child welfare, education and other services. The Iowa Department of Social Services is appropriated Indian Relief monies which totaled $34,000 in 1981. Determining eligibility for and the disbursement of these funds are the responsibility of the Sac and Fox.

Wisconsin in 1979 contracted with both the Oneida and Stockbridge-Munsee for them to administer AFDC, medical assistance and food stamps. Relief to needy Indians is entirely state funded and administered by the tribes. Wisconsin works with BIA, the Indian Health Service (IHS), the counties and the tribes on a regular basis.[45]

The Wisconsin Legislative Council has a Native American Study Committee consisting of four senators, four representatives and six public members to study problems and develop recommendations and legislative proposals relating to Indians and tribes within the state.[46] Wisconsin also has an innovative statewide plan for Indian library services.[47] This project was proposed to the Great Lakes Inter-Tribal Council and the state's Division of Library Services in 1974 by the National Indian Education Association. The plan presents data on the status of Indian people as well as proposals for improving library services to Indian citizens.

Wyoming reported that all of its health and social services programs are available to the Federally recognized Indians on the Wind River Indian Reservation, resulting in an expenditure of approximately $100,000 in the month of January 1982, for AFDC, SSI, Food Stamps, social services, and low income energy assistance.[48]

SUMMARY

Many states have no BIA-recognized Indians and a relatively small Indian population. In these states no distinction is made between Indian and other citizens. However, some Federal agencies other than BIA may provide services or funds to these Indians, as Indians, on occasion, e.g., in North Carolina, for example, in the foregoing discussion.

The Federal form of government under the Constitution provides for a division of responsibilities between the central and state governments. Clear-cut delineation of the responsibilities and services to Indian citizens by the state and Federal governments has been difficult because of the constitutional provisions regarding Indians, the location of many governmental functions at the state level for most citizens, and constantly changing circumstances. The foregoing review makes clear that the states and their subdivisions are very important governments to Indians, including those Indians residing on Federal reservations. [49]

FOOTNOTES

[1]As indicated in chapter 1, of the 1,421,400 Indians counted in the 1980 census only 53 percent have any relation with BIA. The other 47 percent receive most of their governmental services from the state and Federal governments in the same manner as other citizens. Even many Indian groups having some connection with BIA receive many services through the state. When the 90-95 percent of Indian education provided by the state (both reservation and non-reservation Indians) and the high ratio of state provision of law and order and other services to Indians are considered, the estimate that states furnish 80-85 percent of the government services received by Indians seems reasonable.

[2]American Indian Policy Review Commission, *Final Report*, 2 vols. (Washington, D.C.: GPO, 1977), vol. 1, p. 5. Hereafter referred to as AIPRC *Final Report.* The Senate Select Committee has sought to further this objective by introducing legislation in the sessions since 1977, for example, S. 563, 97th Cong. 1st. sess., February 24, 1981, "Tribal-State Compact Act of 1981".

[3]S. Lyman Tyler, "European-American Relations With the Indigenous Americans: Crown to Congress to Executive, and Colony to State", Lecture, University of Utah, 1978.

[4]Theodore W. Taylor, *The States and Their Indian Citizens* (Washington: U.S. Department of the Interior, Bureau of Indian Affairs, 1972), pp. 27-62 for details. Hereafter referred to as Taylor, *States.*

[5]Johnson-O'Malley Act of 1934, 48 Stat. 596.

[6]39 Stat. 127.

[7]Telephone conversation with Raymond Butler, Division of Social Services, March 8, 1982.

[8]Taylor, *States*, particularly pp. 89-106.

[9]As of January 1982, forty one states had responded by letter or telephone to the letter sent by Kenneth Payton, Acting Deputy Assistant Secretary for Indian Affairs (Operations), October 16, 1981, to the governors of the fifty states. Those not responding were: Alabama, Connecticut, Georgia, Kentucky, Massachusetts, New Jersey, Pennsylvania, Vermont and West Virginia. *Federal/State Indian Reservations and Indian Trust Areas* (Washington, D.C.: U.S. Department of Commerce, 1974) indicates several states with state reservations for Indians for states not responding to Payton's inquiry or which were not mentioned in the responses received:

State	Tribe or group	Population	Land (acres)
Connecticut	Eastern Pequot	19	220
	Western Pequot	2	175
	Golden Hill	2	.26
	Schaghticoke	2	400
Massachusetts	Hassanamisco	1	12
Michigan	Huron Potowatomi Band	50	120

[10]Letters from Governor Bruce Babbitt, December 3, 1981, and from Clinton M. Pattea, November 27, 1981, and enclosed material.

[11]Material received from Rachel Bluestone, Coordinator, in February 1982. No transmittal letter and no indication of funding.

[12]*Annual Report*, Colorado Commission of Indian Affairs, for fiscal years 1979-1980 and 1980-1981.

[13]Ibid.

[14]Letter from Governor Harry Hughes, November 23, 1981.

[15]Letter from Governor William C. Milliken, November 18, 1981.

[16]Letter from Governor Albert H. Quie, December 8, 1981.

[17]Reports of the Indian Affairs Intertribal Board for the years 1977, 1979, and 1981, received from O. J. Doyle, Jr., Special Assistant to the Governor, February 23, 1982.

[18]Letter from James Parker Shield, State Coordinator of Indian Affairs, January 7, 1982.

[19]Memorandum from Leo Berry to Governor Ted Schwinden, January 20, 1982, about BIA book, *The States and Their Indian Citizens*, transmitted by James Parker Shield, February 11, 1982.

[20]Letter from Marvin Buzzard, Executive Director, Nebraska Indian Commission, October 26, 1981.

[21]Letter from Governor Robert List, November 18, 1981.

[22]*Biennial Report*, 1979-1980, Nevada Indian Commission, transmitted by letter from Elwood Mose, Executive Director, February 22, 1982.

[23]Letter from Governor Bruce King, November 13, 1981.

[24]*Federal Programs and North Carolina Indians*, North Carolina Commission of Indian Affairs, 1981. Letter from Janet Y. Jacobs, Commission Staff, February 16, 1982 with comments.

[25]Letters from Juanita J. Helphrey, Executive Director, North Dakota Indian Affairs Commission, November 5, 1981 and January 18, 1982.

[26]*Oregon Directory of American Indian Resources*, Katherine Greene, Commission on Indian Services, 1981-1982.

[27]Rules Division 26, Children's Services Division, State of Oregon, transmitted by letter from Dennis Mulvihill, February 19, 1982.

[28]The Washington Post, May 10, 1979. Telephone conversation with Commission office. February 3, 1982.

[29]*1980 Annual Report*, Rhode Island Commission on Indian Affairs, transmitted with other materials by letter from Paulla Dove Jennings, Executive Director, February 22, 1982.

[30]Letter from Marcella Prue, Coordinator, South Dakota Indian Affairs Office, February 18, 1982.

[31]47 Stat. 1418, March 1, 1933.

[32]Letter from Bruce G. Parry, Director, Division of Indian Affairs, Utah, January 29, 1982, with the accompanying documents: Utah Code Annotated, 1953; a table on royalty income and expenditure information; and a functional statement for the division of Indian Affairs.

[33]*Are You Listening Neighbor?* and *The People Speak, Will You Listen?* Revised, 1978, Indian Task Force, State of Washington. Hereafter cited as *Task Force Report.*

[34]*Task Force Report*, p. 103

[35]Ibid. p. 104.

[36]Letter from Joe A. Quetone, Executive Director, Florida Governor's Council on Indian Affairs, December 2, 1981, and subsequent telephone conversations.

[37]Letters from Elma R. Patterson, Indian Services Specialist, New York State Department of Social Services, November 6, 1981 and February 26, 1982.

[38]Letter from Rudy Long, Office of the Governor, South Carolina, November 19, 1981.

[39]Letter from Walt Broemer, Executive Director, Texas Indian Commission, December 22, 1981.

[40]Telephone conversation with G. Warren Cook, Coordinator, Native American Programs, Governor's Office, Virginia, January 27, 1982, and letter from Cook dated March 2, 1982. House Document No. 10 of the General Assembly of Virginia, 1983, contained a report of a subcommittee recommending that Indian tribes be recognized officially and assisted in securing "available governmental benefits reserved for Indians." Four groups other than the Pumunkey and Mattaponi now connected with state reservations are mentioned: Chickahominy in Charles City County; East Chickahominy in New Kent County; Rappahannock of Caroline, Essex, and King and Queen Counties; and the Upper Mattaponi of King William County.

[41]Letter from Susan S. Green, Special Assistant to the Governor of Alaska, December 4, 1981, and subsequent telephone conversation.

[42]Letter from Alice E. Sproul, Legal Assistant, Department of the Attorney General, State of Maine, Jan. 6, 1982, and the following documents transmitted by that letter: Report of the Joint Select Committee on Indian Land Claims of the Maine Legislature; Attorney General's Opinion, August 30, 1981, re: Indian Education Financing for FY 1981; and Attorney General's Opinion, October 30, 1981, re: Applicability of General Assistance Laws within Indian Territory. For further reference there are the House and Senate Reports on the Maine Indian Claims Settlement Act and two volumes of testimony and documents presented to the Senate Select Committee on Indian Affairs.

43Letter from Michael V. Reagen, Commissioner, Iowa Department of Social Services, November 19, 1981.

44*Race Relations in Tama County*, Iowa Advisory Committee to the U.S. Commission on Civil Rights, August 1981.

45*State-Tribal Agreements: A Comprehensive Study*, Commission on State-Tribal Relations, of the National Conference of State Legislators, American Indian Law Center, May 1981, pp. 74-75.

46*Wisconsin Blue Book*, 1981-1982. Forwarded by H. Rupert Theobald, Chief, Legislative Reference Bureau, Wisconsin, February 22, 1982.

47"Statewide Plan for the Development of Indian Library Services in the State of Wisconsin", Wisconsin Department of Public Instruction, Revised 1981.

48Letter from C. Richard Skinner, Administrative Assistant to the Governor, Wyoming, February 15, 1982.

49More detailed information on state Indian activities and interface with the tribes and the Federal Government as of 1971 can be found in Taylor, *States,* especially in appendices B, C, E, F and H. Appendix J, Taylor, *States,* indicates state reservations in Massachusetts, Connecticut, Michigan and Pennsylvania which are not included in this book. They had very small groups with little land in 1971. None of these states reported reservations in response to the Payton letter. See footnote 9.

CHAPTER 5
INDIAN INTEREST GROUPS

INTRODUCTION

Indians and Indian interest groups participate in the creation and execution of Indian policy. Clientele of all government agencies have an impact on agency programs. Indians are no different. Navajo has a Washington office and for a while so did the Alaska Federation of Natives.

General Indian interest groups such as the National Congress of American Indians or the Association of American Indian Affairs are concerned with many aspects of Indian policy, whereas special Indian interest groups such as the Council of Energy Resource Tribes or the Association of American Indian Physicians concentrate primarily on a single or limited subject matter area.

Students of government have long recognized that the individual citizen or his representative has an important place in the governmental process. Citizens of course are represented in the state and Federal government by their elected representatives and elected executives. But they also can deal directly with these individuals rather than just through the ballot box. Indians do this at Congressional hearings, in letters and in legislative proposals as well as in communications with the elected executive, whether it be a governor or the President.

Most individuals, however, interact with the local governmental officials carrying out programs throughout the country. For Indians the two primary agencies with field personnel are the Bureau of Indian Affairs (BIA) and the Indian Health Service (IHS). An Indian wanting to lease his trust land needs the approval of the Indian superintendent at the agency. If a member of his family is sick he uses the services of the IHS, either through outpatient facilities or by admittance to an Indian hospital.

Indians as clients interact with service programs continually. This interaction affects both the Indian and the agency. The government employee learns what is and is not acceptable in the nature of a service or the way in which it is provided. The Indian client becomes aware of the necessary information required for a particularly desired action and of the limits of personnel time or funds available. Changes in policy may result from this interaction. The agency may propose a regulation change or a legislative change on the basis of the experiences of its field personnel. Clients may band together to implement such an action directly with agency national offices or with Congress. Both the agency and its clients may also strive to increase resources available through increased funds and personnel, e.g., for improved education or health services.

Indians have discovered that in unity there is strength. Thus the National Congress of American Indians (NCAI) states "that a prime purpose is to help achieve unity among tribes to address issues and concerns common to all so that Indians can speak with one voice on national issues."

Indian interest groups can be classified in different ways—by purpose, by size, by whether all-Indian or both Indian and non-Indian, by source of funding and by general effectiveness. Indian interest groups deserve to be the subject of a special study all by themselves. Here we can indicate only some of their characteristics and present examples to illustrate their relation to BIA and other participants in the Indian policy process.

In order to obtain specific data about Indian interest groups the writer sent a letter to approximately 60 non-profit groups or organizations. From those responding, examples of various types are profiled below.

GENERAL NATIONAL INDIAN ORGANIZATIONS

These organizations are concerned with several aspects of Indian social, economic, political, and governmental relationships. They generally do not restrict membership or services to just a part of the United States and they involve may different tribes and groups. Some seek to achieve consensus among Indian tribes and individuals on major policy issues and act as Indian advocates. They frequently lobby at all levels of government with administrative agencies and elected representatives. Most of them obtain as much private financial help as possible. One of the following, the Association on American Indian Affairs (AAIA), is funded completely by private funds. Most, however, are heavily dependent on Federal grants and contracts.

Association on American Indian Affairs (AAIA) (Founded in 1923)
432 Park Avenue South, New York, N.Y. 10016

Purpose: To "assist American Indian and Alaska Native communities in their efforts to achieve full economic, social, and civil equality, and to defend their rights. . . . The Association conducts continuing programs in Indian economic and community development; health, education and welfare; legal defense; arts and crafts; and public education. It aids Indian tribes in mobilizing all available resources—Federal, state, and private—for a coordinated attack on the problems of poverty and injustice."

Organization: The AAIA is a private, non-profit, national citizens' organization. Officers are: president, three vice presidents, secretary and treasurer; an executive director is one of six full-time and two part-time employees in the New York office. The Association also has an office of general counsel in Washington, D.C. The "policies and programs of the Association are formulated by a Board of Directors, the majority of whom are Indian and Alaska Native." The board of directors is composed of: (1) an executive committee of 13 members including the officers listed above, and (2) 12 directors. This is a total of 26 persons, not including three honorary directors.

Budget: "The Association's annual operating budget is approximately $500,000. The Association is completely dependent upon contributions from its members and contributors."

Budget for the year ending February 28, 1981:

Income

Contributions and dues	$364,110
Legacies	229,537
Trusts	35,080
Investment Income	31,808
Unrealized loss (securities)	(30,800)
Sales of literature	2,439
Total Income	$632,174

Expenses

Program services:		
Indian community development	$160,738	
Public education	57,888	
Health	8,286	
Education	27,429	
Legal defense	24,733	
		$279,074
Supporting services:		
General and administrative	$109,507	
Fundraising	113,417	
		$222,924
Total Expenses		$501,998

Major Accomplishments: AAIA worked with the Alaska Federation of Natives in achieving the Alaska Land Claims Settlement Act of 1971;

purchased 15 acres in 1975 for the landless Coushatta in Louisiana; with grant funds from AAIA as a down payment, the landless Wittenberg Band of Winnebagos of Wisconsin acquired a 160-acre working farm.

AAIA made suggestions to the House Interior Committee in 1979 that were incorporated into the Archaeological Resources Protection Act.

In 1961 it helped the Miccosukee Tribe of Florida gain recognition as a Federal tribe and similarly helped the Payson Band of Tonto Apache of Arizona in 1972, the Coushattas of Louisiana in 1973, and two bands of Indians in California in 1975 and 1978.

The Association was a leader in seeking a change in Indian child welfare procedures and stimulated the Senate Subcommittee on Indian Affairs to hold hearings in 1974, and, in 1976, AAIA drafted an Indian Child Welfare Act to protect the rights of Indian parents and children. A child-welfare law was passed in 1978 and the Association worked closely with the BIA in drafting Federal regulations to implement the law.

In 1978 AAIA helped the Sisseton-Wahpeton Sioux Tribe negotiate an agreement with the state of South Dakota enabling the tribe to operate social services programs under Title XX of the Social Security Act.

A series of articles on Indian child welfare entitled *The Destruction of American Indian Families* was published in 1977 and reprinted in 1978 and 1979. The AAIA also publishes a quarterly bulletin, *Indian Family Defense*.

The AAIA has helped the following tribes with negotiations for self-determination contracts (contracts to operate services formerly provided by BIA or IHS): Miccosukee, Shoshones and Arapahoes of Wyoming, Northern Cheyennes, Menominees, Southern Cheyennes, Oneidas of Wisconsin, several Navajo communities, Cook Inlet Native Association, Tanana Chiefs' Conference, Metlakatla Village, Havasupai, Oglala Sioux, and others.

In 1977 the Association assisted nine Eskimo whaling villages in reaching a temporary quota on the taking of bowhead whales thus helping avert clashes between the Eskimos and the Federal government.

Assistance in improving health has included financial aid to help organize the Association of American Indian Physicians (1971) and the American Indian Nurses Association (1973).

AAIA also has participated in many court cases to defend treaty rights and to assist in the objectives of full economic, social and civil equality.[1]

Friends Committee on National Legislation (FCNL)
245 Second Street, N.E., Washington, D.C. 20002

Purpose: "The Friends Committee on National Legislation began in 1943 to work toward a nonmilitary world order based so firmly on justice, spiritual unity, and voluntary cooperation that there is no place for war." A portion of the total effort is devoted to work with minorities, including American Indians. "Through Congressional testimony, direct lobbying, and publications, FCNL's legislative staff and constituency inform members of Congress, their staffs, and colleague organizations about issues of concern to the Religious Society of Friends."

The Indian concern of FCNL was stated as follows in 1981:

American Indians, Alaskan Natives, and other peoples with whom the Federal government has special trust relations should be free to direct their own lives, their lands, resources, and the government of their tribal communities. The cultural and political diversity among and within tribes should be respected. Many tribal groups are recognized as distinct nations by the treaties they signed with the United States. The United States should honor the provisions of these treaties and other agreements made with them. When arrangements are unsatisfactory, resolution should be negotiated rather than imposed.

Most groupings of these people, both on and off reservations, face critical difficulties from inadequate employment, health care, and housing. Adequate Federal programs, in keeping with the Federal trust responsibility, should be available to all Indians. Tribal governments should administer these programs for tribal members on their reservations. Organized groups of Indians in urban areas should participate in directing these programs for members of their communities. The Bureau of Indian Affairs should limit itself to an assistance role.

Organization: The staff for Native American Affairs consists of two full-time legislative advocates, one a volunteer appointed by the Mennonite Central Committee and the other a Jesuit who shares his time with the National Office of Jesuit Social Ministries.

Budget: Only a fraction of the FCNL budget of around $450,000 goes toward Native American issue work. FCNL's budget is raised entirely from constituency contributions.

Major Accomplishments: The Legislative Advocate, Steve Linscheid, wrote an article "Native America vs. the MX Missile" concerning the Western Shoshones' struggle to protect their land rights in Nevada, which was published in *grapevine*, March 1981. This article was sent to members of the House and Senate Appropriations Committees.

FCNL:

Participated in the planning for the National Tribal Governments Conference held in Washington, D.C. in May 1981 to interface with administration officials on Indian policy.

Prepared a summary of "Economical Alternatives to Orme Dam" which would flood much of the reservation of the Fort McDowell Tribe (March 1981). Initiated a letter signed by 17 religious offices to the Interior Department asking for support of an alternative to Orme Dam.

Opposed the bill limiting the taking of steelhead trout to sport fishing as being contrary to Indian treaty rights in the Pacific Northwest.

Worked with others to clarify the status of Texas Kickapoos.

Supported reauthorization of the Indian Health Care Improvement Act and adequate funding for Administration for Native Americans, especially in view of CETA cuts for 1982.

Published two issues of the *FCNL Indian Report* in 1981 and the September/October issue of the *FCNL Washington Newsletter* in 1981 was devoted to Native American issues.[2]

National Congress of American Indians (NCAI) (Organized in 1944)
202 E Street, N.E., Washington, D.C. 20002

Purpose: To help achieve unity among tribes in order to address issues and concerns common to all so that NCAI can speak with one voice on national issues. Primary service to its approximately 150-member tribes with 400,000 Indians and Alaska Natives is through policy analysis, policy development, and information dissemination. NCAI seeks to influence government agencies and Congress through strong advocacy and lobbying for its views.

Recent policy issues have included:

1. Indian housing including concern over reduced funding for HUD and recommending the consolidation of Indian housing functions now located in HUD, BIA, and IHS.
2. Employment of Indians, with particular reference to Indian preference. Expressed concern over persons obtaining employment through Indian preference with doubtful ability to demonstrate tribal affiliation.
3. Economic development for Indians and expression of concern over limiting the economic development initiative of the Interior Department to resource development projects. The initiative should be comprehensive and long range.
4. Recommendation of a guaranteed health package for every Indian, reservation or urban, without arbitrary funding limits and opposition to cuts in direct health services.
5. Declaration of war on Indian alcoholism and drug abuse; seeking of funds from IHS and World Health Organization to step up this battle.
6. Strong stand on trust responsibility of the Federal government, expansion of tribal jurisdiction to include criminal jurisdiction over non-

Indians, removal of any provisions in IRA limiting tribal self-government, resolution of trust status relationship of Alaskan natives under the Alaska Native Claims Settlement Act.
7. Strengthening of Indian education.
8. Opposition to impact of budget reductions on human resources eg. loss of CETA funds and employment in the face of unemployment rates on some reservations as high as 70 percent.

Organization: President, 12 vice presidents (for BIA areas, except Navajo, and two for Eastern area), first vice president, recording secretary, and treasurer. Chairmen of nine issue committees. Membership is by tribe (150) and individuals.

There were 12 paid staff as of January 1982.

Budget: The budget for 1980 derived from two sources:

Private income and expenses for calendar year 1980

Revenue		Expenses	
Tribal dues	$32,648.94	Executive Director	$36,000.00
Dues - Individual & Organization	9,915.00	Consultant Attorneys	3,702.43
Registration	53,290.00	Travel - staff	6,909.73
Other	22,968.62	Committee Travel	7,286.77
Total	$118,822.56	Other	7,454.69
		Total	$61,353.62

Excess of revenue over expenses: $57,468.94

Federal Contract and Grant Funds as of April 1981:

Community Services Administration
—Training and technical assistance to tribes in
developing community action programs $300,000
—Planning grants to establish 13 community
action programs   280,000

Department of Interior, for policy analysis and development	228,000	
Law Enforcement Assistance Agency		
—Juvenile justice project	100,000	
—Funding for tribal law enforcement	260,000	
Total		$1,168,000

Foundation Grant:
Ford Foundation—Planning grant to establish
  Tribal education departments   30,000

Summary of funds:

Private	$ 118,823	
Federal	1,168,000	
Foundation	30,000	
	Total	$1,316,823

Note: Necessary administrative expenses for staff, rent and other overhead items are obtained from the above contracts and grants. The executive director is funded from NCAI dues and other private income as he is the primary lobbyist for the organization.

Current Priority Projects: Indicated above.

Major Accomplishments: NCAI has succeeded in obtaining consensus on many areas of Indian policy and in being a vigorous advocate with an influence on policy. As a recent example NCAI helped obtain exemption for Indian tribes from the Windfall Profit tax on oil.[3]

National Tribal Chairmen's Association (NTCA) (Organized in 1970)
1010 Vermont Avenue, N.W., Washington, D.C. 20005

Purpose:

The National Tribal Chairmen's Association was formed in 1970 to represent the interest of the Federally-recognized tribes and the officials of those tribes on a national level, chiefly as a mechanism to aid the "government-to-government" relationship between the Federal government and the tribal governments implied in the Constitution of the United States, and also to encourage the Federal government not to lose sight of its trust responsibility to the recognized tribes. NTCA has concentrated on developing and maintaining a good working relationship with the Federal government, especially the Bureau of Indian Affairs and the Indian Health Service, and has fulfilled its role

in the development of positions, the monitoring of Federal actions and policy developments, the holding of regional and national conferences for Indian input into governmental decisions, and serving as a general advocate for recognized tribes and emphasizing the necessity of consultation with tribes.
Recent policy issues have included:

1. ". . .consultation (is) where we have the most problems with the new national Administration. They do not want to talk. When they do talk, they do not want to listen."
2. March from White House to the Capitol in September 1980 to protest proposed FY 1982 cutbacks in Indian funds.
3. Education of public and government officials on Indian policy.

Organization: Membership is restricted to the chief elected official of each Federally recognized tribe. The board of directors has representatives of the 12 BIA areas who serve one-year terms, four officers serving two-year terms, an executive director and two other staff persons.
Budget: NTCA "depends in large part for support from grants and contracts to perform specific projects for the Federal government concerning Indians." The budget averages about $150,000 each year, about 85 percent from Federal sources and the rest from contributions.

Major Accomplishments:

The major accomplishment of NTCA has been the establishment of a communications linkage among the recognized tribes, especially in terms of getting out up-to-date information on pending legislation and regulations, and information on non-BIA and IHS programs. Before NTCA, there was a large "information gap" in these areas, especially in the case of the smaller and mid-sized recognized tribes.

Another accomplishment of the organization recently has been the successful campaign to limit the proposed budget cuts for fiscal year 1982 in the Interior appropriations bill, which was carried out in conjunction with NCAI.[4]

National Urban Indian Council (Organized in 1976)
1805 South Bellaire, Suite 525, Denver, Colorado 80222

Purpose

—To promote the social and economic self-sufficiency of off-reservation American Indians and Alaska Natives.

—To establish the unified voice that will represent off-reservation American Indians and Alaska Natives.

x x x

—To develop a national office to work primarily with and address itself to the needs of off-reservation American Indians and Alaska Natives.

—To develop a mechanism of legislative activity for off-reservation American Indians and Alaska Natives at various levels of government; city, county, state, and Federal.

—To establish communication with all American Indian and Alaska Native organizations at a national level to present a unified consensus of their concerns.

The National Urban Indian Council is the only national community-based organization to help provide information, technical assistance, and advocacy and to help coordinate the work of over 200 off-reservation service groups.

Organization: There are 15 employees headed by a chief executive.

Budget:

Income:
1981 - Federal contracts, grants	$500,000
Private	30,000
1982 - (Estimated) Federal contracts, grants	$600,000
(Estimated) Private	50,000

Expenses: Not Provided

Major Accomplishments:

—Leveraged local funding for off-reservation corporations, 1981—approximately $2,500,000.

—Providing a national organization for 200 member groups.

—Provision of information to Congress.

—Providing a vehicle for communication for off-reservation Indian groups.

—Monitoring off-reservation activities of Federal officials and programs.

Thoughts on Policy: Federal agencies do not recognize their responsibilities for Natives living off-reservation.

For future "we would submit that the government of the United States could enhance its standing by honoring its responsibilities through extending full policy inclusion and services to the entire American Indian and Alaska Native population and discontinue its exclusion by virtue of residency in off-reservation areas."[5]

REGIONAL TRIBAL ORGANIZATIONS

Tribes in various states or regions have banded together in organizations to help each other and to increase their bargaining position with the private sector, states, and the Federal government.

The National Congress of American Indians furnished the writer with the following list:

Affiliated Tribes of Northwest Indians (20 tribes)

Alaska Federation of Natives (13 Alaska Native Regional Corporations, 12 non-profit associations)

All Indian Pueblo Council (18 pueblos)

Arizona Inter-Tribal Council (19 tribes)

Great Lakes Inter-Tribal Council (5 tribes)

Inter-Tribal Council of California (28 tribes or groups)

California Tribal Chairman's Association (?)

Southern California Tribal Chairman's Association (18 tribes and groups)

Inter-Tribal Council of Michigan (5 tribes)

Montana Inter-Tribal Policy Board (7 tribes)

Nevada Indian Tribal Council (24 tribes and groups)

United Sioux Tribes of South Dakota (11 tribes)

United South and Eastern Tribes (10 tribes)

United Tribes of North Dakota (5 tribes)

United Indian Tribes of Western Oklahoma and Kansas (20 tribes)

Inter-Tribal Council (Oklahoma - 8 tribes)

A whole book could be devoted to the activities and influence of these groups. Often, for policy matters affecting their respective areas, they are more influential than the national groups. Their interests are more uniform and concentrated and they can focus clearly on the consensus of their membership.

As an example of this group the Alaska Federation of Natives (AFN) is described. AFN is also discussed in Chapter 2 on Alaska Native Claims.

Alaska Federation of Natives (AFN) (Organized in 1967)
411 West 4th Avenue, Suite 1A, Anchorage, Alaska 99501

Purpose: The purpose of AFN is to work for the welfare and best interests of Alaska Native groups. This involves:

1. Cooperating with various villages and Native corporations in developing policy and approaches to: BIA, BLM, the State of Alaska, private companies interested in Native resources or rights-of-way over Native land, other Native and Indian interest groups (including the Lower 48) and the U.S. Congress.

2. Maintaining surveillance of legislative and executive actions in Juneau and Washington, D.C., to be alert to and testify on items of importance to Alaska Natives.
3. Testifying before executive agencies or legislative hearings on initiatives of Alaska Natives.
4. Supplying information on Alaska Native matters to state and Federal policy makers.
5. Operating as an informal clearing house for matters of concern to one or more Native groups.
6. Establishing working relationships with state, Federal, and private groups by becoming involved in businesses and forming business relationships.

Organization: Officers are: president, vice president, land manager, human resources specialist, legal counsel and support staff.

Budget: About $400,000 annually; funds come from dues paid by regional and individual Native corporations.

Current Priority Projects:

—Monitoring land transfer to Alaska Natives by BLM as provided in the Alaska Native Claims Settlement Act (ANCSA) (85 Stat. 688).
—Monitoring amendments to ANCSA (1976) P.L. 94-204.
—Monitoring Alaska National Interest Lands Conservation Act of 1980 (P.L. 96-487, 16 USC 3101) which includes further amendments and new legislation based on the 1971 Claims Act provisions, problems, and technical considerations.

Major Accomplishments: AFN obtained the cooperation of Alaska Native groups to present united front on key issues and employed top flight attorneys to help guide the Alaska Native Claims Settlement Act through the Congress. The Natives succeeded in obtaining about 95 percent of what they wanted in the Settlement Act. Chapter 2 relates this effort in more detail. Alaska Natives will be the largest private landowners in Alaska after the conveyance of the 40 million acre settlement in the 1980s. The Federal government and state will hold more land than the Natives, but the first selection of all lands went to Alaska Natives.

General: The Alaska Natives are participating effectively in state and local government. There are seven Natives in the Alaska House of Representatives out of a total of 40 members, and two Natives in the Senate out of a total of 20 members. The chairman of the House Finance Committee is a Native. Two Natives are members of the Senate Finance Committee.

The Natives are primarily from rural areas and cooperate with other rural legislators in the "Bush Caucus" to increase their influence in the legislature.

Anchorage and Fairbanks have over 50 percent of Alaska's population. The Natives constitute about 16 percent of the total population.

The Alaska Native strategy has been to hold back to see what the various factions were and the issues they were fighting over. In such situations sometimes the Natives have the balance of power. They bargain and often work out compromise solutions that are in the Natives' interest. Examples are:

1. The Senate leadership and Committee assignments are made to balance rural interests with Anchorage, Fairbanks, and Juneau because of their urban populations and differing constituents.
2. The Bush Caucus supports urban legislators to key committees only after bargaining concessions and assignments to further rural districts in all committee structures and assignments.

The Native Corporations are vulnerable to takeover 20 years after the date of the Settlement Act (1971), when Native shareholders will be free to sell their shares. One of the educational challenges to AFN is to help the shareholders understand the value of their shares and the advantages of holding on to them.

AFN is carefully watching and participating in discussions on what degree of trust responsibility resides in the Interior Department under the Alaska Land Claims Settlement Act. The AFN position is that the Natives want to be on their own in due time, but do not want an abrupt change that would not be in the best interests of Alaska Natives.

The overall philosophy is to be fully participating citizens in the local, state, and Federal governments. Also the objective is for Natives to be fully participating shareholders in the Native corporations and active in the economic life of the villages and the state. The Alaska Natives may lead other Native groups in reaching a successful, non-subsidized accommodation with the non-Native population.[6]

INDIAN INTEREST ORGANIZATIONS WITH A SPECIALIZED INTEREST

Groups concerned with a single discipline such as health care, education, energy, housing, or with a specific tribe or group of Indians have been placed under this heading. These groups may sometimes emphasize their professional activity and improvement and at other times engage in vigorous lobbying with tribes, Federal agencies, the Congress, and state governments for funds or desired legislation. Many also seek funding support from private sources such as foundations.

Not all active organizations of this type are listed both because of space and because some are primarily social or limited in function. Others, perhaps important enough to be included, did not answer the questionnaire. The following examples are indicative of activity under this category.

Legal organizations, because of their number and importance, have been placed in a separate group.

American Indian Higher Education Consortium (AIHEC) (Founded 1972)
1582 South Parker Road, Suite 204, Denver, Colorado 80231

Purpose: To provide an organization through which member institutions can help one another; to promote improvement of postsecondary education for American Indians and Alaska Natives "so they can receive the educational tools necessary for a productive life in whatever field they choose while retaining their unique cultural aspects."

"If American Indian tribes are to survive as a people, they must develop and control their own institutions. This, in its simplest form, is the basic reason for AIHEC colleges existence."

Organization:

The American Indian Higher Education Consortium was formed in October 1972 by six Indian community colleges with a view toward mobilizing a concerted effort to deal with developmental problems common to them all. By April 1974, membership in the Consortium had grown to 12. As of May 1981, there were 18 tribally-chartered colleges comprising the AIHEC membership, 15 which are regular (voting) members, and 3 associate (non-voting) members. These institutions are two-year community colleges offering degree programs at the Associate of Arts level. They are in varying stages of development and their needs differ accordingly. However, they all have definite similarities: they are tribally-chartered; their governing boards are comprised of Indian people; their student bodies are predominantly Indian; they are in isolated locations; they actively reinforce unique tribal cultures while offering pragmatic curricula geared to contemporary lifestyles; and they are community service oriented.

The Consortium Board of Directors is made up of designees from the member institutions who elect the following officers which act as the executive committee: president, vice-president, secretary, treasurer, and member-at-large.

The staff is headed by an executive director who is assisted by six staff members. The staff is responsible for helping in: (1) accreditation, (2) financial resources, (3) curriculum, (4) human resource development, and (5) research.

Budget:

Dues for 1980 were:

Regular membership	$2500 per year
Associate and affiliated members	1500 per year

Other funds from Federal appropriations and grants.
No specific budget presented.

Major Accomplishments:

—Many consulting services, workshops, and seminars.
—Accreditation work with members—Navajo Community College and D-Q University, California, have achieved full accreditation (The General Accounting Office [GAO] has recently questioned the status, activities, procedures and funding of D-Q.).
—Surveyed extent and need for tribally chartered colleges.
—Special Seminars in staff development, training for board of trustees, mid-level college administrators, and student leaders.
—Helped member institutions obtain training and technical assistance money under the "Tribally Controlled Community College Assistance Act of 1978."
—Development of a *Directory of American Indian Private Funding Sources*, e.g., foundations, corporations, and government agencies.
—Workshops in grantsmanship skills.[7]

Arrow, Inc. (Founded 1949)
1000 Connecticut Avenue, N.W., Suite 401, Washington, D.C. 20036

Purpose: Arrow is a non-profit, tax exempt, charitable and welfare organization dedicated to direct aid, training, and research for American Indians.

Organization:

Arrow . . .[was] founded in 1949 by Will Rogers, Jr., Robert L. Bennett and other prominent Indians. Most of the Board is Indian; the rest are well versed in Indian affairs, a balance proved practical in the decision-making process. Arrow initiates constructive efforts at the reservation level, embracing direct aid, education, health and training; offers scholarship assistance; recruits physicians and RN's from the private sector to help fill shortages at Indian hospitals; conducts training for Indian Court Judges and helps them improve their system of law and order and justice. Arrow meets high standards of accountability . . .[and] has a . . . tax-exempt status. . . .

Major Accomplishments:

—Helped organize the National American Indian Court Judges Association; serves as its secretariat and co-sponsors its programs.
—Sponsors Indian youth participation in national and international seminars.
—Helps Indian high school and college youth with supplemental funds for clothing or other extra costs which their parents cannot afford.
—Recruited and continues to recruit physicians and RN volunteers from the private sector who donate 2 or more weeks work at Indian hospitals to fill shortages of doctors and nurses. Arrow undertakes logistics and provides travel costs. Cooperates with IHS.[8]

Council of Energy Resource Tribes (CERT)
(Organized in 1975)

Technical Assistance Center: 5660 South Syracuse Circle, Suite 206, Englewood, Colorado 80111

Purpose:

1. "To ensure that the Indian people receive an equitable return for their resources, and are able to utilize those resources as a foundation upon which to develop stable tribal economies."
2. "To assist the tribes in protecting their natural, social, and cultural environment from the adverse impacts of energy resource development."
3. "To aid each tribe in acquiring the capability to manage its resources for itself."

CERT sponsors meetings with persons central to Indian energy policy—Washington lawmakers, Western state governors, business and financial leaders, and other Indian organizations—to build communication and enable Indians to speak with one voice.

CERT provides technical help to tribes on the quality and quantity of their energy resources, evaluates development options, develops feasibility studies, trains tribal personnel, and assists tribes in selecting and initiating discussions with possible industrial and financial partners.

CERT is available to advise tribes on effective management.

CERT provides education through stimulation of the young by talks to high schools students, by designing and distributing motivational materials to students and through supervision of Indian intern and apprenticeship programs for college students.

With consultation and technical assistance, CERT helps tribes achieve a balance between development and protection of the environment, social structures, traditions and cultural values.

Organization: The chief elected officer of the 29-member tribes form the council. The nine member executive committee includes the chairman, vice-chairman, secretary, treasurer and five other members of the council. The operating organization of 50 to 60 individuals is under the supervision of an executive director, who has a communications coordinator, special legal counsel, office of policy analysis, and office of administration in Washington, D.C. The Technical Assistance Center in Denver, Colorado has the following offices: assessment and development, environmental analysis, planning and management services, and education and resource development.

Budget:

The CERT Annual Report for FY 1980 cites:

Interagency grant	$1,200,000
Health and Human Services (ANA)	721,000
Education, HHS, BIA & private	
sector contributions	240,000
	$2,161,000

[CERT did not provide a detailed budget. Telecon December 22, 1981, with J. Pete Segall, Communications Coordinator]

Major Accomplishments:

In 1980:
—The Jicarilla Apache Tribe became the first to acquire 100 percent ownership of producing oil and gas wells on Indian land. Production is administered by the tribe's own Oil and Gas Administration.
—The Navajo Nation established its own Navajo Energy Department Authority, an independent, for-profit entity that will compete with private developers in offering project proposals.
—The Northern Cheyenne Tribe is permitting a search for oil and gas on its reservation.
—CERT conducted a study of regulatory authority desirable in mining and reclaiming Indian lands. In 1980 the Interior Department's proposed draft legislation included virtually all of CERT's recommendations.
—In 1980 CERT mounted a "heavy lobbying campaign of tribal telegrams, newspaper editorials, and knocking on Capitol Hill doors" to help exempt oil produced on Indian reservations from the Oil Windfall Profits Tax.

—CERT publishes a biweekly newsletter, "The CERT Report" and a
companion annual "Tribal Energy Directory," providing current energy
resource information.

—In 1977 the Jicarilla Apache instituted a severance tax on energy
companies. The case was appealed to the Supreme Court and CERT
joined a coalition of other tribes and Indian organizations in supporting
the tax which was upheld by the Supreme Court.

—In 1979 the Administration for Native Americans (HHS) introduced a
program to strengthen tribal governments. With funds from the Administration for Native Americans, CERT worked with the government of the
Fort Berthold reservation to develop a new government structure based
on a model developed by CERT's Office of Planning and Management
Services.[9]

Housing Assistance Council, Inc. (HAC) (Established in 1971)
1025 Vermont Avenue, N.W., Suite 606, Washington, D.C. 20005

Purpose: The Housing Assistance Council is a non-profit housing
organization providing housing assistance to the rural poor, including Indians
on reservations. Information, technical assistance, and advocacy for Indian
housing by HAC are coordinated with local and national Indian organizations,
appropriate agency staff and the broader coalition of persons and
organizations interested in housing. The objective is to strengthen the
commitment and capability of government and housing organizations at all
levels to provide decent housing for the rural poor.

Organization: The Council is governed by a 40-member board of directors
representing public and non-profit housing agencies, public interest
organizations, unions, and minorities at the national, state, and local levels.
The staff includes professional housing technicians and specialists in
government housing programs, research, information and training. One
Indian Housing Specialist works under the executive director and spends
full-time providing information, technical assistance, and advocacy for Indian
housing.

Budget: HAC is funded primarily by HUD, but has some revolving funds
of its own.

Major Accomplishments:

—For FY 1982 the Reagan administration proposed termination of HUD
Indian housing funds and IHS water and sanitation facilities
construction funds. HAC's Indian Housing Specialist helped inform
interested groups and worked with others to try to save the Indian
housing program. The final action for the 1982 budget keeps 4,000

Indian housing units in HUD's budget, but no funds are in the Office of Management and Budget's plans for 1983.

—The Indian Housing Specialist works with HUD, BIA, IHS, and Indian organizations to promote Indian housing, and enclosed a NARF (Native American Rights Fund) Indian housing fact sheet in the materials sent to the writer.[10]

INDIAN LEGAL INTEREST ORGANIZATIONS

Indian law is a very complicated and specialized area. As indicated in the profile of the Legal Services Corporation which follows, low income and disadvantaged persons often lack access to our system of justice which requires trained attorneys. Although many tribes can now afford competent attorneys, general interest groups such as AAIA provide legal services to tribes, and NCAI provides a yearly update on important court cases with their policy implications. Also the Federal government has been assigned the responsibility of representing Indians (Department of Justice) when Indian treaty or legal rights are concerned. Of the many actors in the Indian legal arena, here we consider only non-governmental organizations active in the field of Indian law.

Some of these organizations tend to place primary emphasis on research and legal policy as well as in providing legal services in support of Indian causes such as tribal jurisdiction, Indian preference, or land claims.

Indian Law Resource Center (Established in 1978)
601 E Street, S.E., Washington, D.C. 20003

Purpose: A non-profit public interest legal organization devoted to the protection of the legal rights of American Indians.

The goal of the Center is to assist Indian people to achieve self-sufficiency and to overcome the terrible poverty and suffering characteristic of reservation life. To this end, the Center gives legal help, free of charge, to Indian communities and governments in order to secure human and legal rights such as the right to own property, the right to self-government, the right to freedom of religion and the right to cultural survival. Through a coordinated program of research, public education, and litigation, the Center seeks to enable Indian people to survive as distinct peoples with unique, living cultures.

x x x

The program of the Center is national in scope. The Center represents Indian tribes and governments throughout the country, including Seminoles in Florida, the Iroquois in New York, traditional Hopis in Arizona, Western Shoshone in Nevada and the Sioux in South Dakota. The Center's law reform efforts are also national in scope and are designed to change the fundamental legal disabilities facing Indians and to combat discrimination and injustice in the law.

The Center carries on a program of public education directed nationwide to foster understanding and support for Indian needs, to combat discrimination and to bring about much-needed changes. The Center has consultative status with the United Nations Economic and Social Council, enabling the Center to extend its educational efforts in behalf of Indian people.

Organization: The Center has an Indian-controlled board of directors and an executive director. The staff includes four full-time attorneys, one historical researcher, a legal investigator, an administrative assistant/paralegal, and one clerical worker. There is one volunteer full-time researcher/writer.

Budget: The 1981 budget was approximately $257,000 and was expected to be about the same in 1982. Funding sources include foundations, churches, and individual contributors. The Center receives no funds from the Federal or state governments.

Major Accomplishments:

Some of the Center's accomplishments include defending the Mohawk community of Ganienkeh which sought to recover a portion of their homeland in upstate New York. We were able to resolve that volatile conflict and help make new lands available where today Ganienkeh still carries on and grows. Another success involved the resolution of a jurisdictional conflict in Akwesasne (Mohawk Nation) which had developed into an armed confrontation and over twenty criminal indictments. Through extensive legal research, investigation, community organizing and negotiations, all of the indictments were dismissed and a community resolve developed to resist corruption and reject state and Federal interference in internal Mohawk affairs.

x x x

For several years, the Center has been working to convince the United Nations Commission on Human Rights to establish a Working Group on Indigenous Populations x x x

The center has focused attention on the systematic destruction of Indian land rights through the Indian claims process; our reports on the claims brought in the name of the Hopis and the Seminoles have received national attention.[11]

Legal Services Corporation (LSC)(Established in 1974)
733 15th Street, N.W., Washington, D.C. 20005

Indian Desk of LSC: 1726 Champa Street, Suite 500, Denver, Colorado 80202

Purpose: To provide low-income people access to the legal system.

Organization: The LSC is an outgrowth of the legal services program added to the Office of Economic Opportunity in 1965. When partisan politics crippled OEO in the 1970s, legal services clients, the American Bar Association, and other groups urged Congress to create the private non-profit LSC as the successor to the OEO poverty law program.

There is an 11-member board of directors and the president ex-officio. The president is assisted by 11 senior staff and approximately 260 employees in the Washington office and nine regional offices. The main work sponsored and funded by LSC is in the over 300 independent local legal service programs, employing over 6,000 attorneys. These local field programs are supervised by independent program boards made up of attorneys, clients, and other representatives of the local community. Most of the LSC appropriation goes into funding the actual work with disadvantaged people performed by these local groups. LSC funds support a core program of staff attorneys and paralegals and attorneys in private practice supplement this effort both "for free" in some instances and "for pay" in other instances.

There is a one-man coordinating desk, the Indian Desk, in Denver for Indian programs. As of 1981, LSC funded 29 Indian legal services programs and Indian components of regular programs (local field programs described above) in 22 states. These programs employ more than 185 attorneys and 80 paralegals and tribal court advocates, as well as having the assistance of 13 attorneys of the Indian Law Support Center of the Native American Rights Fund (discussed later in this section).

During FY 1981 more than $6 million went to legal services for Indians. These services were provided only $5.5 million in 1982. In all instances the local organization receiving the funds was under a local board of directors drawn from the local community which established policy, priorities, and follow-through to see that the programs provided efficient, quality services to eligible clients in the community.

LSC has designated support centers for specific areas of law to provide centralized research, training, counseling, library, and coordinating capability to aid local programs in a more economical and efficient way than if each did its own. The Native American Rights Fund (NARF) is the support center for Indian law.

Budget: (As of February 5, 1982, LSC was operating on a continuing resolution at the $241 million level.)

Revenue, FY 1982 projected

Federal appropriation	$300,000,000
Grants	765,327
Donated services	74,123
Interest income	437,413

$301,276,863

Expenses

Program activities	$302,791,957
Supporting activities	5,029,041

$307,820,998

Excess of Expenses over Revenue   6,544,135

The excess was covered by fund balance at beginning of the year.
In FY 1981 Congress appropriated $321 million to LSC.

Major Accomplishments:

—In 1980 free legal services for the poor became a reality in most counties
in the United States. This included Indian poor.
—The Burns Paiute Indian Reservation is in Harney County, Oregon,
where there are six private attorneys serving clients whose interests
conflict with the tribe. Until the Oregon Legal Services (an LSC funded
field group) expanded service to the county "the tribe was virtually without legal representation." Legal help has been given to assist the tribe in
implementing the Indian Child Welfare Act by conducting training for
both the state and the tribe, thus avoiding wasteful conflict and
litigation.
—Legal service programs funded by LSC serve Indian country. For
example, DNA-People's Legal Services ($1,882,314 in 1980) serves the
Navajo, Hopi and White Mountain Apache reservations. Anishinable
Legal Services serve the Leech Lake, White Earth and Red Lake
reservations. Indian Pueblo Legal Services serves 19 pueblos and reservations in northern New Mexico. The Alaska Native Component of the
Anchorage Legal Services Corporation was $273,675 in 1980; for
Southern Arizona Legal Aid in Tucson the American Native Component
was $115,121; and for the North Dakota Legal Services at New Town,
out of $104,108, $93,570 was for Indians.[12]

Native American Rights Fund (NARF) (Organized in 1970)
1506 Broadway, Boulder, Colorado 80302

Purpose: NARF grew out of the concept of providing legal services to the poor and disadvantaged pioneered by the Office of Economic Opportunity in the mid-1960s. It soon became obvious that Indian law was a specialty and in 1970 the Ford Foundation funded a pilot program with California Indian Legal Services (CILS), which was OEO funded, to expand Indian legal services on a national basis. The project was called the Native American Rights Fund (NARF). It separated from CILS and moved to Colorado and incorporated under an all-Indian board called the NARF Steering Committee. Its purpose is to help Indians with "cases involving major national issues of Indian law" by a program sufficiently funded to follow through on important cases. The subject matter priorities are:

1. Preservation of tribal existence by considering matters dealing with Federal recognition, restoration of terminated tribes, self-government, tax immunity rights, Indian preference, and land claims cases.
2. Protection of tribal resources such as land, water, minerals, hunting and gathering rights and environmental protection.
3. Promotion of human rights such as educational rights, adequate health care, rights of Indian inmates and religious freedom.
4. Holding all levels of government accountable under existing laws and regulations.
5. Development and dissemination of Indian law.

Organization: NARF's Steering Committee has 13 members and a staff of about 40. The Steering Committee has an executive committee of four members. The corporate officers are: executive director, development officer, treasurer, and secretary. There are sixteen staff attorneys, two legislative liaisons, a law library staff, project staff, law clerks and interns, and support staff.

Budget:

For the year ended September 30, 1980:

Income:		
Grants	$1,943,017	
Contributions	163,958	
Other	77,399	
Loss, disposal of fixed assets	(550)	
Total		$2,183,824
Expenses:		
Program		
—Litigation & client services	$1,649,939	
—National Indian Law Library	87,344	
Total		$1,737,283

Support		
—Management	$ 228,274	
—Fund raising	150,559	
Total		$ 378,833
Total expenses		$2,116,116
Net Income over expenditures		67,708

Revenue by source:

Government agencies	68%
Private foundations	21%
Contributions from individuals and corporations	8%
Other sources	3%

Major Accomplishments:

—The 1980 settlement act passed by Congress "concluded a case brought by NARF in 1972 on behalf of the Passamaquoddy and Penobscot tribes." There was a cash settlement of $27 million and $54 million for the purchase of 300,000 acres of land.

—NARF's effort begun in 1975 resulted in the Siletz Tribe of Oregon receiving a 3,600 acre reservation by act of Congress.

—In 1980 Congress settled a claim brought by NARF on behalf of the Pamunkey Tribe of Virginia against a railroad right-of-way.

—NARF was co-counsel in the Supreme Court case holding that "states cannot impose their sales taxes on sales transactions concluded on Indian reservations regulated by Federal trade laws."

—NARF worked with a broad coalition of tribes and organizations to secure exemption from the Oil Windfall Profits Tax for production on Indian lands.

—"NARF played the lead role in securing a Congressional extension of the Federal statute of limitations on pre-1966 Indian damage claims against third parties for trespass."

—NARF drafted legislation and pushed for passage of the law that restored Menominee's tribal status.

—Major new cases in 1980 included a case concerning water rights for seven Sioux tribes, in which NARF represented the Rosebud Sioux; and "the traditional Kickapoo Indians of Texas who need citizenship and tribal status."

—Filed a lawsuit on behalf of the Catawba Tribe of South Carolina for 140,000 acres.[13]

ORGANIZATIONS BELIEVING INDIAN POLICY DISCRIMINATORY AGAINST NON-INDIANS

The Interstate Congress for Equal Rights and Responsibilities is the main organization stating that Federal laws and tribal ordinances have created a special citizen exempt from paying many taxes and providing for unconstitutional controls by tribal governments over Indians and non-Indians alike and over land, water, and other resources.

Interstate Congress for Equal Rights and Responsibilities (ICERR)
(Organized in 1976)
P.O. Box 6, Walthill, Nebraska 68067

Purpose:

...a non-profit corporation to insure that all citizens of this country shall have equal rights and bear equal responsibilities under the law. It opposes the current trend of Federal Indian policy which infringes on the property and civil rights of citizens, be they non-tribal or tribal members. x x x ...legislation is continuously introduced in Congress which would take away your constitutional rights and enlarge the powers of racial groups in the name of tribal sovereignty. Only continued support and concerted efforts by citizen groups such as ICERR can turn the trend around.

Specific objectives are:

—"Insure that the United States shall remain One Nation with no sovereign subdivisions to deny any of its citizens their rights (tribal or non-tribal) as guaranteed under the U.S. Constitution."
—"Provide that Indian Reservations diminished by Congressional action or previous tribal land sales not be returned to their original boundaries by any means."
—"Provide that no Indian Reservation boundaries be enlarged by grants, Power of Eminent Domain or any other means."
—"Prevent jurisdiction of Tribal governments over non-members who have no vote or voice in that government."
—"Prevent grants of public funds to any group based solely upon their race which excludes their neighbors whose need is equal."
—"In the event of legal action by the U.S. Government on behalf of Indian Tribes, provide equal financial and legal support for non-members."
—"Provide that members of Indian Tribes shall not have the right to

participate in non-tribal governments unless they are subject to the laws and responsibilities of that non-tribal government.

—"Encourage members of Indian tribes to participate in Local, State and Federal Government by assuming the rights and responsibilities of those governments and not to be endangered by their own tribal governments."

—"Taxes for all—or none at all."

Organization: Organizations and groups from 13 states formed ICERR at Salt Lake City, Utah, February 1976. Since then others have joined. "ICERR is a national organization made up of various state organizations. It is open to any state organization that is concerned with protecting and advancing the principles of the Declaration of Independence, the Constitutional rights of U.S. citizens to the end that no Federal, state or local government shall make distinction in civil or political rights on account of race, color or national origin." Individual memberships are also available.

Budget: Not submitted.

Major Accomplishments: Not submitted.[14]

SUMMARY

There are many groups not included in the above examples. Some of these, but by no means all of them, are briefly mentioned at this point to indicate their variety. The American Indian Historical Society (1451 Masonic Avenue, San Francisco, California 94117) strives to preserve the philosophy, human values, and languages of Indians and to promote their culture, education, and general welfare. It took the lead in eliminating Indian stereotypes from school textbooks in California and published material on the history and culture of American Indians. The American Indian Movement (Box 262, White Earth, Minnesota 56591) is an activist organization. The American Indian Lawyers Training Program (319 MacArthur Boulevard, Oakland, California 94610) provides training resources to Indian attorneys and law students. There are associations for Indian and Native nurses, physicians and school boards. Americans for Indian Opportunity which recently moved to Washington, D.C. assists tribes and individuals in areas such as natural resources, development, justice, and education. There is the Lumbee Regional Development Association (P.O. Box 68, Pembroke, North Carolina) concerned with the advancement of the 40,000 Lumbees. The Maryland Indian Heritage Society (5408 Silver Hill Road, Suite 502, Forestville, Maryland 20747) researches and makes available the history and culture of Maryland's native Indian people. The Haskell Indian School Alumni Association of the Nation's Capitol strives to maintain contact with Haskell graduates and generate support for the school. On February 8, 1982, the American Indian National Republican Federation was organized and planned a national membership campaign. Former Indian Commissioner Louis Bruce, first vice president of the new group, said: "Our members will be a consistent Indian voice in Republican party councils." This political organization is a member of the National Republican Heritage Groups Council. Dartmouth College has a Native American Science Resource Center, and the American Association for the Advancement of Science has prepared "A Resource Guide to Native American Scientific and Technical Development."

Many readers of this book will have received over the years solicitations for contributions from organizations such as the St. Francis Indian Mission, South Dakota; the Navajo Health Foundation, Arizona; St. Joseph's Indian School, South Dakota; St. Labre Indian School, Montana; American Indian Development Association, Bellingham, Washington; and the National Indian Youth Council, Albuquerque, New Mexico.

As will be discovered by reviewing the activities and claimed accomplishments of the pro-Indian groups above, several may be working for the same objective, such as exemption of oil produced on Indian lands from the Windfall Profits Tax. (AAIA, NCAI, FCLN, CERT, NARF and perhaps others.)

It is also clear that these organizations act to a limited extent as sounding boards for both the Federal organizations charged with carrying out Indian policy as well as for Congressional committees concerned with Indian policy and funding.

Not specifically mentioned above is the use by BIA, IHS and other agencies of such groups as NCAI and NTCA in the consultation process. The current emphasis on "self-determination" and "participation and involvement of Indians in Indian policy formation and execution" requires some mechanism or methods for accomplishment. Presenting an administrative proposal to NCAI or NTCA for evaluation and comment may help achieve this end. However, consultation is generally through direct contact with individual tribes.

It is obvious that Indian interest organizations provide a channel to and from government for Indian tribes, groups, and individuals. Also ICERR provides a possible channel for Indians and non-Indians dissatisfied with specific actions or current trends. The 1978 Supreme Court decision that tribal governments did not have criminal jurisdiction over non-Indians on a reservation eliminated one of the primary issues providing impetus to ICERR (Oliphant v. Suquamish, 435 U.S. 191 (1978)).

Some organizations are large and have greater expertise available which obviously will have a greater impact over various policy matters. However, single purpose or regional organizations may have larger impact on policy relating to their particular subject matter or regional area. The AFN role in the settlement of Alaska Native Claims is an example.

Review of the funding arrangements of the various organizations indicates a wide difference in dependence on public funding. It could be postulated that dependence on Federal funding might compromise independence. However, officials dealing with organizations do not find that NCAI, NTCA, and CERT are any less vitriolic, critical, or reluctant to lobby vigorously against a BIA or administration stand than AAIA or FLC which are privately funded. These influences, of course, are subtle and difficult to determine. More important, perhaps, is the indication of grass roots support found in the source and amount of funding. Strong funding support from memberships and contributions is one indication of degree of support. Contract funding may in part result from the Congressional policy of turning execution of programs insofar as possible over to Indians. It may not be based on an evaluation and determination that a particular Indian organization is the most effective mechanism to achieve a given program result.

FOOTNOTES

[1]Letter from Ruth Alterman of the AAIA, October 30, 1981, and accompanying material.

[2]Letters from Steve Linscheid, Legislative Advocate, Native American Affairs, FCNL, November 19, 1981 and February 1, 1982, with accompanying material.

[3]Interview with Ronald P. Andrade, Executive Director, and Annette Traversie Bagley, Editor/Legislative Coordinator, NCAI, November 26, 1981, and accompanying material.

[4]Letters from Phillip Martin, President, NTCA, January 4 and March 2, 1982.

[5]Letter from Gregory W. Frazier, Chief Executive, National Urban Indian Council, December 30, 1981.

[6]Interview with Dennis J. Tiepelman, Director, Governmental and Legislative Affairs, AFN, October 21, 1981. Tiepelman was then located in Washington, D.C., but has moved back to Alaska.

[7]American Indian Higher Education Consortium (flyer), revised September 22, 1981; Membership Handbook; and interview with Leroy V. Clifford, Executive Director, February 1982.

[8]Letter from E. Thomas Colosimo, Executive Director, Arrow, October 22, 1981, and review of first draft.

[9]Letter from J. Pete Segall, Communications Coordinator, CERT, November 3, 1981.

[10]Letter from Virginia E. Spencer, Indian Housing Specialist, HAC, November 12, 1981, and material transmitted. Telephone conversation with Spencer December 22, 1981.

[11]Letters and material from Robert T. Coulter, Executive Director, Indian Law Resource Center, October 19, 1981 and February 5, 1982.

[12]Letter from Clint Lyons, Director, Office of Field Services, LSC, December 2, 1981; letter from Britt E. Clapham, Assistant Regional Director, Indian Desk, February 5, 1982.

[13]Letter and material from John E. Echohawk, Executive Director, NARF, November 2, 1981.

[14]Letter from W. H. Matthies, President of Montanans Opposing Discrimination (MOD), June 12, 1979, which transmitted an ICERR brochure. MOD was organized in 1974 at a public meeting held at Ronan, Montana, attended by over 2000 concerned citizens. MOD helped organize ICERR.

CHAPTER 6
THE FUTURE

SELF-DETERMINATION

The reservation system is largely the result of Federal policy. The way in which it has evolved has been influenced in recent years by Indian reservation leadership and Indian interest groups. Indian leaders seem to be supportive of the Indian Self-Determination and Education Assistance Act of 1975[1] which is largely concerned with Indian governments on Indian reservations and emphasizes the strengthening of tribal government through tribal administration of Federal funds for tribal operations and services. As indicated in Chapter 1 the objective is to develop tribal governmental independence, but it may instead lead to increased financial dependence on the non-Indian society unless there are sufficient reservation resources and a balance between such resources and population to provide the possibility of economic viability. This may not be the case on some reservations.

The 1977 *Final Report* of the American Indian Policy Review Commission[2] endorsed the philosophy of the Self-Determination Act. This commission was established by Congress and charged with the responsibility of reviewing the history and law related to the Indians' relationship with the Federal government and to make recommendations for the benefit of Indians. The Chairmen of the Indian committees of the Senate, James Abourezk, and of the House, Lloyd Meeds, were Chairman and Vice Chairman respectively of the Commission. The Commission also included two senators, three Congressmen, and five Indians. The executive director, Ernest L. Stevens, was Indian (Oneida) as were many of the staff and task force members.

The *Report* states that a damaging policy of the past was the effort "through the first three-quarters of the 19th century to remove the Indian people from the midst of European settlers by isolating them on reservations . . .," and then goes on to emphasize sovereignty of tribal governments, the importance of Indian land, and the desirability of the Federal government's trust responsibility.[3] The *Report's* concept of trust responsibility includes Indian resources and other things but did not attempt to spell it out in "statutory specificity."

The *Report* outlined the great resources of Indian lands and asked why, then, were many reservations poverty-stricken. A part of the *Report's* answer was the practice of Indian leasing of land primarily to non-Indians, fractionated ownership of land due to the BIA heirship procedures, inadequate credit, lack of technical skills, and dearth of adequate infrastructure such as roads and communications systems.[4]

Tribal governments should be developed into "fully operational governments exercising the same powers and shouldering the same responsibilities as other local governments," said the *Report*, but it dodged the issue of tribal jurisdiction over non-Indians.[5] As can be surmised from the above, the Commission emphasized the Federal-tribal relationship, trust responsibility for Indian resources, development of tribal government, and the goal of tribal economic self-sufficiency. This is one of the historic approaches to Indian policy and was a part of the philosophy of the Indian Reorganization Act in 1934.[6] It is the current official policy.

UTILIZING CONSTITUTIONAL STRUCTURE

The other approach, adopted from time to time, has been that Indians, as American citizens, should be assisted in adjusting to the basic U.S. governmental structure, which of course includes the states, and be served eventually by the same governments that serve other citizens as well as paying the same taxes. The Allotment Act of 1887 provided that Indians receiving an allotment of formerly tribal land would become citizens and after the expiration of 25 years of Federal trust on the land would take their place among other citizens with the same rights and responsibilities.[7] The Meriam Report of 1928 recommended that Indians be helped to adjust to the surrounding white society and eventually pay the same taxes and be served by the same governments.[8] House Concurrent Resolution 108, adopted in 1953, expressed the same philosophy.[9]

It is likely that Indian policy will continue to fluctuate between these two emphases. No matter which approach is stressed at any given time there probably will be little change in the current state responsibilities for Indians and in the free movement of Indians in and out of reservations to live and work.

THE QUESTION OF SIZE AND POPULATION BALANCE

There are two aspects of the current reservation scene that need further attention. One is the tremendous variation in size and resources of the various Indian groups and the other is the balance between population and reservation resources.

Size and Resources

A casual review of the geographical distribution of Indians (Appendix B) indicates that many reservation groups are very small in numbers and in many cases have very little land in trust. The Federal government and Indian interest groups have tended to think in terms of a uniform policy for all groups—large and small. Since very small groups often have entirely different governmental and economic needs than do large groups consideration should be given to how best to give them help. Recognition of this problem by the Bureau of Indian Affairs is seen in the current "small tribes initiative" which proposes to place several groups together under one governmental tent to increase viability. Further serious study of this question of size related to viability would possibly result in concentration of effort and yield more positive outcomes than at present. It will be remembered from Chapter 3 that the National Highway Traffic Safety Administration (NHTSA) analyzed the Indian reservation situation to see how its limited funds could result in maximum benefit. Of the 496 Indian groups identified by NHTSA, 326 had populations of fewer than 300 and 82.9 percent had populations of fewer than 1000. NHTSA decided to concentrate its efforts on eleven of the larger tribes. Indian leadership, Interior Department officials, and Congressional committees concerned with Indian affairs might well follow this lead and take a hard look at Indian entities and see which ones have any chance of self-government or economic viability.

The smaller Indian groups will probably increasingly become dependent on, and parts of, the state and local government service system. Such small groups will continue to live together if they desire and have their own customs, but it might make sense to help them integrate economically and governmentally into the state system with whatever variations of government organization seem to make the most sense to the Indians concerned and the state involved. State legislatures have a great deal of flexibility in legislating for local governing bodies.

Arrangements might also be worked out with the Federal Government for symbolic recognition of each particular group's historic sovereignty and identity, perhaps in the form of a joint resolution which would have no benefits or relationship to the current situation except to recognize their ancestral and tribal origin as a matter of identity and pride. Formal tribal government and the Federal trust over Indian land are the current symbols of original sovereignty for such small groups. The basic question is whether these current policies are of real practical assistance in meeting the groups' future needs.

Population - Resource Ratio

The second question that requires serious attention is the population resource ratio on some of the larger reservations which might have the potential of economic and governmental self-sufficiency if there were an appropriate relationship or balance between the two factors. A first step in such an analysis might be to research each of the larger reservation's "human carrying capacity," that is, how many families could a reservation support at a decent standard of living? Such a study would of course take into account the resource base, the feasible development of the economy utilizing the available resources, and the number of families that such a development could sustain. In the early 1950s I heard a discussion of Pine Ridge in which, with the grazing-farming resource base, it was estimated that the reservation could support perhaps one-fifth of its population at a decent standard of living. I do not know how accurate this estimate was but it illustrates the nature of the question to be investigated.

This question has been studied in the past. For example, the Commissioner's *Annual Report* for 1951 presented the results of a study of 16 reservations with overpopulation problems indicating that "resources available within the reservation can support only 46 percent of the reservation population even at a minimum standard of subsistence." For a standard of living comparable to the national average, ". . .it is probable that more than half of all Indians (on reservations) would have to seek their livelihood off reservation."[10] A study of various facets of the Indian situation in 1952[11] considered overpopulation a problem on many reservations. The situation may be worse today.

NEED FOR RESEARCH AND DATA

The American Indian Policy Review Commission complained about the lack of data at BIA, particularly on employment, but said, also, "There is an urgent need to develop a uniform, consistent, and accurate data base now, so that the effects of Government programs and all expenditures on development can be measured."[12] There currently is no base line for each of the larger reservations or criteria for measuring reservation progress toward economic or governmental self-sufficiency. There is data for some of the subject-matter programs, such as jobs and income provided by forestry operations, but no across-the-board procedure for considering all aspects of the reservation economy and coming up with how close it is to being self-sufficient. When I asked for such data, I not only did not get it because it apparently is non-existent, but I received the same impression as did the AIPRC that such data was not considered necessary.[13] The Interior Department apparently sees no need for across-the-board summary data for the larger reservations and developing measures of progress toward economic independence. AIPRC stated, "Good statistics are not ends in themselves but invaluable to evaluation of Federal programs and policy."[14]

OPTIONAL APPROACHES

If such studies of reservation human carrying capacity were instituted and indicated that some of the larger reservations with potential economic self-sufficiency had from two to perhaps ten times the number of people who could be supported from reservation resources, there would be at least two optional approaches to resolution of the problem. One route would be to increase the carrying capacity by increasing income and jobs through a different utilization of reservation resources. The other would involve assisting excess population to find decent jobs in other places. Both approaches have been utilized in the past.

Development of Reservation

The Economic Development Administration (until recently) and the Bureau of Indian Affairs have poured millions of dollars into industrial parks, tourist facilities, and subsidization of industry and business on the reservation. Indian tribes have participated by providing land and other aids and a pool of labor. Often Indians have not only had opportunities for jobs in such enterprises but also for training in management and for opportunities to move up the ladder, and some have done so. Various subject-matter programs of the Bureau of Indian Affairs such as forestry, farming, irrigation, recreation and fossil fuel programs have sought in cooperation with Indian tribes and individual Indians to increase utilization of these resources and to stimulate increased income and payroll with some success.

But joblessness on reservations is currently at an all-time high. Population increase seems to be outstripping any increased economic opportunities.

Incentives for Relocation

The other obvious option of helping Indians move from high unemployment reservation situations to greener pastures was tried in the voluntary employment assistance and relocation program of the 1950s and 1960s. During this period Indians wishing to use the program were funded for training, were provided living expenses for themselves and their families while in training and until they obtained a job, were helped to find adequate housing, and the worker and family were assisted in becoming acquainted with a new community.

Perhaps a revival of this program with improvements that might come from current research and experience would help relieve reservation-job ratio pressure where it is needed. Of course, one of the main incentives for relocation is the lack of opportunity on the reservation. Many Indians in spite of incentives to stay on the reservation have migrated out in search of greener pastures without special relocation incentives. But it is also obvious that many have not. If there is a need to reduce some reservations' population, thought might be given as to how to counter the perverse incentives discussed in Chapter 1. In addition to the relocation subsidy mentioned above, termination of the Federal trust responsibility has been tried on several reservations. This had the effect of taking Indian land out of its tax free status and subjecting it to state real estate taxes. However, Indian resistance to the termination of the Federal trust resulted in the abandonment of this policy.

Hopefully, Indian leadership can discover other options that would help reduce overpopulation where it exists.

Reservation stagnation is very likely to continue in many places until the population-resource-job ratio problem is faced clearly by Indian groups and government policy makers and programs. Reservation-wide summary data and bench marks will be needed to measure progress toward the goal and to determine which policies yield results and which do not.

Muddling Through

Another option is to muddle on with programs based on precedent or conventional wisdom without guidance based on research studies and evaluation and see what develops. No matter what research is accomplished and what policy options based on such research might be adopted, people and programs tend to change incrementally. Even though a sharp and dramatic change might seem to be desirable it may not be feasible to carry out rapid change. If there were better defined goals and ways of reaching them, actions could be taken in line with such guidelines for a consistent total result over time which might result in reservation self-sufficiency sooner than by a hit-or-miss approach.

EDUCATION

Education of the Indian young may be making a major contribution to the eventual resolution of reservation and tribal dependency. The vast majority of Indian young people are being educated in state public school systems. Frequently state schools with Indian children have special courses related to Indian culture which both the Indian and non-Indian students in the school may take. As Indian parents, Indian communities and Indian young people themselves take education seriously it certainly will have an impact on the future. A high school diploma is a key to many job options as well as a qualifier for continuing education in a university, as many Indian young people are doing. Even though university graduates may face bleak employment prospects, trained Indian professionals increase their own personal options. There are many Indian attorneys, doctors, teachers, artists, businessmen, and governmental leaders who have made good use of educational opportunities. Affirmative action employment programs often give a well-qualified Indian an edge in employment.

The ever changing nature of culture is presented in Chapter 1. Education is certainly having an impact on traditional Indian culture. This has caused uneasiness among many people, Indian and non-Indian, who do not want to see valuable aspects of Indian culture and tradition lost. But, apparently, it is not necessary that they disappear.

> "I'm not familiar with tribal organizations and customs" Thomas Jimboy, a Haskell (Indian School) graduate and a Lawrence (Kansas) resident said. "My family didn't function within a tribe. But nevertheless I take pride in Indian tradition and don't want to see it lost." Most of the Indians attending the reorganizational meetings in Lawrence insist being an Indian is more than having a sense of customs and traditions, and that participation in business and industry off the reservation cannot damage the Indian identity.
>
> "These kids can retain their culture and still make it in the white man's world," Wesley Benito, education director of the Apache tribe at Whiteriver, Arizona said. "They don't want to be assimilated by the white man's society, but they want to compete in it. We want to be better than the white man. We've been playing a tax-eating role for too long."[15]

James Wilson, an Oglala Sioux on the Pine Ridge Reservation, who was director of the Office of Economic Opportunity Indian Desk in Washington, D.C., has stated:

> Many of the concerns of the traditional Indians about the changing values of the young Indians were relieved when these young Indians found that they could be productive members of this society, and still Indian in every sense of the word. This was a real breakthrough for a lot of us.[16]

As is clear, education has made and can make a difference. It may be a major factor in helping achieve the goal of Indian and reservation self-sufficiency sought by both Indians and non-Indians.

SUMMARY

Indian individuals, tribal governments, Indian interest groups, state governments, and the Federal government all will be involved in the formulation and application of Indian policy in the future. If appropriate solutions can be developed for small Indian groups, if a balance between reservation resources and population can be achieved for large tribes, and if continued support for education and scholarships for Indian young people can be maintained, the future holds much promise. Indians will play a major part in considering and deciding on such policy issues and in helping carry through the policies that are adopted. Chief Joseph, quoted in Chapter 1, sought no special favors or laws for Indians. He sought freedom and equal opportunity. Indians are citizens of the United States and they have equal opportunity and responsibility.

The setting for Indian Affairs and Indian policy is the total American society. As indicated throughout the book, especially in Chapter 2, the limits of Indian policy and program are determined in the last analysis by public opinion. If there is to be change or improvement in Indian policy the general public, and well as the direct participants, must have a concept of the big picture. Appreciation of the complex forces, special interests, and existing programs and their interrelationships would seem to be necessary for the development of Indian policy that represents the considered goals of society in general as well as of the Indian citizens most directly affected.

FOOTNOTES

[1] Indian Self-Determination and Education Assistance Act, January 4, 1975, 25 USC 450.

[2] American Indian Policy Review Commission, *Final Report* Two volumes. (Washington, D.C.: Government Printing Office, 1977). Hereafter referred to as AIPRC *Final Report*. My views on the preliminary report are included in Volume 2 of the *Final Report*, pp. 809-819.

[3] AIPRC *Final Report*, pp. 3-6.

[4] *Ibid.*, p. 6.

[5] *Ibid.*, pp. 13-14.

[6] Indian Reorganization Act, 1934, 48 Stat. 984.

[7] Allotment Act, 1887, 24 Stat. 388; sometimes referred to as the Dawes Act.

[8]Lewis Meriam and others, *The Problem of Indian Administration*, Institute for Government Research Studies in Administration. (Baltimore: Johns Hopkins Press, 1928).

[9]House Concurrent Resolution 108, adopted August 1, 1953; frequently referred to as the "termination policy."

[10]Commissioner of Indian Affairs, *Annual Report,* 1951. p. 375.

[11]"Investigation of BIA, Pursuant to H. res. 698," *Report No. 2503* (Washington, D.C.: 82nd Cong., 2nd sess., U.S. House of Representatives, Dec. 15, 1952), pp. 29-30.

[12]AIPRC *Final Report*, p. 349.

[13]*Ibid.*, p. 348 ("What good are accurate statistics?").

[14]*Ibid.*

[15]Robert W. Butler, "Haskell Molds Indian Identity," Kansas City, Missouri, *Times*, February 18, 1971. Quoted in Taylor, *The States and Their Indian Citizens*, pp. 128-129.

[16]Stan Steiner, *The New Indian* (New York: Dell Publishing Co., 1968), p. 94.

APPENDIX A

MAP OF INDIAN LANDS AND COMMUNITIES

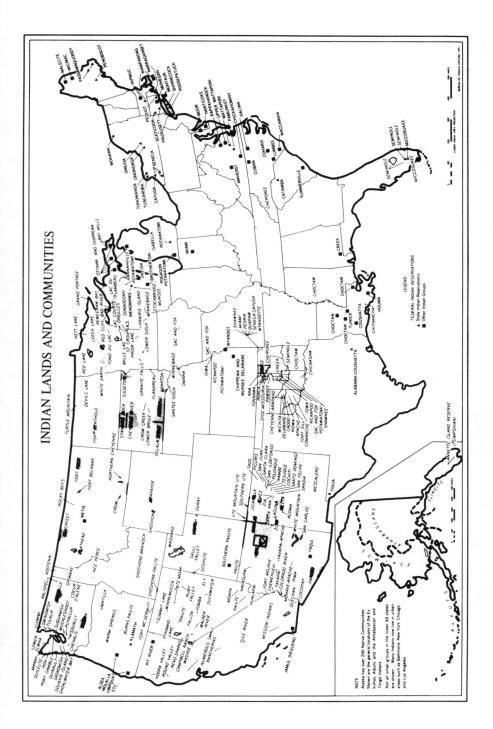

INDIAN LANDS AND COMMUNITIES

NOTE

Alaska has over 200 Native Communities.
Shown are the general locations of the Es-
kimos, Aleuts and the Athabascan and
Tlingit Indians

Not all small groups in the lower 48 states
are shown. Many Indians now live in urban
areas such as Baltimore, New York, Chicago
and Los Angeles.

LEGEND

FEDERAL INDIAN RESERVATIONS
State Indian Reservations
Other Indian Groups

APPENDIX B

RESIDENT INDIAN POPULATION BY BIA AREA OFFICE, STATE, AND BIA RESERVATION AGENCY

DOI
August 1983

Financial Management

LOCAL ESTIMATES OF RESIDENT INDIAN POPULATION AND LABOR FORCE STATUS: JANUARY 1983

INTRODUCTION

Coverage: The term "resident Indian" means Indians living on Federal reservations or nearby who are considered part of the service population of the Bureau of Indian Affairs. The term "near reservations" is defined in CFR 25 par. 20.1 (r). Special legislation governs eligibility in Alaska and Oklahoma. In Alaska the figures include all Alaska Natives, i.e. Aleuts, Eskimos, as well as Indians. Since very few are actually living on reservations, the term "nearby" refers to all the rest of Alaska. In Oklahoma, the area covered encompasses former reservations. Thus, in both states the bureau's responsibility extends almost entirely to the total Indian population of those states.

The statistics compiled herein refer basically to the population of a geographic area; they do not necessarily refer to tribal membership. These latter figures are maintained by the individual tribes according to their specific rules of membership, which may include members wherever they may be living. The few cases where membership rather than residency was used are so indicated in the appropriate table.

In certain instances the figures for individual Reservations are higher than the figures shown in the 1980 census for the counties where these reservations are located. Some of the reasons for these differences are: (1) the tribes may have included in their count members that have left the reservation on a temporary basis (students, employment, etc.); (2) or, as stated above the tribes may have included tribal membership in their count; (3) possible variance of tribal population counts among tribes residing in the same county; and (4) not all members may have been counted in the 1980 census. Consequently, in this report the total Indian population in some States differs somewhat from the 1980 census. In addition there has been a slight increase in the Indian population since the census was taken.

The total of approximately 755,000 Indians covered in these tables represents over half of the total Indian population of the United States, which in the 1980 U.S. census numbered 1,421,367. This figure includes 42,162 Eskimos, and 14,205 Aleuts. The remainder consists of members of federally recognized tribes who live off-reservation, or Indian people who are not members of any federally recognized tribe, or those who claimed Indian ancestry. The above census count differs slightly from that reported by the census initially. The change reflects correction of errors found after the advanced census reports were prepared.

Estimated Figures: The Local Agency offices of the Bureau of Indian Affairs estimate the data using whatever information may be available for the reservation. Accuracy varies from place to place; it is relatively high at small, isolated locations where everyone's activity is common knowledge. On the other hand, the labor force status can be difficult to estimate for Alaska, Oklahoma, and the Navajo reservation where Indians are scattered over enormous geographic areas. Household surveys of labor force status are conducted but infrequently because of the considerable cost that such a procedure involves.

Labor Force Status: Considered in this category are all those 16 years old and over (493,880) representing about 65% of the total population. This category is divided into three major groups for the purposes of this report--unable to work, employed, and able to work but not employed.

(1) Unable to work (column 5 and 6). The total 150,531, or 30% of those 16 years old and over, includes those who are prevented from working by attending school, caring for children, or unable to work by reasons of disability, retirement, or age. Students make up some 41% of this group. Reservations differ considerably in the proportion estimated to fall into this category.

(2) Employed (column 7). The total, 168,084, or 34% of those 16 years old and over includes full-time and part-time employees. Of those close to two-thirds earn 7,000 or more (column 8)--the $7,000 figure being based on the annual income of a worker earning minimum wage. In other words, one-third of the employed are earning less than the minimum wage for a full-time job.

It could be argued that employment, excluding marginal jobs, provides a better picture of the economic health of a reservation than the total employment. As one possible index of this condition, column 9 shows the number of employed Indians earning $7,000 or more as a percent of a labor force which is in the 16 to 65 population range (column 4 minus column 2). [NOTE: The 1981 report calculated this percentage as a function of the 16 years old and older population, including those over 65. That calculation overstated the real economic labor force and should not be compared with the similar data in this compilation].

(3) Not employed but able to work (column 10). The total, 175,265, or 35% of those 16 years old and over, includes persons actually seeking work and those not seeking work. This distinction underlies two concepts of labor force: (a) The "potential labor force" consisting of all those 16 years old and over who are able to work, whether employed or not (columns 7 and 10 totaling 343,349). Fifty-one percent of the "potential labor force" are not employed (column 11); (b) those not seeking work and who are omitted from the standard Labor Department definition of labor force and unemployed. By this definition the labor force consists of columns 7 and 12, totaling 275,031 and the unemployment rate is 39 percent (column 13). [NOTE: Unlike the national statistics, we include persons not seeking work, because of difficulty of estimating this group without expensive surveys. There are also problems in developing a useful concept of those seeking work in places where few jobs are available, as on many reservations. In any case, including persons not wanting work in the labor force results in a higher unemployment rate than would be found in a standard household survey].

Table Format: The basic data is compiled in Table 3. They are arranged by BIA Area Offices and within Area, by Agency or equivalent unit of organization below the Area level, the Reservation, and State.

Table 1 and 2 are summary tables. The former shows the totals for each State. The latter shows totals for each of the areas into which the BIA is administratively divided.

Additional Comments: In the compilation of this Labor Force Report, a conscious effort was made to present as accurately as possible the resident Indian population on and near reservations. It should be noted, however, that there are problems with statistics on Indian reservations. The collection of statistics in Indian urban areas is particularly difficult since household surveys are infrequent or non-existent. Also in isolated rural areas, it is difficult to separate the job-seekers from those not seeking jobs because there are not jobs available to draw out this distinction. Were jobs available, the unemployment rate would be somewhere between the two measures given in this report notably 39 percent and 51 percent. In either case these rates show a considerable increase (9% and 5% respectively) from the last reporting period, which is attributed to the fact that the local and regional economies have been significantly affected by national recession.

Any questions pertaining to this report should be directed to the Office of Financial Management, Bureau of Indian Affairs, Washington, D.C.

Table 1. – LOCAL ESTIMATES OF RESIDENT INDIAN POPULATION AND LABOR FORCE STATUS; INDIANS LIVING ON AND ADJACENT TO RESERVATIONS; SUMMARY BY STATE; JANUARY 1983

State	BIA TOTAL	Years of Age			Unable to Work		Labor Force Status, 16 Years Old & Over							1980 Census TOTAL
		65 & Over	Under 16	16 & Over	Students	Others	Employed			Not Employed, Total		Able to Work, Seeking Work		
							Total	Number Earn $7000+	% of 16-65	Number	% 7+10	Number	% 7+12	
	(1)	(2)	(3)	(4)	(5)	(6)	(7)	(8)	(9)	(10)	(11)	(12)	(13)	
BIA TOTAL	755,201	46,190	261,321	493,880	62,321	88,210	168,084	109,886	25%	175,265	51%	106,947	39%	1,421,367
ALASKA (AK)	64,970	2,899	25,618	39,352	5,832	7,236	9,991	6,409	18%	16,293	62%	10,822	52%	64,103
ARIZONA (AZ)	154,818	7,440	57,086	97,732	11,515	16,627	28,290	18,125	20%	41,300	59%	24,320	46%	152,745
CALIFORNIA (CA)	23,625	1,352	7,344	16,281	1,396	2,257	4,496	2,613	18%	8,132	64%	4,999	53%	201,369
COLORADO (CO)	2,661	128	852	1,809	382	180	485	246	15%	762	61%	654	57%	18,068
FLORIDA (FL)	1,921	81	723	1,198	114	143	598	416	37%	343	36%	241	29%	19,257
IDAHO (ID)	7,108	407	2,626	4,482	478	726	1,108	774	19%	2,170	66%	1,039	48%	10,521
IOWA (IA)	662	28	285	377	43	24	100	88	25%	210	68%	205	67%	5,455
KANSAS (KS)	2,243	172	902	1,341	71	239	796	538	46%	235	23%	158	17%	15,373
LOUISIANA (LA)	717	43	253	464	32	141	196	157	37%	95	33%	54	23%	12,065
MAINE (ME)	2,261	114	860	1,401	171	279	545	279	22%	406	43%	268	33%	4,087
MICHIGAN (MI)	5,829	267	1,984	3,845	351	588	1,155	671	19%	1,751	60%	1,229	52%	40,050
MINNESOTA (MN)	18,260	1,220	6,803	11,457	1,363	2,762	2,532	1,706	17%	4,800	65%	3,892	61%	35,016
MISSISSIPPI (MS)	4,487	147	1,750	2,737	213	418	1,428	677	26%	678	32%	352	20%	6,180
MONTANA (MT)	27,529	1,087	10,111	17,418	2,057	2,777	5,579	4,043	25%	7,005	56%	4,043	42%	37,270
NEBRASKA (NE)	4,404	347	1,329	3,075	281	413	629	535	20%	1,752	74%	950	60%	9,195
NEVADA (NV)	8,259	509	2,610	5,649	567	626	1,835	1,299	25%	2,621	59%	1,662	48%	13,308
NEW MEXICO (NM)	105,973	6,204	31,511	74,462	9,329	8,334	30,207	24,342	36%	26,592	47%	15,860	34%	106,119
NEW YORK (NY)	11,167	935	2,942	8,225	872	1,885	2,463	1,260	17%	3,005	55%	2,502	50%	39,582
NORTH CAROLINA (NC)	5,971	424	1,819	4,152	884	710	1,092	828	22%	1,466	57%	659	38%	64,652
NORTH DAKOTA (ND)	21,552	853	8,025	13,527	1,461	2,946	3,384	3,025	24%	5,736	63%	3,893	53%	20,158
OKLAHOMA (OK)	159,852	15,406	49,715	110,137	16,293	25,729	52,451	28,353	30%	15,664	23%	8,716	14%	169,459
OREGON (OR)	4,301	194	1,547	2,754	326	541	990	571	22%	897	48%	614	38%	27,314
SOUTH DAKOTA (SD)	46,101	2,035	19,545	26,556	2,665	4,593	4,977	4,406	18%	14,321	74%	6,003	55%	45,968
UTAH (UT)	7,140	313	2,607	4,533	631	643	1,412	1,045	25%	1,847	57%	902	39%	19,256
WASHINGTON (WA)	39,726	2,220	14,091	25,635	2,557	4,413	6,986	4,215	18%	11,679	63%	8,711	55%	60,804
WISCONSIN (WI)	18,279	1,156	6,689	11,590	1,542	1,994	3,777	2,843	27%	4,277	53%	3,300	47%	29,499
WYOMING (WY)	5,385	189	1,694	3,691	895	986	582	422	12%	1,228	68%	899	61%	7,094
OTHER STATES														187,400

NOTE: 1. The 1980 Census data are shown for references only. They may differ somewhat from those reported by the census initially. The changes reflect correction of errors found after the initial census reports were prepared.

2. The difference in Indian population between the Census Bureau figure and the BIA total, represents Indian People of federally recognized tribes but living off reservation, or Indian people who are not members of any federally recognized tribe, and all those who claimed Indian ancestry.

Table 2. - LOCAL ESTIMATES OF RESIDENT INDIAN POPULATION AND LABOR FORCE STATUS; INDIANS LIVING ON AND ADJACENT TO RESERVATIONS; SUMMARY BY BIA AREA AND WITHIN AREA BY STATE: JANUARY 1983

Area & State	TOTAL	YEARS OF AGE			UNABLE TO WORK		LABOR FORCE STATUS, 16 YEARS OLD & OVER						
		65 & Over	Under 16	16 & Over	Students	Others	EMPLOYED			NOT EMPLOYED, ABLE TO WORK			
							Total	Earn $7000+ Number	% of 16-65	Total Number	% of 7&10	Seeking Work Number	% of 7 + 12
	(1)	(2)	(3)	(4)	(5)	(6)	(7)	(8)	(9)	(10)	(11)	(12)	(13)
BIA TOTAL	755,201	46,190	261,321	493,880	62,321	88,210	168,084	109,886	25%	175,265	51%	106,947	39%
ABERDEEN	[72,160]	[3,230]	[28,947]	[43,213]	[4,412]	[7,956]	[9,010]	[7,988]	[20%]	[21,835]	[71%]	[10,875]	[55%]
Nebraska (NE)pt.	4,345	338	1,308	3,037	276	398	618	527	20%	1,745	74%	946	60%
North Dakota (ND)	21,552	853	8,025	13,527	1,461	2,946	3,384	3,025	24%	5,736	63%	3,893	53%
South Dakota (SD)	46,101	2,035	19,545	26,556	2,665	4,593	4,977	4,406	18%	14,321	74%	6,003	55%
Montana (MT)pt.	162	4	69	93	10	19	31	30	33%	33	52%	33	52%
ALBUQUERQUE	[46,639]	[2,838]	[16,263]	[30,376]	[4,176]	[5,001]	[10,103]	[5,863]	[21%]	[11,096]	[52%]	[8,246]	[45%]
Colorado (CO)	2,661	128	852	1,809	382	180	485	246	15%	762	61%	654	57%
New Mexico (NM)pt.	43,978	2,710	15,411	28,567	3,794	4,821	9,618	5,617	22%	10,334	52%	7,592	44%
ANADARKO	[37,285]	[2,296]	[10,848]	[26,437]	[3,779]	[6,795]	[9,988]	[7,411]	[32%]	[5,875]	[37%]	[4,679]	[32%]
Kansas (KS)	2,243	172	902	1,341	71	239	796	538	46%	235	23%	158	17%
Oklahoma (OK)pt.	34,983	3,115	9,925	25,058	3,703	6,541	9,181	6,865	31%	5,633	38%	4,517	33%
Nebraska (NE)pt.	59	9	21	38	5	15	11	8	L	7	L	4	L
BILLINGS	[29,527]	[1,233]	[10,059]	[19,468]	[2,830]	[3,400]	[5,378]	[4,076]	[22%]	[7,860]	[59%]	[4,608]	[46%]
Montana (MT)pt.	24,142	1,044	8,365	15,777	1,935	2,414	4,796	3,654	25%	6,632	58%	3,709	44%
Wyoming (WY)	5,385	189	1,694	3,691	895	986	582	422	12%	1,228	68%	899	61%
EASTERN	[26,524]	[1,744]	[8,347]	[18,177]	[2,286]	[3,576]	[6,322]	[3,617]	[22%]	[5,993]	[49%]	[4,076]	[39%]
Florida (FL)	1,921	81	723	1,198	114	143	598	416	37%	343	36%	241	29%
Louisiana (LA)	717	43	253	464	32	141	196	157	37%	95	33%	54	23%
Maine (ME)	2,261	114	860	1,401	171	279	545	279	22%	406	43%	268	33%
Mississippi (MS)	4,487	147	1,750	2,737	213	418	677	677	26%	678	32%	352	20%
New York (NY)	11,167	935	2,942	8,225	872	1,885	2,463	1,260	17%	3,005	55%	2,502	50%
North Carolina (NC)	5,971	424	1,819	4,152	884	710	1,092	828	22%	1,466	57%	659	38%
JUNEAU	[63,858]	[2,860]	[25,211]	[38,647]	[5,746]	[7,153]	[9,782]	[6,209]	[17%]	[15,966]	[62%]	[10,495]	[52%]
Alaska (AK)pt.	63,858	2,860	25,211	38,647	5,746	7,153	9,782	6,209	17%	15,966	62%	10,495	52%

Table 2 - Continued

Area & State	TOTAL	YEARS OF AGE			UNABLE TO WORK		LABOR FORCE STATUS, 16 YEARS OLD & OVER						
		65 & Over	Under 16	16 & Over	Students	Others	EMPLOYED			NOT EMPLOYED, ABLE TO WORK			
							Total	Number	Earn $7000+ % of 16-65	Total Number	% of 7&10	Seeking Work Number	% of 7+12
	(1)	(2)	(3)	(4)	(5)	(6)	(7)	(8)	(9)	(10)	(11)	(12)	(13)
MINNEAPOLIS	[43,030]	[2,671]	[15,761]	[27,269]	[3,299]	[5,368]	[7,564]	[5,308]	[22%]	[11,038]	[59%]	[8,626]	[53%]
Iowa (IA)	662	28	285	377	43	24	100	88	25%	210	68%	205	67%
Michigan (MI)	5,829	267	1,984	3,845	351	588	1,155	671	19%	1,751	60%	1,229	52%
Minnesota (MN)	18,260	1,220	6,803	11,457	1,363	2,762	2,532	1,706	17%	4,800	65%	3,892	61%
Wisconsin (WI)	18,279	1,156	6,689	11,590	1,542	1,994	3,777	2,843	27%	4,277	53%	3,300	47%
MUSKOGEE	[124,869]	[12,291]	[39,790]	[85,079]	[12,590]	[19,188]	[43,270]	[21,488]	[30%]	[10,031]	[23%]	[4,199]	[9%]
Oklahoma (OK)pt.	124,869	12,291	39,790	85,079	12,590	19,188	43,270	21,488	30%	10,031	23%	4,199	9%
NAVAJO	[158,917]	[8,138]	[50,895]	[108,022]	[13,278]	[10,651]	[34,894]	[29,678]	[30%]	[49,199]	[59%]	[28,155]	[45%]
Arizona (AZ)pt.	92,574	4,435	33,251	59,323	7,291	6,870	13,439	10,281	19%	31,723	70%	19,124	70%
New Mexico (NM)pt.	61,995	3,494	16,100	45,895	5,535	3,513	20,589	18,725	44%	16,258	44%	8,268	29%
Utah (UT)pt.	4,348	209	1,544	2,804	452	268	866	672	26%	1,218	58%	763	47%
PHOENIX	[76,251]	[3,763]	[28,305]	[47,946]	[5,084]	[11,044]	[18,105]	[9,934]	[22%]	[13,713]	[43%]	[7,432]	[29%]
Arizona (AZ)pt.	62,244	3,025	23,835	38,409	4,224	9,757	14,851	7,844	22%	9,577	39%	5,196	26%
California (CA)pt.	2,657	108	723	1,934	103	267	819	373	20%	745	48%	310	27%
Idaho (ID)pt.	299	17	74	225	11	19	54	45	22%	141	72%	125	69%
Nevada (NV)	8,259	509	2,610	5,649	567	626	1,835	1,299	25%	2,621	59%	1,662	48%
Utah (UT)pt.	2,792	104	1,063	1,729	179	375	546	373	23%	629	54%	139	20%
PORTLAND	[55,173]	[2,882]	[20,274]	[34,899]	[3,548]	[6,088]	[9,991]	[6,074]	[19%]	[15,272]	[60%]	[10,867]	[52%]
Alaska (AK)pt.	1,112	39	407	705	86	83	209	200	30%	327	61%	327	61%
Idaho (ID)pt.	6,809	390	2,552	4,257	467	707	1,054	729	19%	2,029	66%	914	46%
Montana (MT)pt.	3,225	39	1,677	1,548	112	344	752	359	24%	340	31%	301	29%
Oregon (OR)	4,301	194	1,547	2,754	326	541	990	571	22%	897	48%	614	38%
Washington (WA)	39,726	2,220	14,091	25,635	2,557	4,413	6,986	4,215	18%	11,679	63%	8,711	55%
SACRAMENTO	[20,968]	[1,244]	[6,621]	[14,347]	[1,293]	[1,990]	[3,677]	[2,240]	[17%]	[7,387]	[67%]	[4,689]	[56%]
California (CA)pt.	20,968	1,244	6,621	14,347	1,293	1,990	3,677	2,240	17%	7,387	67%	4,682	56%

Table 3. Local Estimates of Resident Indian Population and Labor Force Status;
Indians Living On and Adjacent to Reservations; Compiled by BIA Area,
and within Area by Agency, Reservation, and State: January 1983

AREA, AGENCY, RESERVATION, & STATE	TOTAL	YEARS OF AGE			UNABLE TO WORK		LABOR FORCE STATUS, 16 YEARS OLD & OVER						
		65 & Over	Under 16	16 & Over	Students	Others	Total	EMPLOYED		NOT EMPLOYED, ABLE TO WORK			
								Earn $7000+		Total		Seeking Work	
								Number	% of 16-65	Number	% of 7+10	Number	% of 7+12
	(1)	(2)	(3)	(4)	(5)	(6)	(7)	(8)	(9)	(10)	(11)	(12)	(13)
BIA TOTAL	755,201	46,190	261,321	493,880	62,321	88,210	168,084	109,886	25%	175,265	51%	106,947	39%
Aberdeen (MT,NE,ND,SD)	72,160	3,230	28,947	43,213	4,412	7,956	9,010	7,988	20%	21,835	71%	10,875	55%
Cheyenne River Agcy. & Res. (SD)	4,649	192	2,128	2,521	500	230	894	858	37%	897	50%	897	50%
Crow Creek Agcy. & Res. (SD)	2,384	88	1,046	1,338	129	283	390	377	28%	536	58%	344	47%
Flandreau F.O. & Res. (SD)	415	21	166	249	15	83	124	107	47%	27	18%	27	18%
Ft. Berthold Agcy. & Res. (ND)	3,081	123	915	2,166	274	538	770	680	33%	584	43%	400	34%
Ft. Totten Agcy. & Res. (ND)	3,109	65	1,736	1,373	128	127	425	395	30%	693	62%	550	56%
Lower Brule Agcy. & Res. (SD)	971	28	436	535	64	17	171	156	13%	283	62%	86	33%
Pine Ridge Agcy. & Res. (NE,SD)	18,397	846	8,444	9,953	354	1,896	1,532	1,345	15%	6,171	80%	1,500	49%
Est. NE Pt. (3%)	(552)	(25)	(253)	(299)	(11)	(57)	(46)	(40)	(15%)	(185)	(80%)	(45)	(47%)
Est. SD Pt. (97%)	(17,845)	(821)	(8,191)	(9,654)	(343)	(1,839)	(1,486)	(1,305)	(15%)	(5,986)	(80%)	(1,455)	(49%)
Rosebud Agcy. & Res. (SD)	9,674	540	3,676	5,998	734	601	1,141	926	17%	3,522	76%	1,255	52%
Sisseton Agcy. & Res. (ND,SD)	3,735	100	1,647	2,088	150	488	272	185	9%	1,178	81%	353	56%
Est. ND Pt. (8%)	(299)	(8)	(132)	(167)	(12)	(39)	(22)	(15)	(9%)	(94)	(81%)	(28)	(56%)
Est. SD Pt. (92%)	(3,436)	(92)	(1,515)	(1,921)	(138)	(449)	(250)	(170)	(9%)	(1,084)	(81%)	(325)	(56%)
Standing Rock Agcy. & Res. (ND,SD)	8,197	286	2,906	5,291	955	1,267	637	609	12%	2,432	79%	2,068	76%
Est. ND Pt. (49%)	(4,017)	(140)	(1,424)	(2,593)	(468)	(621)	(312)	(298)	(12%)	(1,192)	(79%)	(1,013)	(79%)
Est. SD Pt. (51%)	(4,180)	(146)	(1,482)	(2,698)	(487)	(646)	(325)	(311)	(12%)	(1,240)	(79%)	(1,055)	(76%)

Table 3 - Continued

AREA, AGENCY, RESERVATION, & STATE	TOTAL	YEARS OF AGE			LABOR FORCE STATUS, 16 YEARS OLD & OVER								
					UNABLE TO WORK		EMPLOYED			NOT EMPLOYED, ABLE TO WORK			
		65 & Over	Under 16	16 & Over	Stu-dents	Others	Total	Earn $7000 +		Total		Seeking Work	
								Number	% of 16-65	Number	% of 7+10	Number	% of 7+12
	(1)	(2)	(3)	(4)	(5)	(6)	(7)	(8)	(9)	(10)	(11)	(12)	(13)
Aberdeen – Continued													
Trenton F.O. (MT,ND)	1,625	38	690	935	105	190	305	300	33%	335	52%	335	52%
Est. MT Pt. (10%)	(162)	(4)	(69)	(93)	(10)	(19)	(31)	(30)	(33%)	(33)	(52%)	(33)	(52%)
Est. ND Pt. (90%)	(1,463)	(34)	(621)	(842)	(95)	(171)	(274)	(270)	(33%)	(302)	(52%)	(302)	(52%)
Turtle Mt. Agcy. & Res. (ND)	9,583	483	3,197	6,386	484	1,450	1,581	1,367	23%	2,871	64%	1,600	50%
Yankton Agcy. & Res. (SD)	2,547	107	905	1,642	255	445	196	196	13%	746	79%	559	74%
Winnebago Agency	[3,791]	[313]	[1,055]	[2,738]	[265]	[341]	[572]	[487]	[20%]	[1,560]	[73%]	[901]	61%
Omaha Res. (NE)	2,188	189	474	1,714	171	167	249	202	13%	1,127	82%	606	75%
Santee Sioux Res. (NE)	422	27	161	261	25	57	89	89	38%	90	50%	90	50%
Winnebago Res. (NE)	1,183	97	420	763	69	117	234	196	29%	343	59%	205	47%

NOTES:

1. Data in brackets and parentheses, non-add.

2. Percentages assigned to each State for Reservations extending into more than one state are based on the proportions of Indian populations in the 1980 census for the counties in which the Reservations are located, except for the Trenton Field Office where the proportions were provided by the Program Director.

3. The Pine Ridge Reservation count reflects Oglala Sioux Indians residing in adjacent to Reservation areas encompassing counties in South Dakota (including Rapid City) and Nebraska. They were omitted from the 1981 estimates but are now included in the service population.

Table 3 - Continued

AREA, AGENCY, RESERVATION, & STATE	TOTAL	YEARS OF AGE			LABOR FORCE STATUS, 16 YEARS OLD & OVER								
		65 & Over	Under 16	16 & Over	UNABLE TO WORK		Total	EMPLOYED		NOT EMPLOYED, ABLE TO WORK			
					Stu-dents	Others		Earn $7000+ Number	% of 16-65	Total Number	% of 7+10	Seeking Work Number	% of 7+12
	(1)	(2)	(3)	(4)	(5)	(6)	(7)	(8)	(9)	(10)	(11)	(12)	(13)
ALBUQUERQUE (CO, NM)	46,639	2,838	16,263	30,376	4,176	5,001	10,103	5,863	21%	11,096	52%	8,246	45%
Jicarilla Agcy. & Res. (NM)	2,344	190	876	1,468	60	112	834	373	29%	462	36%	150	15%
Laguna Agcy. & Res. (NM)	6,525	455	2,113	4,412	538	843	855	685	17%	2,176	72%	1,818	68%
Mescalero Agcy. & Res. (NM)	2,481	75	1,205	1,276	159	215	512	282	23%	390	43%	255	33%
Northern Pueblos Agcy.	[7,574]	[507]	[1,835]	[5,739]	[699]	[869]	[2,379]	[1,495]	[29%]	[1,792]	[43%]	[1,290]	[35%]
Nambe (NM)	382	15	133	249	15	28	136	129	55%	70	34%	7	5%
Picuris (NM)	162	17	44	118	6	20	47	23	23%	45	45%	13	22%
Pojoaque (NM)	81	5	21	60	7	16	20	9	16%	17	46%	8	29%
San Ildefonso (NM)	550	23	148	402	45	41	144	120	32%	172	54%	126	47%
San Juan (NM)	1,871	144	329	1,542	171	234	858	473	34%	279	25%	206	19%
Santa Clara (NM)	2,466	105	486	1,980	237	324	886	544	29%	533	38%	419	32%
Taos (NM)	1,762	183	592	1,170	191	177	193	158	16%	609	76%	446	70%
Tesuque (NM)	300	15	82	218	27	29	95	39	14%	67	41%	65	41%
Ramah-Navajo Agcy. & Res. (NM)	1,793	102	466	1,327	28	63	375	244	20%	861	70%	688	65%
Southern Pueblos Agcy.	[15,973]	[1,003]	[5,912]	[10,061]	[1,843]	[2,308]	[3,213]	[1,936]	[21%]	[2,697]	[46%]	[1,924]	[27%]
Acoma (NM)	2,809	205	1,033	1,776	811	378	137	107	7%	450	77%	423	76%
Cochiti (NM)	970	63	314	656	51	101	257	221	37%	247	49%	47	15%
Isleta (NM)	3,184	280	1,222	1,962	365	593	673	377	22%	331	33%	285	30%
Jemez (NM)	2,298	102	861	1,437	155	54	293	262	20%	935	70%	468	64%
Sandia (NM)	247	18	84	163	27	45	73	66	45%	18	20%	11	13%
San Felipe (NM)	2,051	86	843	1,208	156	202	716	393	35%	134	16%	134	16%
Santa Ana (NM)	529	38	142	387	49	129	167	104	30%	42	20%	37	18%
Santo Domingo (NM)	3,257	164	1,208	2,049	167	786	724	279	15%	372	34%	351	33%
Zia (NM)	628	47	205	423	62	20	173	127	34%	168	49%	168	49%

Table 3 — Continued

AREA, AGENCY, RESERVATION, & STATE	TOTAL	YEARS OF AGE			LABOR FORCE STATUS, 16 YEARS OLD & OVER								
					UNABLE TO WORK		EMPLOYED			NOT EMPLOYED, ABLE TO WORK			
		65 & Over	Under 16	16 & Over	Stu-dents	Others	Total	Earn $7000 +		Total		Seeking Work	
								Number	% of 16-65	Number	% of 7+10	Number	% of 7+12
	(1)	(2)	(3)	(4)	(5)	(6)	(7)	(8)	(9)	(10)	(11)	(12)	(13)
ALBUQUERQUE - (Continued)													
Southern Ute Agcy. & Res. (CO)	1,107	50	292	815	226	72	188	167	22%	329	64%	329	64%
Ute Mt. Agcy. & Res. (CO)	1,554	78	560	994	156	108	297	79	9%	433	59%	325	52%
Zuni Agcy. & Res. (NM)	7,288	378	3,004	4,284	467	411	1,450	602	15%	1,956	57%	1,467	50%

NOTES:

1. Data in brackets non-add.

Table 3 - Continued

AREA, AGENCY, RESERVATION, & STATE	TOTAL	YEARS OF AGE			UNABLE TO WORK		LABOR FORCE STATUS, 16 YEARS OLD & OVER						
		65 & Over	Under 16	16 & Over	Stu-dents	Others	Total	EMPLOYED Earn $7000+ Number	% of 16-65	NOT EMPLOYED, ABLE TO WORK Total Number	% 7+10	Seeking Work Number	% of 7+12
	(1)	(2)	(3)	(4)	(5)	(6)	(7)	(8)	(9)	(10)	(11)	(12)	(13)
ANADARKO (KS,NE,OK)	37,285	3,296	10,848	26,437	3,779	6,795	9,988	7,411	32%	5,875	37%	4,679	32%
Anadarko Agcy.	[10,554]	[565]	[3,893]	[6,661]	[853]	[1,516]	[2,392]	[1,574]	[26%]	[1,900]	[44%]	[1,682]	[41%]
Apache Tribe (OK)	520	17	230	290	37	44	84	49	18%	125	60%	85	50%
Caddo Tribe (OK)	1,216	71	310	906	169	235	347	236	26%	155	31%	120	26%
Comanche Tribe (OK)	3,602	209	1,439	2,163	289	396	803	451	23%	675	46%	642	44%
Delaware Tribe (OK)	525	19	222	303	45	33	132	111	39%	93	41%	62	32%
Ft. Sill Apache Tribe (OK)	68	8	17	51	7	7	19	13	L	18	L	L	L
Kiowa Tribe (OK)	4,009	210	1,422	2,587	255	701	865	587	25%	766	47%	721	45%
Witchita Tribe (OK)	614	31	253	361	51	100	142	127	38%	68	32%	41	22%
Concho Agency (OK)	5,303	153	1,726	3,577	304	204	997	717	21%	2,072	67%	1,243	55%
Arapaho Tribe	(1,750)	(50)	(570)	(1,180)	(100)	(67)	(329)	(237)	(21%)	(684)	(67%)	(410)	(55%)
Cheyenne Tribe	(3,553)	(103)	(1,156)	(2,397)	(204)	(137)	(668)	(480)	(21%)	(1,388)	(67%)	(833)	(55%)
Horton Agency	[2,302]	[181]	[923]	[1,379]	[76]	[254]	[807]	[546]	[46%]	[242]	[23%]	[162]	[17%]
Iowa Reservation (KS,NE)	331	45	119	212	30	89	60	40	24%	33	35%	21	26%
Est. KS Pt. (83%)	(275)	(37)	(99)	(176)	(25)	(74)	(50)	(33)	(24%)	(27)	(35%)	(17)	(26%)
Est. NE Pt. (17%)	(56)	(8)	(20)	(36)	(5)	(15)	(10)	(7)	(24%)	(6)	(35%)	(4)	(26%)
Kickapoo Reservation (KS)	595	36	238	357	22	27	231	184	57%	77	25%	60	21%
Prairie Potawatomi Res. (KS)	1,330	90	555	775	20	137	495	310	45%	123	20%	75	13%
Sac & Fox Reservation (KS,NE)	46	10	11	35	4	1	21	12	L	9	L	6	L
Est. KS Pt. (94%)	(43)	(9)	(10)	(33)	(4)	(1)	(20)	(11)	(L)	(8)	(L)	(6)	(L)
Est. NE Pt. (6%)	(3)	(1)	(1)	(2)	(0)	(0)	(1)	(1)	(L)	(1)	(L)	(0)	(L)
Pawnee Agency	[7,316]	[494]	[1,828]	[5,488]	[517]	[1,353]	[2,352]	[1,767]	[35%]	[1,266]	[35%]	[1,245]	[35%]
Kaw Tribe (OK)	527	36	132	395	24	113	168	126	35%	90	35%	88	34%
Otoe-Missouria Tribe (OK)	1,191	80	297	894	91	258	354	270	33%	191	35%	187	35%
Pawnee Tribe (OK)	2,093	141	523	1,570	135	380	686	514	36%	369	35%	365	35%
Ponca Tribe (OK)	2,221	150	555	1,666	170	361	738	553	36%	397	35%	392	35%
Tonkawa Tribe (OK)	1,284	87	321	963	97	241	406	304	35%	219	35%	213	34%

American Indian Policy

Table 3 — Continued

AREA, AGENCY, RESERVATION, & STATE	TOTAL	YEARS OF AGE			UNABLE TO WORK		LABOR FORCE STATUS, 16 YEARS OLD & OVER						
							EMPLOYED			NOT EMPLOYED, ABLE TO WORK			
		65 & Over	Under 16	16 & Over	Stu-dents	Others	Total	Earn $7000 +		Total		Seeking Work	
								Number	% of 16-65	Number	% of 7+10	Number	% of 7+12
	(1)	(2)	(3)	(4)	(5)	(6)	(7)	(8)	(9)	(10)	(11)	(12)	(13)
ANADARKO — Continued													
Shawnee Agency	[11,810]	[1,903]	[2,478]	[9,332]	[2,029]	[3,468]	[3,440]	[2,807]	[38%]	[395]	[11%]	[347]	[9%]
Absentee - Shawnee Tribe (OK)	1,384	208	290	1,094	183	451	407	357	40	53	11%	42	11%
Citizen Potawatomi Tribe (OK)	6,439	1,050	1,352	5,087	1,131	1,739	2,001	1,607	40	216	10%	198	9%
Iowa Tribe (OK)	210	31	44	166	35	44	75	55	41	12	L	8	L
Mexican Kickapoo Tribe (OK)	726	122	152	574	94	221	233	174	38	26	10%	21	8%
Sac & Fox Tribe (OK)	1,379	224	289	1,090	173	449	413	354	41	55	12%	49	11%
Other Tribes * (OK)	1,672	268	351	1,321	413	564	311	260	25	33	10%	29	8%

NOTES:

1. Data in brackets and parentheses non-add.

2. Percentages assigned to each State for Reservations extending into more than one State are based on the proportions of Indian populations in the 1980 census for the counties in which the Reservations are located.

3. L means base for percentage is less than 50; percentage not shown.

4. The Indians of other tribes (*) include the Five Civilized Tribes residing in areas under the jurisdiction of the Shawnee Agency.

Table 3 - Continued

AREA, AGENCY, RESERVATION, & STATE	TOTAL	YEARS OF AGE			LABOR FORCE STATUS, 16 YEARS OLD & OVER								
		65 & Over	Under 16	16 & Over	UNABLE TO WORK		EMPLOYED			NOT EMPLOYED, ABLE TO WORK			
					Students	Others	Total	Earn $7000 + Number	% of 16-65	Total Number	% of 7+10	Seeking Work Number	% of 7+12
	(1)	(2)	(3)	(4)	(5)	(6)	(7)	(8)	(9)	(10)	(11)	(12)	(13)
BILLINGS (MT,WY)	29,527	1,233	10,059	19,468	2,830	3,400	5,378	4,076	22%	7,860	59%	4,608	46%
Blackfeet Agcy. & Res. (MT)	6,555	340	2,073	4,482	621	295	1,682	1,128	27%	1,884	53%	471*	22%
Crow Agcy. & Res. (MT)	5,288	182	1,993	3,295	391	851	724	517	17%	1,329	65%	1,063	59%
Fort Belknap Agcy. & Res. (MT)	2,223	94	718	1,505	243	50	326	326	23%	886	73%	355	52%
Fort Peck Agcy. & Res. (MT)	5,022	238	1,682	3,340	495	815	1,076	844	27%	954	47%	820	43%
No. Cheyenne Agcy. & Res. (MT)	3,197	126	1,139	2,058	20	257	767	644	33%	1,014	57%	700	48%
Rocky Boys Agcy. & Res. (MT)	1,857	64	760	1,097	165	146	221	195	19%	565	72%	300	58%
Wind River Agcy. & Res. (WY)	5,385	189	1,694	3,691	895	986	582	422	12%	1,228	68%	899	61%

NOTES:

1. Flathead Agency previously listed under jurisdiction of this Area is now listed under the jurisdiction of the Portland Area.

2. Asterisked number indicates a Central Office estimate of incomplete data.

Table 3 - Continued

190   **American Indian Policy**

AREA, AGENCY, RESERVATION, & STATE	TOTAL	YEARS OF AGE			LABOR FORCE STATUS, 16 YEARS OLD & OVER								
					UNABLE TO WORK		EMPLOYED			NOT EMPLOYED, ABLE TO WORK			
		65 & Over	Under 16	16 & Over	Stu-dents	Others	Total	Earn $7000+ Number	% of 16-65	Total Number	% of 7+10	Seeking Work Number	% of 7+12
	(1)	(2)	(3)	(4)	(5)	(6)	(7)	(8)	(9)	(10)	(11)	(12)	(13)
EASTERN (FL,LA,ME,MS,NY,NC)	26,524	1,744	8,347	18,177	2,286	3,576	6,322	3,617	22%	5,993	49%	4,076	39%
Area Field Offices	[2,756]	[128]	[1,039]	[1,717]	[184]	[315]	[559]	[367]	[23%]	[599]	[46%]	[375]	[36%]
Houlton Band of													
Maliseet Indians (ME)	245	5	110	135	7	42	36	11	8%	50	58%	50	58%
Indian Township Passamaquoddy (ME)	406	14	168	238	15	69	77	62	28%	77	50%	20	21%
Miccosukee Res. (FL)	495	14	179	316	13	36	114	88	18%	153	57%	107	48%
Penobscot Reservation (ME)	1,029	62	360	669	108	131	328	135	22%	102	24%	84	20%
Pleasant Point Passamaquoddy (ME)	581	33	222	359	41	37	104	71	22%	177	63%	114	52%
Cherokee Agency & Res. (NC)	5,971	424	1,819	4,152	884	710	1,092	828	22%	1,466	57%	659	38%
Choctaw Agency	[5,204]	[190]	[2,003]	[3,201]	[245]	[559]	[1,624]	[834]	[28%]	[773]	[32%]	[406]	[20%]
Chitimacha Reservation (LA)	325	19	111	214	12	60	99	86	44%	43	30%	19	16%
Choctaw Reservation (MS)	4,487	147	1,750	2,737	213	418	1,428	677	26%	678	32%	352	20%
Coushatta Reservation (LA)	326	22	120	206	17	74	76	60	33%	39	34%	26	25%
Tunica-Biloxi Tribe (LA)	66	2	22	44	3	7	21	11	26%	13	L	9	L
New York Liaison Office	[11,167]	[935]	[2,942]	[8,225]	[872]	[1,885]	[2,463]	[1,260]	[17%]	[3,005]	[55%]	[2,502]	[50%]
Cayuga Nation (NY)	408	20	90	318	32	24	196	125	42%	66	25%	66	25%
Oneida Tribe (NY)	166*	13*	52*	114*	16*	25*	43*	21*	21%	30*	41%	14*	25%
Onondaga Reservation (NY)	631*	50*	173*	458*	56*	114*	181*	88*	22%	107*	37%	53*	23%
St. Regis Mohawk Res. (NY)	2,879	262	615	2,264	350	406	426	120	6%	1,082	72%	1,082	72%
Seneca Nation-Allegany and Cattaraugus Reservation (NY)	5,536	370	1,580	3,956	282	1,040	1,172	689	19%	1,462	56%	1,159	50%
Tonawanda Reservation (NY)	622*	49*	218*	404*	49*	100*	161*	78*	22%	94*	37%	46*	18%
Tuscarora Reservation (NY)	925*	171*	214*	711*	87*	176*	284*	139*	26%	164*	37%	82*	23%

Table 3 - Continued

AREA, AGENCY, RESERVATION, & STATE	TOTAL	YEARS OF AGE			LABOR FORCE STATUS, 16 YEARS OLD & OVER								
					UNABLE TO WORK		EMPLOYED			NOT EMPLOYED, ABLE TO WORK			
										Total		Seeking Work	
		65 & Over	Under 16	16 & Over	Stu-dents	Others	Total	Earn $7000 + Number	% of 16-65	Number	% of 7+10	Number	% of 7+12
	(1)	(2)	(3)	(4)	(5)	(6)	(7)	(8)	(9)	(10)	(11)	(12)	(13)
EASTERN - Continued													
Seminole Agency (FL)	1,426	67	544	882	101	107	484	328	40%	190	28%	134	22%

NOTES:

1. Figures in brackets are non-add.

2. L means base for percentage is less than 50; no percentage shown.

3. Asterisked numbers indicate Bureau Central Office & New York State estimates of incomplete data.

4. The count for the Seminole Agency includes the Reservations of Big Cypress, Brighton, and Hollywood.

Table 3 - Continued

AREA, AGENCY, RESERVATION, & STATE	TOTAL	YEARS OF AGE			LABOR FORCE STATUS, 16 YEARS OLD & OVER								
		65 & Over	Under 16	16 & Over	UNABLE TO WORK		EMPLOYED			NOT EMPLOYED, ABLE TO WORK			
					Students	Others	Total	Earn $7000 + Number	% of 16-65	Total Number	% of 7+10	Seeking Work Number	% of 7+12
	(1)	(2)	(3)	(4)	(5)	(6)	(7)	(8)	(9)	(10)	(11)	(12)	(13)
JUNEAU (AK)	63,858	2,860	25,211	38,647	5,746	7,153	9,782	6,209	17%	15,966	62%	10,495	52%
Anchorage Agency	[20,968]	[940]	[8,278]	[12,690]	[1,885]	[2,350]	[3,212]	[2,039]	[17%]	[5,243]	62%	[3,445]	52%
Aleutian Pribilof Is. Assn-APIA	1,917	86	757	1,160	172	215	294	187	17%	479	62%	314	52%
Bristol Bay Native Assn. - BBNA	4,055	181	1,601	2,454	363	456	621	394	"	1,014	"	666	"
Cook Inlet Native Assn. - CINA	10,479	469	4,137	6,342	943	1,174	1,606	1,020	"	2,619	"	1,722	"
Copper River Native Assn. - CRNA	650	30	257	393	59	72	99	63	"	163	"	107	"
Kodiak Area Native & Assn. - KANA	2,514	113	992	1,522	226	282	385	244	"	629	"	413	"
North Pacific Rim & Assn. - NPRA	1,353	61	534	819	122	151	207	131	"	339	"	223	"
Bethel Agency	12,078	541	4,768	7,310	1,087	1,353	1,850	1,174	"	3,020	"	1,986	"
Fairbanks Agency	[10,578]	[473]	[4,176]	[6,402]	[953]	[1,184]	[1,620]	[1,028]	"	[2,645]	"	[1,739]	"
Barrow	3,979	178	1,571	2,408	358	446	609	386	"	995	"	654	"
Tanna Chiefs Conference	6,599	295	2,605	3,994	595	738	1,011	642	"	1,650	"	1,085	"
Nome Agency	[8,954]	[401]	[3,535]	[5,419]	[806]	[1,002]	[1,372]	[871]	"	[2,239]	"	[1,472]	"
Kawerak	4,483	200	1,770	2,713	403	502	687	436	"	1,121	"	737	"
Maniilaq	4,471	201	1,765	2,706	403	500	685	435	"	1,118	"	735	"
Southeast Agency	[11,280]	[505]	[4,454]	[6,826]	[1,015]	[1,264]	[1,728]	[1,097]	"	[2,819]	"	[1,853]	"
Tlingit & Haida (Centr. Council)	9,311	417	3,676	5,635	838	1,043	1,426	905	"	2,328	"	1,531	"
Sitka (Community Assn.)	1,969	88	778	1,191	177	221	302	192	"	491	"	322	"

NOTES: 1. Data in brackets are non-add.

2. In previous compilations the Native Associations listed under the jurisdiction of the Anchorage Agency corresponded to the following named Areas: APIA - Aleut; BBNA - Bristol Bay; CINA - Ahtna; KANA - Kodiak; NPRA - Chugah. Also Metlakatla Reservation previously under the jurisdiction of the Southeast Agency is listed now under the jurisdiction of the Portland Area Office.

3. Population for each area was derived from the 1980 Distribution of the Native population and the percentage applied to the population in the 1980 census increased by a factor of 1.3% - 1.5% reflecting the average annual population growth rate for the State.

Table 3 - Continued

AREA, AGENCY, RESERVATION, & STATE	TOTAL	YEARS OF AGE			LABOR FORCE STATUS, 16 YEARS OLD & OVER								
		65 & Over	Under 16	16 & Over	UNABLE TO WORK		EMPLOYED			NOT EMPLOYED, ABLE TO WORK			
					Students	Others	Total	Earn $7000+ Number	% of 16-65	Total Number	% of 7+10	Seeking Work Number	% of 7+12
	(1)	(2)	(3)	(4)	(5)	(6)	(7)	(8)	(9)	(10)	(11)	(12)	(13)
MINNEAPOLIS (IA, MI, MN, WI)	43,030	2,671	15,761	27,269	3,299	5,368	7,564	5,308	22%	11,038	59%	8,626	53%
Field Offices	[4,636]	[317]	[1,803]	[2,833]	[312]	[147]	[1,079]	[819]	[18%]	[1,295]	[54%]	[847]	[44%]
Lower Sioux Community (MN)	191	19	73	118	8	58	34	25	25%	18	35%	18	35%
Menominee Res. (WI)	3,373	237	1,284	2,089	248	22	842	650	35%	977	54%	541	39%
Prairie Island Ind. Com. (MN)	144	10	62	82	1	12	16	7	10%	53	77%	53	77%
Sac & Fox Community (IA)	662	28	285	377	43	24	100	88	25%	210	68%	205	67%
Shakopee Sioux Com. (MN)	131	8	46	85	6	9	54	32	42%	16	23%	16	23%
Upper Sioux Com. (MN)	135	15	53	82	6	22	33	17	25%	21	39%	14	L
Great Lakes Agency (WI)	[14,906]	[919]	[5,405]	[9,501]	[1,294]	[1,972]	[2,935]	[2,193]	[26%]	[3,300]	[53%]	[2,759]	[49%]
Bad River Res.	1,314	82	456	858	115	270	242	186	24%	231	49%	231	49%
Forest County Potawatomi Com.	451	13	188	263	27	89	32	21	8%	115	78%	98	75%
Lac Courte Oreilles Res. (1981 Data)	1,811	81	654	1,157	223	172	296	222	21%	466	61%	185	38%
Lac Du Flambeau Res.	1,500	69	577	923	109	167	320	276	32%	327	50%	304	49%
Mole Lake Res.	271	9	97	174	14	31	12	8	5%	117	91%	117	91%
Oneida Res.	4,393	373	1,577	2,816	428	735	949	712	29%	704	43%	633	40%
Red Cliff Res.	1,381	65	460	921	169	206	234	177	21%	312	57%	300	56%
St. Croix Res.	1,139	67	398	741	49	144	254	197	29%	294	54%	294	54%
Stockbridge-Munsee Res.	928	87	272	656	76	63	295	145	25%	222	43%	210	42%
Wisconsin-Winnebago Res. (1981 Data)	1,718	73	726	992	84	95	301	249	27%	512	63%	387	56%
Michigan Agency (MI)	[5,829]	[267]	[1,984]	[3,845]	[351]	[588]	[1,155]	[671]	[19%]	[1,751]	[60%]	[1,229]	[52%]
Bay Mills Res.	540	14	264	276	51	25	124	85	32%	76	38%	64	43%
Hannahville Res.	348	4	149	199	14	26	36	18	9%	123	77%	98	73%
Grand Traverse Band	834	78	168	666	10	40	294	160	27%	322	52%	130	31%
Isabella Res. (1981 Data)	768	24	307	461	71	35	132	82	19%	223	63%	207	61%
Keewenaw Bay Res.	1,027	35	334	693	120	101	139	83	13%	333	71%	240	63%
Sault Ste. Marie Tribe	2,312	112	762	1,550	85	361	430	243	17%	674	61%	490	52%

Table 3 - Continued

AREA, AGENCY, RESERVATION, & STATE	TOTAL	YEARS OF AGE			LABOR FORCE STATUS, 16 YEARS OLD & OVER								
		65 & Over	Under 16	16 & Over	UNABLE TO WORK		EMPLOYED			NOT EMPLOYED, ABLE TO WORK			
					Students	Others	Total	Earn $7000+ Number	% of 16-65	Total Number	% of 7+10	Seeking Work Number	% of 7+12
	(1)	(2)	(3)	(4)	(5)	(6)	(7)	(8)	(9)	(10)	(11)	(12)	(13)
MINNEAPOLIS (Continued)													
Minnesota Agency (MN)	[12,877]	[926]	[4,599]	[8,278]	[992]	[2,067]	[1,709]	[1,170]	[17%]	[3,510]	[67%]	[3,291]	[66%]
Fond Du Lac Res.	1,497	83	549	948	154	142	387	231	27%	265	41%	250	39%
Grand Portage Res.	321	30	107	214	5	75	76	63	34%	58	43%	58	43%
Leech Lake Res.	4,838	315	1,855	2,983	380	846	526	388	15%	1,231	70%	1,231	70%
Mille Lacs Res.	897	71	371	526	15	95	205	138	30%	211	51%	99	33%
Net Lake Res.	1,449	90	400	1,049	90	347	220	120	13%	392	64%	300	58%
White Earth Res.	3,875	337	1,317	2,558	348	562	295	230	10%	1,353	82%	1,353	82%
Red Lake Agcy. & Res. (MN)	4,782	242	1,970	2,812	350	594	686	455	18%	1,182	63%	500	42%

NOTES:

1. Data in brackets non-add.

2. L means base for percentage is less than 50; no percentage shown.

Table 3 - Continued

AREA, AGENCY, RESERVATION, & STATE	TOTAL	YEARS OF AGE			LABOR FORCE STATUS, 16 YEARS OLD & OVER								
					UNABLE TO WORK			EMPLOYED		NOT EMPLOYED, ABLE TO WORK			
		65 & Over	Under 16	16 & Over	Stu-dents	Others	Total	Number	Earn $7000+ % of 16-65	Total Number	% of 7+10	Seeking Work Number	% of 7+12
	(1)	(2)	(3)	(4)	(5)	(6)	(7)	(8)	(9)	(10)	(11)	(12)	(13)
MUSKOGEE (OK)	124,869	12,291	39,790	85,079	12,590	19,188	43,270	21,488	30%	10,031	23%	4,199	9%
Ardmore Agcy. (Chickasaw Tribe)	8,757	942	2,244	6,513	1,350	1,582	2,685	1,774	32%	896	25%	862	24%
Miami Agency	[3,983]	[294]	[1,244]	[2,739]	[328]	[462]	[1,736]	[1,512]	[62%]	[213]	[11%]	[190]	[10%]
Eastern Shawnee Tribe	349	20	115	234	30	43	145	128	60%	16	10%	14	9%
Miami Tribe	364	23	128	236	33	54	132	122	57%	17	11%	16	11%
Modoc Tribe	156	8	61	95	10	11	67	60	69%	7	9%	7	9%
Ottawa Tribe	349	45	109	240	29	61	134	117	60%	16	11%	15	10%
Peoria Tribe	369	45	96	273	36	60	153	135	59%	24	16%	20	12%
Quapaw Tribe	1,241	59	371	870	86	88	621	562	69%	75	11%	65	9%
Seneca-Cayuga Tribe	697	47	181	516	69	81	326	260	55%	40	11%	36	10%
Wyandotte Tribe	458	47	183	275	35	64	158	128	56%	18	10%	17	10%
Okmulgee Agcy. (Creek Tribe)	39,432	1,921	15,226	24,206	3,702	5,301	12,132	7,339	33%	3,071	20%	763	6%
Osage Agcy. & Tribe	5,999	762	1,526	4,473	480	1,243	2,243	2,204	59%	507	18%	129	5%
Tahlequah Agcy. (Cherokee Tribe)	42,992	4,815	13,671	29,321	4,077	4,054	17,085	4,771	19%	4,105	19%	1,323	7%
Talihina Agcy. (Choctaw Tribe)	19,913	3,178	4,779	15,134	2,369	5,803	5,917	2,784	23%	1,045	15%	887	13%
Wewoka Agcy. (Seminole Tribe)	3,793	379	1,100	2,693	284	743	1,472	1,104	48%	194	12%	45	3%

NOTES:

1. Data in parentheses - non-add.

Table 3 - Continued

AREA, AGENCY, RESERVATION, & STATE	TOTAL	YEARS OF AGE			LABOR FORCE STATUS, 16 YEARS OLD & OVER								
					UNABLE TO WORK		EMPLOYED			NOT EMPLOYED, ABLE TO WORK			
		65 & Over	Under 16	16 & Over	Stu-dents	Others	Total	Earn $7000+ Number	% of 16-65	Total Number	% of 7+10	Seeking Work Number	% of 7+12
	(1)	(2)	(3)	(4)	(5)	(6)	(7)	(8)	(9)	(10)	(11)	(12)	(13)
NAVAJO (AZ,NM,UT)	158,917	8,138	50,895	108,022	13,278	10,651	34,894	29,678	30%	49,199	59%	28,155	45%
Chinle Agency (AZ)	23,629	1,050	6,630	16,999	2,686	3,131	2,510	2,408	15%	8,672	78%	5,637	69%
Eastern Navajo Agcy. (NM)	33,247	2,021	6,581	26,666	2,560	1,160	14,758	13,558	55%	8,188	36%	3,737	20%
Fort Defiance Agcy. (AZ)	40,360	2,195	15,160	25,200	1,611	3,081	5,438	4,810	21%	15,070	73%	7,500	58%
Shiprock Agcy. (NM,UT)	31,591	1,619	10,460	21,131	3,269	2,586	6,408	5,678	29%	8,868	58%	4,979	44%
Est. NM Pt. (91%)	(28,748)	(1,473)	(9,519)	(19,229)	(2,975)	(2,353)	(5,831)	(5,167)	(29%)	(8,070)	(58%)	(4,531)	(44%)
Est. UT Pt. (9%)	(2,843)	(146)	(941)	(1,902)	(294)	(233)	(577)	(511)	(29%)	(798)	(58%)	(448)	(44%)
Western Navajo Agcy. (AZ,UT)	30,090	1,253	12,064	18,026	3,152	693	5,780	3,224	19%	8,401	59%	6,302	52%
Est. AZ Pt. (95%)	(28,585)	(1,190)	(11,461)	(17,124)	(2,994)	(658)	(5,491)	(3,063)	(19%)	(7,981)	(59%)	(5,987)	(52%)
Est. UT Pt. (5%)	(1,505)	(63)	(603)	(902)	(158)	(35)	(289)	(161)	(19%)	(420)	(59%)	(315)	(52%)

NOTES:

1. Data in parentheses - non-add.

2. Percentages assigned to each State for Reservations extending into more than one State are based on the proportions of Indian populations in the 1980 census for the counties in which the Reservation is located.

Table 3 - Continued

AREA, AGENCY, RESERVATION, & STATE	TOTAL	YEARS OF AGE			UNABLE TO WORK		LABOR FORCE STATUS, 16 YEARS OLD & OVER						
							EMPLOYED			NOT EMPLOYED, ABLE TO WORK			
										Total		Seeking Work	
		65 & Over	Under 16	16 & Over	Stu-dents	Others	Total	Earn $7000 + Number	% of 16-65	Number	% of 7+10	Number	% of 7+12
	(1)	(2)	(3)	(4)	(5)	(6)	(7)	(8)	(9)	(10)	(11)	(12)	(13)
PHOENIX - (AZ,CA,ID,NV,UT)	76,251	3,763	28,305	47,946	5,084	11,044	18,105	9,934	22%	13,713	43%	7,432	29%
Colorado River Agency	[2,829]	[112]	[1,096]	[1,733]	[201]	[259]	[713]	[642]	40%	[560]	[44%]	[292]	[29%]
Chemehuevi Res. (CA)	144	4	56	88	2	15	31	19	23%	40	56%	28	47%
Colorado River Res. (AZ,CA)	2,139	95	850	1,289	174	207	580	580	49%	328	36%	200	26%
Est. AZ Pt. (98%)	(2,096)	(93)	(833)	(1,263)	(170)	(203)	(568)	(568)	(49%)	(322)	(36%)	(196)	(26%)
Est. CA Pt. (2%)	(43)	(2)	(17)	(26)	(4)	(4)	(12)	(12)	(49%)	(6)	(36%)	(4)	(26%)
Fort Mojave Res. (AZ,CA)	546	13	190	356	25	37	102	43	13%	192	65%	64	39%
Est. AZ Pt. (37%)	(202)	(5)	(70)	(132)	(9)	(14)	(38)	(16)	(13%)	(71)	(65%)	(24)	(39%)
Est. CA Pt. (63%)	(344)	(8)	(120)	(224)	(16)	(23)	(64)	(27)	(13%)	(121)	(65%)	(40)	(39%)
Eastern Nevada Agency	[2,920]	[197]	[944]	[1,976]	[146]	[316]	[564]	[430]	[24%]	[950]	[63%]	[828]	[59%]
Battle Mt. Colony & City (NV)	200	24	42	158	12	39	33	16	12%	74	69%	74	69%
Duck Valley Res. (ID, NV)	1,496	83	368	1,128	53	96	272	226	22%	707	72%	624	69%
Est. ID Pt. (20%)	(299)	(17)	(74)	(225)	(11)	(19)	(54)	(45)	(22%)	(141)	(72%)	(125)	(69%)
Est. NV Pt. (80%)	(1,197)	(66)	(294)	(903)	(42)	(77)	(218)	(181)	(22%)	(566)	(72%)	(499)	(69%)
Duckwater Res. (NV)	136	18	45	91	11	19	39	32	44%	22	36%	22	36%
Elko Colony & City (NV)	468	24	203	265	33	55	127	98	41%	50	28%	35	22%
Ely Colony & City (NV)	208	15	116	92	24	23	24	14	18%	21	47%	21	47%
Goshute Res. (NV, UT)	211	11	109	102	6	37	24	17	19%	35	59%	20	L
Est. Neveda Pt. (24%)	(50)	(3)	(26)	(24)	(1)	(9)	(6)	(4)	(19%)	(8)	(59%)	(5)	L
Est. Utah Pt. (76%)	(161)	(8)	(83)	(78)	(5)	(28)	(18)	(13)	(19%)	(27)	(59%)	(15)	L
South Fork (NV)	123	15	30	93	3	36	31	20	26%	23	43%	14	L
Wells Indian Colony (NV)	78	7	31	47	4	11	14	7	L	18	L	18	L
Fort Apache Agcy. & Res. (AZ)	8,140	276	2,874	5,266	311	1,323	2,335	1,335	27%	1,297	36%	600	20%
Fort McDowell F.O.	[1,156]	[62]	[484]	[672]	[89]	[141]	[217]	[77]	[13%]	[225]	[51%]	[203]	[48%]
Fort McDowell Res. (AZ)	387	29	195	192	30	27	67	32	20%	68	50%	68	50%
Pasqua Yaqui Res. (AZ)	769	33	289	480	59	114	150	45	10%	157	51%	135	47%

Table 3 - Continued

Page 16 of 22

198

American Indian Policy

ARF, AGENCY, RESERVATION, & STATE	TOTAL	YEARS OF AGE			UNABLE TO WORK		LABOR FORCE STATUS, 16 YEARS OLD & OVER						
							EMPLOYED			NOT EMPLOYED, ABLE TO WORK			
		65 & Over	Under 16	16 & Over	Stu-dents	Others	Total	Earn $7000 + Number	% of 16-65	Total Number	% of 7+10	Seeking Work Number	% of 7+12
	(1)	(2)	(3)	(4)	(5)	(6)	(7)	(8)	(9)	(10)	(11)	(12)	(13)
PHOENIX - Continued													
Fort Yuma Agency	[2,819]	[126]	[699]	[2,120]	[90]	[258]	[950]	[395]	[20%]	[822]	[46%]	[375]	[28%]
Cocopah Res. (AZ)	869	41	233	636	20	34	270	110	18%	312	54%	175	39%
Quechan Res. (CA)	1,950	85	466	1,484	70	224	680	285	20%	510	43%	200	23%
Hopi Agency	[8,945]	[669]	[3,915]	[5,030]	[947]	[1,379]	[1,400]	[544]	[12%]	[1,304]	[48%]	[686]	[33%]
Hopi Res. (AZ)	8,755	660	3,813	4,942	939	1,363	1,363	520	12%	1,277	48%	668	33%
Kaibab Res. (AZ)	190	9	102	88	8	16	37	24	30%	27	42%	18	33%
Papago Agency (1981 Data)	[17,651]	[916]	[5,708]	[11,943]	[891]	[2,865]	[6,147]	[2,563]	[23%]	[2,040]	[25%]	[1,257]	[17%]
Gila Band Res. (AZ)	760	26	272	488	52	131	218	82	18%	87	28%	60	22%
Papago Res. Sells (AZ)	10,610	660	3,363	7,247	604	1,751	3,542	1,466	22%	1,350	28%	707	17%
San Xavier Res. (AZ)	6,281	230	2,073	4,208	235	983	2,387	1,015	26%	603	20%	490	17%
Pima Agency	[10,198]	[435]	[4,755]	[5,443]	[703]	[1,628]	[1,943]	[1,283]	[26%]	[1,169]	[37%]	[697]	[26%]
Ak-Chin (Maricopa) Res. (AZ)	414	19	171	243	31	72	101	54	24%	39	17%	25	20%
Gila River Res. (AZ)	9,784	416	4,584	5,200	672	1,556	1,842	1,229	26%	1,130	38%	672	27%
Salt River Agcy. & Res. (AZ)	4,085	146	1,583	2,502	472	521	785	470	20%	724	48%	311	28%
San Carlos Agcy. & Res. (AZ)	6,695	267	2,501	4,194	462	1,367	743	615	16%	1,622	69%	624	46%
Truxton Canyon Agency	[2,207]	[115]	[879]	[1,328]	[150]	[282]	[405]	[263]	[22%]	[491]	[55%]	[423]	[51%]
Camp Verde (Yav.-Apa.) Res. (AZ)	519	44	206	313	34	112	103	69	26%	64	38%	60	37%
Havasupai Res. (AZ)	426	23	159	267	16	42	123	86	35%	86	41%	56	31%
Hualapai Res. (AZ)	1,083	41	452	631	87	108	124	73	12%	312	71%	283	69%
Payson (Tonto-Apa.) Res. (AZ)	103	3	44	59	2	16	25	9	16%	16	L	16	L
Prescott (Yav. Pres.-Ap) Res. (AZ)	76	4	18	58	11	4	30	26	48%	13	L	8	L
Uintah & Quray Agency	[2,318]	[87]	[881]	[1,437]	[125]	[284]	[479]	[327]	[24%]	[549]	[53%]	[83]	[15%]
Skull Valley Res. (UT)	74	3	31	43	10	14	14	11	L	5	L	3	L
Uintah & Quray Res. (UT)	2,244	84	850	1,394	115	270	465	316	24%	544	54%	80	15%

Table 3 - Continued

AREA, AGENCY, RESERVATION, & STATE	TOTAL	YEARS OF AGE			UNABLE TO WORK		LABOR FORCE STATUS, 16 YEARS OLD & OVER						
							EMPLOYED			NOT EMPLOYED, ABLE TO WORK			
		65 & Over	Under 16	16 & Over	Students	Others	Total	Earn $7000+ Number	% of 16-65	Total Number	% of 7+10	Seeking Work Number	% of 7+12
	(1)	(2)	(3)	(4)	(5)	(6)	(7)	(8)	(9)	(10)	(11)	(12)	(13)
Utah-Paiute F.O.													
Paiute Indian Tribe of Utah (UT)	313	9	99	214	49	63	49	33	16%	53	52%	41	45%
PHOENIX - Continued													
Western Nevada Agency	[5,975]	[346]	[1,887]	[4,088]	[448]	[358]	[1,375]	[957]	[26%]	[1,907]	[58%]	[1,012]	[42%]
Fallon Res. (NV)	654	43	125	529	129	29	215	112	23%	156	42%	92	30%
Fort McDermitt Res. (NV)	675	32	216	459	29	27	27	11	3%	376	93%	376	93%
Las Vegas Res. (NV)	74	7	26	48	7	11	10	8	L	20	47%	20	L
Lovelock Res. (NV)	192	12	81	111	9	43	31	23	23%	28	47%	18	L
Moapa Res. (NV)	278	6	117	161	20	1	44	30	19%	96	69%	24	35%
Pyramid Lake Res. (NV)	1,238	53	446	792	77	46	314	247	33%	355	53%	40	11%
Reno-Sparks Res. (NV)	675	44	183	492	11	45	169	158	35%	267	61%	90	35%
Walker River Res. (NV)	996	70	309	687	90	82	315	171	28%	200	39%	144	31%
Washoe Tribe (CA,NV)	(547)	(30)	(205)	(342)	(40)	(5)	(144)	(125)	(40%)	(153)	(51%)	(89)	(38%)
Carson Colony (NV)	199	16	70	129	12	1	63	55	49%	53	46%	35	36%
Dresslerville Colony (NV)	172	5	71	101	17	3	49	40	42%	32	39%	16	25%
Woodfords Colony (CA)	176	9	64	112	11	1	32	30	29%	68	68%	38	54%
Winnemucca Res. (NV)	96	3	26	70	12	8	23	16	24%	27	L	8	L
Yerrington Res. (NV)	400	39	96	304	24	50	57	32	12%	173	75%	55	49%
Yomba Res. (NV)	150	7	57	93	0	11	26	24	28%	56	68%	56	68%

NOTES:

1. Figures in brackets and parentheses are non-add.

2. L means base for percentage is less than 50; no percentage shown.

Table 3 - Continued

AREA, AGENCY, RESERVATION, & STATE	TOTAL	YEARS OF AGE			UNABLE TO WORK		LABOR FORCE STATUS, 16 YEARS OLD & OVER						
							EMPLOYED			NOT EMPLOYED, ABLE TO WORK			
										Total		Seeking Work	
		65 & Over	Under 16	16 & Over	Stu-dents	Others	Total	Earn $7000+ Number	% of 16-65	Number	% of 7+10	Number	% of 7+12
	(1)	(2)	(3)	(4)	(5)	(6)	(7)	(8)	(9)	(10)	(11)	(12)	(13)
PORTLAND – (AK,ID,MT,OR,WA)	55,173	2,882	20,274	34,899	3,548	6,088	9,991	6,074	19%	15,272	60%	10,867	52%
Colville Agcy. & Res. (WA)	3,780	281	1,241	2,539	111	426	833	700	18%	1,169	58%	935	53%
Flathead Agcy. & Res. (MT)	3,225	39	1,677	1,548	112	344	752	359	24%	340	31%	301	29%
Fort Hall Agcy. & Res. (ID)	3,897	167	1,658	2,239	148	315	623	323	16%	1,153	65%	481	44%
Metlakatla F.O.; Anette Isl. Res. (AL)	1,112	39	407	705	86	83	209	200	30%	327	61%	327	61%
Northern Idaho Agcy.	[2,912]	[223]	[894]	[2,018]	[319]	[392]	[431]	[406]	[23%]	[876]	[67%]	[433]	[50%]
Coeur d'Alene Res. (ID)	833	74	198	635	59	137	128	122	22%	311	71%	155	55%
Kootenai Res. (ID)	111	5	29	82	10	24	17	10	13%	31	65%	21	55%
Nez Perce Res. (ID)	1,968	144	667	1,301	250	231	286	274	24%	534	65%	257	47%
Olympic Peninsula Agcy.	[7,616]	[443]	[2,677]	[4,939]	[515]	[701]	[1,736]	[936]	[21%]	[1,987]	[53%]	[1,678]	[49%]
Chehalis Res. (WA)	742	46	264	478	65	55	231	96	22%	127	35%	127	35%
Hoh Res. (WA)	72	3	30	42	0	1	17	4	10%	24	32%	4	L
Jamestown Clallam Tribe (WA)	336	36	89	247	6	84	106	97	46%	51	80%	46	30%
Lower Elwah Res. (WA)	1,189	58	363	826	47	72	141	53	7%	566	51%	430*	75%
Makah Res. (WA)	982	40	314	668	25	69	281	180	29%	293	58%	217	44%
Quileute Res. (WA)	326	6	134	192	10	17	69	29	16%	96	30%	30	30%
Quinault Res. (WA) (1981 Data)	2,013	165	744	1,269	243	238	554	294	15%	234		225	29%
Shoalwater Bay Res. (WA)	63	8	18	45	7	10	22	11	30%	6	L	6	L
Skokomish Res. (WA)	1,008	40	433	575	35	115	140	87	16%	285	67%	285	67%
Squaxin Island (WA)	885	38	288	597	77	40	175	85	34%	305	64%	305	64%

Table 3 - Continued

AREA, AGENCY, RESERVATION, & STATE	TOTAL	YEARS OF AGE			UNABLE TO WORK		LABOR FORCE STATUS, 16 YEARS OLD & OVER						
								EMPLOYED		NOT EMPLOYED		ABLE TO WORK	
		65 & Over	Under 16	16 & Over	Stu-dents	Others	Total	Earn $7000+ Number	% of 16-65	Total Number	% of 7+10	Seeking Work Number	Work % of 7+12
	(1)	(2)	(3)	(4)	(5)	(6)	(7)	(8)	(9)	(10)	(11)	(12)	(13)
PORTLAND - Continued													
Puget Sound Agcy.	[17,767]	[760]	[6,899]	[10,868]	[1,525]	[1,718]	[2,632]	[1,311]	[13%]	[4,993]	[65%]	[3,970]	[60%]
Lummi Res. (WA)	2,435	167	1,169	1,266	190	342	284	248	23%	486	40%	250	25%
Muckleshoot Res. (WA)	2,300	65	1,058	1,242	97	174	350	130	11%	621	64%	464	57%
Nisqually Res. (WA)	1,326	27	562	764	61	155	177	97	13%	371	68%	371	68%
Nooksack Res. (WA)	856	49	418	438	55	54	82	27	7%	247	75%	85	51%
Port Gamble Res. (WA)	490	13	101	389	17	82	84	77	20%	206	71%	150	64%
Port Madison Res. (WA)	534	46	159	375	20	139	156	83	25%	60	28%	60	28%
Puyallup Res. (WA)	6,990	245	2,390	4,600	966	427	981	245	6%	2,226	69%	2,003	67%
Sauk-Suiattle Res. (WA)	219	11	87	132	11	36	28	13	11%	57	67%	53	65%
Stillaguamish Res. (WA)	464	17	188	276	7	43	74	67	26%	152	67%	78	51%
Swinomish Res. (WA)	635	38	200	435	31	92	189	130	33%	123	39%	77	29%
Tulalip Res. (WA)	1,007	31	437	570	69	164	182	161	30%	155	46%	125	41%
Upper Skagit Res. (WA)	511	51	130	381	1	10	81	33	10%	289	78%	201	71%
Siletz Agcy. & Tribe (OR)	791	35	250	541	48	52	229	154	30%	212	48%	180	44%
Spokane Agency	[2,168]	[122]	[641]	[1,527]	[126]	[208]	[644]	[192]	[14%]	[549]	[46%]	[339]	[26%]
Kalispel Res. (WA) (1981 Data)	205	8	82	123	8	15	40	27	23%	60	60%	45	53%
Spokane Res. (WA)	1,963	114	559	1,404	118	193	604	165	13%	489	45%	294	33%
Umatilla Agcy. & Res.	1,500	103	541	959	165	176	277	117	14%	341	55%	139	33%
Warm Springs Agcy.	[2,010]	[56]	[756]	[1,254]	[113]	[313]	[484]	[300]	[25%]	[344]	[41%]	[295]	[38%]
Burns Paiute Res. (OR)	220	7	92	128	16	19	38	22	45%	55	59%	55	59%
Warm Springs Res. (OR)	1,790	49	664	1,126	97	294	446	278	26%	289	39%	240	35%
Yakima Agcy. & Res. (WA)	8,395	614	2,633	5,762	280	1,360	1,141	1,076	21%	2,981	72%	1,789	61%

NOTES:
1. Figures in brackets are non-add.
2. Asterisked numbers indicate Central Office estimates of incomplete or missing data.
3. The count for the Flathead Res. & the Anette Island Res. was previously included in the Billings & Juneau Area Offices compilations respectively.

Table 3 - Continued

AREA, AGENCY, RESERVATION, & STATE	TOTAL	YEARS OF AGE			UNABLE TO WORK		LABOR FORCE STATUS, 16 YEARS OLD & OVER						
								EMPLOYED		NOT EMPLOYED, ABLE TO WORK			
										Total		Seeking Work	
		65 & Over	Under 16	16 & Over	Stu-dents	Others	Total	Earn $7000+ Number	% of 16-65	Number	% of 7+10	Number	% of 7+12
	(1)	(2)	(3)	(4)	(5)	(6)	(7)	(8)	(9)	(10)	(11)	(12)	(13)
SACRAMENTO (CA)	20,968	1,244	6,621	14,347	1,293	1,990	3,677	2,240	17%	7,387	67%	4,689	56%
Central California Agency	[7,311]	[452]	[2,475]	[4,836]	[327]	[795]	[1,746]	[934]	[21%]	[1,968]	[53%]	[1,059]	[38%]
Alturas Rancheria	12	0	5	7	0	2	4	2	29%	1	L	0	L
Benton Paiute Reservation	48	9	19	29	3	18	2	2	L	3	L	3	L
Berry Creek Rancheria	154	6	61	93	0	6	49	12	14%	38	44%	24	33%
Big Pine Reservation	400	24	136	264	52	49	104	53	22%	59	36%	47	31%
Big Sandy Rancheria	131	15	50	81	7	7	25	11	17%	45	64%	19	L
Bishop Rancheria	1,016	80	276	740	78	109	362	212	32%	191	35%	159	31%
Bridgeport Reservation	81	7	19	62	4	6	21	14	25%	31	60%	29	58%
Cedarville Rancheria	14	2	3	9	1	4	2	0	L	2	L	2	L
Cold Springs Rancheria	210	13	92	118	10	2	62	23	22%	44	42%	9	13%
Colusa Rancheria	44	5	15	29	2	3	18	10	L	6	L	6	L
Cortina Rancheria	78	5	12	66	0	6	44	24	41%	16	27%	8	15%
Coyote Valley Rancheria	216	7	105	111	0	13	46	22	21%	52	53%	36	44%
Dry Creek Rancheria	126	9	48	78	0	17	50	28	40%	11	18%	11	18%
El-Em Indian Colony (1981 Data)	157	3	81	76	1	15	46	26	36%	14	23%	11	19%
Enterprise Reservation (1981 Data)	18	2	5	13	0	0	4	3	L	9	L	2	L
Fort Bidwell Reservation	182	13	64	118	11	34	36	10	10%	37	51%	24	40%
Fort Independence Reservation	90	3	30	60	3	6	15	12	44%	36	71%	20	L
Grindstone Rancheria	173	5	31	142	13	13	40	26	19%	86	68%	48	55%
Hopland Band	136	8	61	75	8	25	17	3	15%	25	L	14	L
Jackson Rancheria	19	1	5	14	8	2	4	3	L	3	L	0	L
Laytonville Rancheria	196	10	73	123	13	55	33	24	21%	22	40%	22	40%
Lone Pine Reservation	196	11	86	110	6	28	35	15	15%	41	54%	32	48%
Lookout Rancheria	13	1	3	10	2	2	0	0	L	7	L	2	L
Manchester Pt. Arena Rancheria	100	6	24	76	0	22	10	6	9%	44	81%	44	81%
Middletown Rancheria	62	5	11	51	1	10	24	12	L	16	L	6	L
North Fork Allotment (1981 Data)	29	8	13	16	4	4	5	5	L	7	L	0	L
Robinson Rancheria	68	5	33	35	0	18	3	0	L	14	L	11	L
Round Valley Reservation	749	35	315	434	25	81	114	42	11%	214	65%	205	64%
Rumsey Rancheria	47	1	20	27	2	11	14	8	L	0	L	0	L
Santa Rosa Rancheria	313	14	142	171	4	27	39	28	18%	101	72%	40	51%
Sherwood Valley Rancheria	173	6	49	124	18	8	60	35	30%	38	39%	16	21%

Table 3 - Continued

AREA, AGENCY, RESERVATION, & STATE	TOTAL	YEARS OF AGE			LABOR FORCE STATUS, 16 YEARS					OLD & OVER			
					UNABLE TO WORK		EMPLOYED			NOT EMPLOYED, ABLE TO WORK			
		65 & Over	Under 16	16 & Over	Stu-dents	Others	Total	Earn $7000+ Number	% of 16-65	Total Number	% of 7+10	Seeking Work Number	% of 7+12
	(1)	(2)	(3)	(4)	(5)	(6)	(7)	(8)	(9)	(10)	(11)	(12)	(13)
SACRAMENTO - Continued													
Central California Agency - Cont'd.													
Stewarts Point Rancheria	204	26	59	145	0	26	95	45	38%	24	20%	12	11%
Susanville Rancheria	376	8	135	241	31	77	75	26	11%	58	44%	29	28%
Table Mountain Reservation	78	7	22	56	4	19	16	15	31%	17	52%	17	52%
Tule River Reservation	566	18	215	351	4	27	116	67	20%	204	64%	52	31%
Tuolumne Rancheria	649	60	82	567	28	4	105	79	16%	430	80%	86	45%
Upper Lake Rancheria	133	7	66	67	0	23	32	12	20%	12	L	3	L
X-L Ranch Reservation (1981 Data)	54	7	7	47	5	16	16	12	L	10	L	10	L
Northern California Agency	[7,446]	[399]	[2,183]	[5,263]	[536]	[485]	[817]	[575]	[12%]	[3,425]	[81%]	[2,457]	[75%]
Big Bend Reservation	6	0	0	6	0	0	1	1	L	5	L	2	L
Big Lagoon Reservation	17	0	6	11	5	0	2	2	L	4	L	0	L
Hoopa Valley (Square) Res.	2,423	81	787	1,636	179	115	306	198	13%	1,036	77%	570	65%
Hoopa Extension (Yurok) Res.	1,850	138	465	1,385	85	60	187	160	13%	1,053	87%	900	85%
Montgomery Creek Rancheria	30	0	19	11	0	0	4	0	L	7	L	7	L
Orleans Karuk Tribe	2,096	122	571	1,525	136	227	221	179	13%	941	81%	612	73%
Resighini Rancheria	844	45	281	563	115	70	76	25	5%	302	80%	302	80%
Roaring Creek Rancheria	40	4	6	34	4	4	5	2	L	21	L	10	L
Table Buff Rancheria	71	5	21	50	6	5	7	2	L	32	L	30	L
Trinidad Rancheria	69	4	27	42	6	4	8	6	L	24	L	24	L
Palm Springs F.S. (Agua Caliente)	203	3	68	135	18	50	30	30	23%	37	55%	0	L
Southern California Agency	[6,008]	[390]	[1,895]	[4,113]	[412]	[660]	[1,084]	[701]	[19%]	[1,957]	[64%]	[1,173]	[52%]
Barona Reservation	304	7	136	168	21	49	40	30	19%	58	59%	47	54%
Cabazon Reservation	25	0	7	18	0	0	16	13	L	2	L	1	L
Cahuilla Reservation (1981 Data)	148	8	51	97	2	13	28	22	25%	54	66%	15	L
Campo Reservation	213	23	102	111	8	32	27	18	20%	44	62%	44	62%
Cuyapaipe Reservation	25	2	7	18	0	7	7	3	L	4	L	3	L
Inaja-Cosmit Reservation	10	0	3	7	0	0	3	3	L	1	L	1	L
Jamul Reservation	66	2	25	41	0	3	11	8	21%	20	L	10	L
LaJolla Reservation	246	17	94	152	17	24	59	39	29%	52	47%	47	44%
LaPosta Reservation	14	0	9	5	1	0	2	0	L	2	L	1	L

Table 3 - Continued

		YEARS OF AGE			LABOR FORCE STATUS, 16 YEARS OLD & OVER								
	TOTAL				UNABLE TO WORK		EMPLOYED			NOT EMPLOYED, ABLE TO WORK			
AREA, AGENCY, RESERVATION, & STATE		65 & Over	Under 16	16 & Over	Stu-dents	Others	Total	Earn $7000+ Number	% of 16-65	Total Number	% of 7+10	Seeking Work Number	% of 7+12
	(1)	(2)	(3)	(4)	(5)	(6)	(7)	(8)	(9)	(10)	(11)	(12)	(13)
SACRAMENTO - Continued													
Southern Calif. Agency - Cont'd.													
Los Coyotes Reservation	185	5	60	125	12	20	34	12	10%	59	63%	49	59%
Manzanita Reservation	40	4	18	22	10	4	6	2	L	2	L	0	L
Mesa Grande Reservation	28	4	7	21	1	5	12	9	L	3	L	1	L
Morongo Reservation	743	40	215	528	82	75	183	127	26%	188	51%	120	40%
Pala Reservation (1981 Data)	455	24	139	316	30	82	156	154	53%	48	23%	23	13%
Pauma Reservation	107	2	41	66	21	12	22	22	34%	11	33%	5	19%
Pechanga Reservation	433	27	152	281	9	77	45	20	8%	150	77%	29	39%
Ramona Reservation	3	0	0	3	0	0	2	1	L	1	L	0	L
Rincon Reservation	390	23	153	237	27	30	60	22	10%	120	67%	120	67%
San Manuel Reservation	89	1	31	58	10	12	18	13	23%	18	L	14	L
San Pasqual Res. (1981 Data)	347	70	99	248	8	50	45	19	11%	145	75%	25	36%
Santa Rosa Reservation	107	3	40	67	0	9	19	16	25%	39	67%	39	67%
Santa Inez Reservation	195	15	78	117	20	28	45	28	6%	24	35%	24	35%
Santa Ysabel Reservation	892	79	69	823	11	17	79	41	6%	716	90%	420	84%
Soboba Reservation	555	22	189	366	102	29	114	42	12%	121	51%	60	34%
Sycuan Reservation	72	0	30	42	5	14	19	19	L	4	L	4	L
Torres-Martinez Reservation	81	2	46	35	14	5	12	7	L	4	L	4	L
Twenty-Nine Palms Reservation	18	2	8	10	1	5	4	3	L	0	L	0	L
Viejas Reservation	217	8	86	131	0	48	16	8	6%	67	81%	67	81%

NOTES:

1. Figures in brackets non-add.

2. L means base for percentage is less then 50; no percentage shown.

APPENDIX C

STATUS OF NONINTERCOURSE ACT CLAIMS

Connecticut

Suits filed in Connecticut seeking recovery of lands allegedly alienated in violation of the Trade and Intercourse Act are still pending for:

(1) the Schaghticoke tribe for several thousand acres of land (1975);
(2) the Western Pequot tribe (1976);
(3) the *Mohegan Tribe* v. *Zaugg* (1977); and
(4) the *Mohegan Tribe* v. *the State of Connecticut* (1977)

In the second instance legislation was passed by the Congress in 1982 but was vetoed on April 5, 1983. A slightly modified bill was reintroduced in the summer of 1983 after discussion with the Office of Management and Budget and it is expected to pass and be signed by the President. In the fourth instance the district court ruled that the Trade and Intercourse Act was applicable. On appeal the district court was upheld, and the Supreme Court denied certiorari. The state had contended that the Trade and Intercourse Act was not intended to apply to Indians such as the Mohegan who, it was alleged, had never resided in Indian country as defined by Federal law.

Florida

In 1978 the Seminole tribe of Florida sued for 16,000 acres, and in 1979 the Muccosukee tribe sued for about 5 million acres under the Trade and Intercourse Act. On December 31, 1982, PL 97-399 (25 USC 1741) became law and completed a state settlement with the Miccosukee in which the state paid the tribe $1,000,000.

Louisiana

A 1977 suit filed by the Chitimacha tribe for 2,000 to 3,000 acres was dismissed by the district court in 1980. The Interior Department has recommended that the Department of Justice sue for 900 acres on behalf of the Chitimacha.

The Tunica-Biloxi tribe was recognized by the BIA in 1981, and the tribe has initiated negotiations for land under the Trade and Intercourse Act.

There has been no final action in either of these cases.

Maine

See chapter 2 of this book. PL 96-420 was signed by President Carter on October 10, 1980.

Massachusetts

In 1976 the Mashpee Tribe (Wampanoag) sought recovery of 17,000 acres alledgedly alienated in violation of the Trade and Intercourse Act. The courts decided the Mashpee were not an Indian tribe and therefore not subject to the act.

In 1974 the Wampanoag Tribe of Gay Head sought recovery of some 5,000 acres of land, and 1976 the Town of Gay Head voted to deed certain lands to the Indians. Some Indians have not agreed to the proposal, and final action must be approved by the state. This matter is still pending.

New York

Oneida. In 1970 the Oneida (New York, Wisconsin, and the Thomas Band Council of Ontario, Canada) sought damages for the use of 100,000 acres purchased by the state in 1795 without Federal approval. Although court action has held that the lands were illegally purchased and damages are due, no formal action has been taken. In 1979 the Oneida filed another suit claiming up to 5 million acres. There has been no final action on this suit.

Cayuga. The Cayuga Indian nation claim to 64,000 acres in New York resulted in a negotiated agreement giving the Cayuga a 5,481 acre reservation and an $8-million trust fund in return for extinguishment of the 64,000-acre claim. The land was to come from a state park and national forestland. In 1980 the House of Representatives failed to pass the legislation based on the negotiation, and the Cayuga filed suit for the return of the 64,000 acres and damages. This case is still pending and further negotiations are in progress.

St. Regis Mohawks. The St. Regis Mohawks have claimed land, and a proposed settlement in 1980 would have given them 9,750 acres of state land and a Federal trust fund of $7.5 million. No final action has been taken.

Rhode Island

Negotiations among the Narraganset Indians, the state of Rhode Island, the town of Charlestown (where claimed land was located), private landholders and representatives of the Carter administration resulted in an agreement that formed the basis for a Federal statute and companion state legislation. PL 95-395, passed on September 30, 1978, provided for the extinguishment of all Narraganset Indian land claims in exchange for approximately 1,800 acres of land—900 from the state and 900 acres to be purchased at Federal expense. A state corporation was created to acquire, hold, and manage the land. A settlement fund of $3.5 million was established in the U.S. Treasury to implement the act.

South Carolina

The Catawba Indian tribe claims 140,000 acres under the Trade and Intercourse Act, and a Federal task force was appointed in 1978 to develop a proposed legislative settlement. There has been no agreement to date. In 1980 the Catawba filed suit for the return of 140,000 acres and damages, the case is still pending.

Virginia

The Pamunkey Indians were successful in claiming 20 acres taken without Federal and state approval for a railroad right-of-way. The Southern Railway will pay the tribe $100,000 in return for the tribe's waiver of any claim for past trespass damages and for a right-of-way for ten years. After that time there would be a lease agreement. If the track were abandoned the land would revert to the Pamunkey.

Sources:
Richard S. Jones, "Indians, Land Claims by Eastern Tribes" (Washington, D.C.: Congressional Research Service, Library of Congress, Issue Brief no. 1B77040, January 15, 1981); telephone conversations with Tim Vollmann and Richard Jones, June 2, 1982; with Peter Taylor and Tim Vollmann on August 12, 1983.

APPENDIX D

STATEMENT BY BRADLEY H. PATTERSON
ON THE IRONY OF THE TRAIL
OF BROKEN TREATIES

There were some supremely ironic features surrounding the Trail of Broken Treaties and its shoddy march on Washington.

It was all unnecessary.

Beginning in the Fall of 1969, the White House was giving unprecedented attention to the problems of Native Americans. At least two White House officers and several in the Vice President's office were deeply involved in pushing for Indian policy reform. As a result, in July of 1970, the President had issued an eloquent Message to the Congress calling for history-making turnabouts: for Indian tribal self-government, for tribal and parental authority over Indian education, for tribally determined health and economic development programs, for protection of trust rights and for restoration of lost lands. The Congress had already enacted some of this legislation and the rest was pending in a sympathetic Congressional Committee.

In 1971, the White House Staff had convinced the President to reject the timid recommendations of OMB and of Interior, and to insist on a very generous Alaska Native Claims Settlement Act—which the Congress enacted that very year.

The most egregious of the "broken treaties" was the one of 1968 with the Sioux—and it was the Congress, exercising its indubitably plenary powers, which committed the injustice by ratifying a new treaty in the heat of the gold-rush and post-Custer emotion. The Sioux themselves were pursuing a legal claim in the Courts—and they were winning.

The leaders of the Trail of Broken Treaties were dissident Sioux—frustrated at not being able to vote the elected Tribal leaders out of office at Pine Ridge, and demanding that the claim action be stopped and that the whole, vast Black Hills area be restored to Indian ownership—a proposal that neither Congress nor the President nor any Court could honor.

All this is adduced to demonstrate what, in the White House view, was the basic point: the Trail of Broken Treaties was not a serious call for change; the needed changes were already taking place and at a faster pace and with the most high-level sponsorship in the history of American Indian Affairs. It was instead a media event—it was guerilla theater. Like the occupations of Alcatraz and of Wounded Knee, it was skillful guerilla theater in terms of its timing and location. As the years since have demonstrated in hundreds of tragic instances, the line between guerilla theater and terrorism is very thin—and now often crossed. It had been crossed in May of 1970 on the campus of Kent State University and the memory of the convulsions in America after the Kent State killings was very fresh in the minds of the responsible White House officers.

Some stolen art, some wrecked typewriters and some busted urinals in the BIA—could all be recouped, but the White House had learned the lessons of two and a half years before and was determined that the United States was not

going to witness another Kent State on Constitution Avenue . . . .
    Yet even as guerilla theater, it was all unnecessary.

Source: Transmitted to author by letter from Bradley H. Patterson, Jr., dated
February 3, 1982. Bradley Patterson represented the White House in many of
its relations with Trail leaders.

BIBLIOGRAPHY

American Indian Policy Review Commission *Final Report*, 2 vol, Washington, D.C.: GPO, 1977.

Arnold, Robert D. et al *Alaska Native Land Claims* Anchorage, Alaska: Alaska Native Foundation, 1978, revised edition.

Cohen, Felix S. *Handbook of Federal Indian Law, with Reference Tables and Index*. Washington, D.C.: Government Printing Office, 1942. Reprinted, Albuquerque: University of New Mexico Press, 1972. See also *Federal Indian Law* and Bernard Strickland for revisions of Cohen's Handbook.

Collier, John *Indians of the Americas*. New York: W. W. Norton, 1947. Collier was Commissioner of Indian Affairs longer than any other Commissioner.

Cushman, Dan *Stay Away, Joe*. Great Falls, Montana: Stay Away Joe Publishers, 1968, 4th ed. A fictional account of an extended Indian family showing various stages of acculturation among the different members. Other excellent fictional accounts are: Harry James *Red Man, White Man*. San Antonio, Texas: Naylor Co., 1957, Hal Glen Borland *When the Legends Die*. New York: J. B. Lippincott Co., 1963, and Thomas Berger *Little Big Man*. New York: The Dial Press, 1964. These books are written by keen observers of the acculturation drama and pathos and give a flavor based on real life which will be helpful to readers who have not had first hand experience is Indian communities.

Deloria, Vine, Jr. *Custer Died for Your Sins*. New York: The Macmillan Co., 1969. A "biting" and "witty" analysis of the causes for and present condition of the American Indian as interpreted by a Sioux Indian. He discusses the problems of Indian leadership, predicts that urban Indians will become the leaders of the Indian movement, and presents a "redefinition" of Indian affairs.

Federal and State Indian Reservations and Indian Trust Areas. Washington, D.C.: United States Department of Commerce, 1974. This is a convenient reference for tribes with Federal or state reservations, organized by state, indicating: number of Indians residing on or adjacent to reservation; labor force and percent of unemployment; average grade level achieved in school; brief history of tribe; short statements on culture, government, economy, climate, transportation, community facilities, and recreation. Does not include Catawba land in South Carolina.

Federal Indian Law. Washington, D.C.: U.S. Department of the Interior, 1958. A revision and updating of Felix Cohen's *Handbook* reflecting the views and policies of the 1950s.

Hagan, William T. *American Indians*, revised edition. Chicago: University of Chicago Press, 1979. This is a brief, readable, and perceptive history of the relations between the Indians and the United States, including the clash of cultures, and relating this clash to the mainstream of American history.

Hodge, Frederick Webb, ed. *Handbook of American Indians North of Mexico*, 2 vols. Washington, D.C.: Smithsonian Institution, Bureau of American Ethnology, Bull. 30, Reprinted, New York: Roman and Littlefield, 1971.

Josephy, Alvin M., Jr. *The Indian Heritage of America*. New York: Alfred A. Knopf, 1968. Presents the archeology, ethnology, and history of the tribes and cultures of the Indians of North and South America from prehistoric times to the present day.

Kappler, Charles J., comp. *Indian Affairs: Laws and Treaties*. 7 vols. Washington, D.C.: Government Printing Office, 1904. Volume 2 contains Indian Treaties.

McNickle, D'Arcy. *Native American Tribalism: Indian Survivals and Renewals*. New York: Oxford University Press, 1973.

Meriam, Lewis, and others. *The Problem of Indian Administration*. Institute for Government Research, Studies in Administration. Baltimore: Johns Hopkins Press, 1928. A survey of the economic, social, educational, health, and other conditions of the American Indians, with a view of what remained to be done to improve services and help the Indians adjust to the prevailing civilization.

Miller, George Frederick. *A Wild Indian*. Washington, D.C.: The Daylion Co., 1942 (Printed by Mt. Vernon Publishing Co., Washington, D.C.) Published anonymously. Miller was one of seven supervisors of Indian education in 1929. His novel reflects the Indian-Agent relationship and presents a description of Indian school operations, the vagaries of policy changes and directives from Washington, and the frustration of the field personnel with the Washington attempts to upgrade services. Many parallels can be seen between this description of the 1920s and 1930s and today.

Prucha, Francis Paul. *American Indian Policy in Crisis: Christian Reformers and the Indian, 1865-1900*. Norman: University of Oklahoma Press, 1976. Prucha has also written about the Trade and Intercourse Acts, Indian policy in the 1840s, and Andrew Jackson's Indian policy in other works. Prucha is the author of *United States Indian Policy: A Critical Bibliography*, Bibliographical Series, The Newberry Library Center for the History of the American Indian. Bloomington: Indiana University Press, 1977.

Report of the Committee on Indian Affairs. Washington, D.C.: Commission on Organization of the Executive Branch of the Government (Hoover Commission) (Mimeograph) October 1948. A 345 page study by Charles J. Rhoads, John R. Nichols, Gilbert Darlington, and George A. Graham, Chairman, on which the majority report of the Hoover Commission based its conclusions. It is a thorough review of Indian programs and discusses the relationships of Indian tribes, states, and the Federal government.

Schmeckebier, Laurence F. *The Office of Indian Affairs: Its History, Activities, and Organization*. Institute for Government Research, Service Monographs of the United States Government, no. 48. Baltimore: Johns Hopkins Press, 1927. A detailed look at the functions and organization of the then Office of Indian Affairs.

Smith, Jane F. and Robert M. Kvasnicka, eds. *Indian-White Relations: A Persistent Paradox*. Washington, D.C.: Howard University Press, 1976. This book contains papers presented at the "National Archives Conference on Research in the History of Indian-White Relations," Washington, D.C., June 16, 1972.

Social Security, Education, Indian Affairs, A Report to the Congress. Washington, D.C.: Commission on Organization of the Executive Branch of the Government (Hoover Commission), March 1949. This report includes the Commission's recommendations and minority reports on Indian policy, reflecting the diverse views often posed in Indian policy considerations.

Sorkin, Alan L. *American Indians and Federal Aid*. Washington, D.C.: Brookings Institution, 1971. An analysis of the effectiveness of Federal aid programs.

Spicer, Edward H. *A Short History of the Indians of the United States*. New York: Van Nostrand-Reinhold Co., 1969. A good short history with some different materials than Hagan.

Steiner, Stan. *The New Indians*. New York: Harper and Row, 1968. A view of the "Red Power" movement.

Strickland, Bernard, et al *Felix S. Cohen's Handbook of Federal Indian Law*. Charlottesville, Va.: Michie Bobbs-Merrill, 1982. The most recent updating of Cohen's Handbook, done by Interior contract with the New Mexico School of Law and Board of Editors. Funding was provided by both the Department of Interior and private foundations.

Swanton, John R. *The Indian Tribes of North America*. Washington, D.C.: Smithsonian Institution, Bureau of American Ethnology, Bull. 145, 1952. A description of tribes and groups about 1650 organized on the boundaries of present states.

Taylor, Theodore W. *The Bureau of Indian Affairs*. Boulder, Co: Westview Press. In publication (1983).

Taylor, Theodore W. *The States and Their Indian Citizens*. Washington, D.C.: Department of the Interior, Bureau of Indian Affairs, 1972. Discusses the services transferred to the states and to the tribes by the Federal government and state organizations concerned with Indian affairs. Includes survey of tribal attitudes and 1970 census data on location of Indians.

Traces Federal policy as it pertains to transferring BIA functions to tribes and to states.

Tyler, S. Lyman. *A History of Indian Policy*. Washington, D.C.: Department of Interior, Bureau of Indian Affairs, 1973. A perceptive review of the history of Indian policy to 1972. Has a very complete bibliography on Indian materials to date of publication.

U.S. Congress. Senate. *Authorizing Funds for the Settlement of Indian Claims in the State of Maine: Report to Accompany S. 2829*. 96th Cong., 2d sess., Sept. 17, 1980. S. Rept. 96-957.

_____Senate. Select Committee on Indian Affairs. *Ancient Indian Land Claims: Hearing on S. 2084*. 97th Cong., 2d sess., June 28, 1982.

_____Senate. Select Committee on Indian Affairs. *Chitimacha and Mashantucket Pequot Indian Land Claims: Hearings on S. 2294 and S. 2719*. 97th Cong., 2d sess., July 14, 1982.

_____Senate. Select Committee on Indian Affairs. *Certain Indian Land Claims Within the State of Florida: Hearing on S. 2893*. 97th Cong., 2d sess., December 7, 1982.

Washburn, Wilcomb E. *The Indian in America*. New York: Harper and Row, 1975. This is the most recent general review of Indian history and Francis Paul Prucha says "in many respects the best".

Watkins, Arthur V. "Termination of Federal Supervision: The Removal of Restrictions over Indian Property and Person." *Annals of the American Academy of Political and Social Science* 311 (May 1957): 47-55.

INDEX OF INDIAN TRIBES, GROUPS AND RESERVATIONS*

*Note: A complete list as of 1972 of tribes and groups by state is in Theodore W. Taylor, *The States and Their Indian Citizens*, Appendices J and K (U.S. Government Printing Office, 1972).

INDEX OF NAMES AND SUBJECTS*

*Index of tribes, groups and reservations is presented separately.

M